Super Baby

By the same author:
Candida
The Complete Book of Men's Health
High Blood Pressure
Irritable Bowel Syndrome
Menopause

Super Baby

BOOST YOUR BABY'S POTENTIAL
FROM CONCEPTION TO YEAR ONE

Dr Sarah Brewer

Thorsons
An Imprint of HarperCollins*Publishers*

This book is dedicated to Richard, Saxon and to all developing babies everywhere – may they reach as full a potential as their genes and enriched environment allow.

Thorsons
An Imprint of HarperCollins*Publishers*
77–85 Fulham Palace Road,
Hammersmith, London W6 8JB
Published by Thorsons 1998

10 9 8 7 6 5 4 3 2 1

A catalogue record for this book
is available from the British Library

ISBN 0 7225 3597 X

Printed in Great Britain by Creative Print and Design
(Wales), Ebbw Vale

Contents

Acknowledgements

I would like to acknowledge the work of all the researchers involved in embryology, fetal neuroanatomy, prenatal stimulation and fetal behaviour whose dedication, findings and leaps of intuition have enhanced our knowledge of how a baby develops – and learns – in the womb.

Author's Note

Throughout the book, I refer to the unborn baby as *he*. This is not designed to be sexist, but the easiest way to distinguish between mother and unborn baby. Apologies to all baby girls, everywhere.

Introduction

At birth, your baby's brain contains over 200 billion brain cells – the same order of magnitude as there are stars in the Milky Way. A quarter of all these cells are in the outer layer of your baby's brain, known as the cerebral cortex. Each brain cell is wired to its neighbours through up to 20,000 different branches, resulting in thousands of trillions of connections – more than the number of stars in all the galaxies of the known universe. Each of these connections can sort and process information, contributing to the immense potential of your newborn baby's brain.

This complex wiring diagram is not predetermined by the genetic information in the fertilized egg, however. Even though half your baby's 100,000 genes are involved in the development of his central nervous system, they do not contain enough information to lay down his entire neural network. Only the basic, main circuits are wired into place through the genetic blueprint. These are the circuits that control breathing and heart-beat, and regulate body temperature and other automatic reflexes. The remaining billions of cells are only loosely wired in – rather like unprogrammed computer chips waiting to be loaded with software. When these cells are excited by a stimulus, they become integrated into the circuitry of your baby's brain and connect up with other brain cells (neurons). If they make enough connections with enough other neurons, they will live. If they do not make enough connections, they are programmed to self-destruct and die.

The way your baby's brain cells interconnect is partly determined through interactions between your baby's senses and his environment. These interactions do not start at birth, as is commonly believed. Your baby is capable of learning in the womb. In fact, this prenatal learning process is a vital part of determining your baby's overall intelligence, his creativity, and some physical characteristics such as strength and even his ability to fight off infections. The more stimulation your baby receives in the womb, the more brain cells are present at birth, and the more connections (synapses) are formed between them. It is the number of brain cells, the number of synapses and the speed at which the synapses work that are now thought to be the biological basis for intelligence. By taking part in a prenatal programme, you are literally shaping your baby's future potential.

During fetal development, your baby's brain produces at least twice as many brain cells as he needs. The excess cells are only loosely wired in. If they do not make a certain minimum number of connections with other brain cells, they will eventually wither and die *just before your baby is born*. At least 40 per cent – and sometimes as many as 75 per cent – of brain neurons are lost during prenatal development, most during the eighth month of pregnancy. You can help to minimize this loss by:

- providing a stimulating womb environment for your baby
- eating a healthy diet providing adequate levels of vitamins, minerals and essential fatty acids needed for healthy brain development
- avoiding stress and ensuring you have regular rest periods to improve the circulation of oxygen and nutrients to your baby
- avoiding excess exposure to toxins, including alcohol, cigarettes and environmental pollutants
- breastfeeding your baby once he is born, to continue providing the correct nourishment for his rapidly growing brain; if you are unable to breastfeed, choosing a formula supplemented with long-chain polyunsaturated fatty acids (LCPs) is the next best thing.
- continuing the process begun in the womb by providing your baby with the right stimulation at the right time to help his brain develop through a series of receptive periods known as 'windows of opportunity'.

Such a programme is likely to give your child a minimum 10-point IQ advantage over what he would otherwise have achieved. This may represent the difference between an A, B or C grade in formal examinations. More importantly, however, it may make the difference between a pass and a fail. That chance has to be worth it for any child. It won't necessarily make him a genius. What he will be, however, is a Super Baby, who has received the best possible start in life to help him become alert, sensitive, good-natured, content, compassionate and as bright as his genes and environment will allow.

1

How Your Baby's Brain Develops

From the moment of conception, when sperm and egg collide, the fertilized egg divides countless times to form a small mass of cells. These cells quickly group themselves into many different types. This process is due to the selective switching on of different genes inside different cells destined for different functions. Each gene codes for the production of a single protein. Some cells make specific enzymes, hormones or sugars, while others develop particular receptors that become embedded in their cell wall. Somehow, each cell knows exactly what it is destined to do, where it should travel, how it should grow, divide – and even when it should die.

Your baby's brain is the most complex organ that will develop over the nine months between his conception and birth.

Your baby is born with all the active brain cells he will ever possess. No more will ever be produced. In fact, a newborn baby has two or three times as many brain cells as he will have by the time he reaches adulthood. Even so, he may be born with between 40 and 75 per cent *fewer* brain cells than were present during the last few months of life in the womb. Sometime just before birth – especially during the eighth month of pregnancy – around half your baby's brain cells may wither and die. This process of programmed cell death is known as *apoptosis*.

Some of the cells that die have already performed their vital function and are no longer necessary. They have secreted chemicals that helped to guide other important neurons into place so they could link up important pathways and shape important structures. Some, however, die because they did not seem to be needed. They did not receive enough stimulation during fetal life to justify their continued existence. By providing the right nutrients and an enriched environment for your baby in the womb, and by avoiding certain cell poisons, you can help to minimize the number of brain cells your baby is destined to lose just before birth.

The number of brain cells your baby is born with are important for defining his intellectual potential. It is the number of connections laid down between them that will eventually determine his ultimate intelligence, however. These connections – known as *synapses* – are formed as a result of learning and stimulation, a process that we now know starts before birth.

If a baby has a low level of stimulation in the womb, fewer synapses are laid down and a larger percentage of cells remain isolated from the developing neural network. They therefore wither and die. If the prenatal environment is stimulating, however, your baby's brain cells become more active and make an increasing number of connections which wire them in more permanently. Your baby will therefore be born with an increased number of brain cells and – more importantly – an increased number of synapses connecting them to neighbouring cells. This is the optimum foundation for allowing your child to develop above-average intelligence. Research suggests, for example, that babies stimulated in the womb with a graded course of heart-rhythm sounds tend to have an intelligence level that is 25 to 50 per cent higher than those whose prenatal environment was not enriched (more on this in Chapter 5).

To help understand this process better, let's take a look at how a baby's brain develops.

How Your Baby's Brain and Senses Develop

The length of your pregnancy is calculated from the first day of your last menstrual period. Conception usually occurs two weeks later, when an egg is released in the middle of your hormone cycle. This means that, throughout your pregnancy, your baby's gestation (developmental age) is two weeks less than the calculated length of your pregnancy. When you are 4 weeks pregnant, for example, the gestation age of your baby is only 2 weeks.

Your baby's development is divided into two stages:

1   the embryonic stage
2   the fetal stage

EMBRYONIC STAGE

During the first 8 weeks of development, while the internal organs, central nervous system and limbs are being laid down, your developing baby is called an *embryo*. This stage of development is one of the most critical periods of your baby's prenatal life. During this stage, he is highly susceptible to the harmful effects of some drugs, toxins and nutritional deficiencies. Most congenital malformations are thought to originate during this time.

0 – 2 Weeks after Conception
Length of embryo: 0.5 – 1 mm

During the first two weeks after conception, the fertilized egg has embedded in the womb lining and started to develop into three layers of cells – *the germ layers*:

1 the ectoderm – which will develop into many things, including the nervous system, brain, pituitary gland, sensory cells of the ears, eye and nose, breasts, skin, sweat glands, hair and tooth enamel
2 the endoderm – which will develop into the intestines, lungs, liver, pancreas, bladder, tonsils and thyroid gland
3 the mesoderm – which will become the skeleton, muscles, cartilage, connective tissues, blood, kidneys, spleen and reproductive organs

These developments start occurring even before you have missed your first period!

3 Weeks Gestation (5 Weeks Pregnant)
Length of embryo: 1 – 2 mm

By now, most women will have noticed that their period seems to be late, although some new mums will still experience a light bleed. During this third week of an embryo's life, a long thickening forms in the area where the future backbone and spinal cord will develop. This is known as the *neural plate* and is pear-shaped, with the widest bit at the head end. The centre of the plate develops a long depression known as the *neural groove*. The walls of the groove grow upwards to form a U-shaped depression similar to a valley surrounded on either side by a range of hills. This neural groove continues to deepen and its walls fold over, until they meet above the groove and begin to fuse. Fusion starts half-way along the length of the neural groove and spreads upwards, towards the future head and brain, and downwards towards the future tail bone (coccyx).

Your baby has already formed a few tiny blood vessels and his heart is starting to develop.

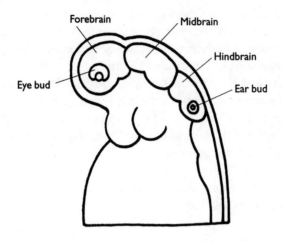

Brain development at 3 weeks

4 Weeks Gestation (6 Weeks Pregnant)
Crown–rump length of embryo: 2 – 4 mm

The crown–rump length is the sitting length from the top of your baby's developing head to his rump or buttocks. This measurement is taken since, as your baby's legs are curled up, his total length is difficult to measure until later in pregnancy.

Fusion of the neural groove is completed with the head end closing first and the tail end closing around two days later. The neural groove has now converted itself into a long, hollow swelling known as the *neural tube*. As cells grow over the surface of the neural tube, it sinks into position where it will develop into the spinal cord. Three membranes, the meninges, develop around the spinal cord and start to secrete cerebro-spinal fluid.

Groups of cells grow around the lower neural tube until they meet and fuse at the back. This encloses the developing spinal cord in a series of rings which will eventually become the protective, bony vertebrae of the spinal column (back bone).

The head end of the neural tube starts to dilate to form three hollow swellings which will eventually develop into the forebrain, midbrain and hindbrain. The remainder of the neural tube elongates and remains smaller in diameter, to form the spinal cord. The main divisions of your baby's central nervous system are now in place.

A tiny liver bud starts to develop. Your baby's heart has now also developed four chambers and starts to beat at a rapid rate of around 180 beats per minute.

Small depressions have appeared where your baby's eyes, ears and mouth will form.

5 Weeks Gestation (7 Weeks Pregnant)
Crown–rump length of embryo: 5 –13 mm (large growth spurt during this week)

By the fifth week, the forebrain starts to divide into two:

1 a front half, which develops two hollow swellings that will become the left and right cerebral hemispheres
2 a rear half, on which the eyes start to form

The wall of the neural tube starts to divide into three layers. The inner layer acts as a structural support, the middle layer becomes the grey substance and is packed full of nerve cells. The outer layer becomes the white substance and is full of nerve fibres.

Later, nerve cells in the central, grey area of the neural tube will grow up through the white substance in the part destined to become the brain. Successive waves of grey cells grow up through the brain to the outer layer, the cortex, so your baby's brain, in effect, forms inside-out compared with the spinal cord.

The eyes start developing as two shallow grooves, one on each side of the expanding forebrain. Each groove expands to form a dilated, cup-shaped swelling (optical vesicle). The tissue behind the swelling constricts to form a stalk that will eventually develop into the optic nerve, which carries signals from light-sensitive cells in the back of the eye to the brain. At the same time, the small area of cells from the 'skin' overlying the optic vesicles sinks inwards and will eventually form the eye lens and pupil. Cells destined to become the lenses rapidly elongate, lose their nuclei and become transparent. An artery passes from the back of each developing eye to nourish the lens, but this will wither away and disappear before birth.

The fluid-filled cavity in each cerebral hemisphere (lateral ventricles) connect up with similar fluid-filled areas inside the midbrain and hindbrain. These spaces are important for allowing cerebro-spinal fluid to bathe and protect your baby's brain and spinal cord.

Blood vessels now extend into the head and throughout the body. The lungs, kidneys, liver and intestines are all forming. The arm and leg buds become visible. The nose has not yet formed, but the nostril openings are appearing. Ridges on your baby's body will eventually develop into muscles and bones.

6 Weeks Gestation (8 Weeks Pregnant)
Crown–rump length of embryo: 14 – 22 mm

Early in development, the neural tube and brain swellings are straight. As your baby's head and tail folds develop, the neural tube becomes gently curved. As the head fold increases, the

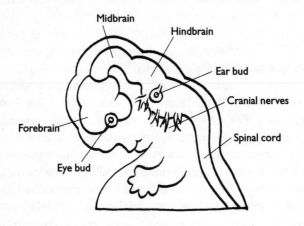

Midbrain

Hindbrain

Ear bud

Cranial nerves

Forebrain

Spinal cord

Eye bud

Brain development at 7 weeks

brain swellings become angled forward from the neural tube to form the neck (cervical) flexure. The brain is now developing at a breath-taking rate.

Your baby's eyelids and ears are now forming. Each ear is divided into three regions: the outer, middle and inner ears. The outer and middle ears develop from pouches in the neck region that resemble primitive gills. The inner ear forms from a depression that sinks into the surface of the developing head near the swelling of the hindbrain. This forms a pit which later closes and disappears deep inside the skull to connect up with the middle ear. Organs of both hearing and balance start to develop in the inner ear during this week.

The beginnings of hands, feet, fingers and toes are now visible. The mouth is becoming recognizable, as the two sides of both the upper and lower jaw fuse. The tongue is also starting to take shape. It will become covered in barrel-shaped collections of cells that form the taste buds. The limbs continue to develop and shoulders, elbows, hips and knees are now apparent. The spine can now make its first tiny bending movements.

7 Weeks Gestation (9 Weeks Pregnant)
Crown–rump length of embryo: 22 – 30 mm/Weight: 2 g

As the different swellings that make up your baby's developing brain grow at different rates, they start to fold up on one another, rather like a concertina. Your baby's brain is now four times larger than it was three weeks ago. Special cells called glial (glue) cells are also forming within the neural tube. These are vital as they support and nourish each neuron, and form scaffolding that guides nerve cells into place so messages can pass between the body and brain.

The eye lenses finish developing during this week. The eyelids now almost cover your baby's eyes. The limbs are growing rapidly and his fingertips are swollen where the touch-sensitive pads are developing.

His neck is developing and, although his head is becoming more erect, it is still bent forward on the chest. His inner ears are taking shape, his nose has appeared and his mouth is continuing to form.

His nervous system is now so well advanced that your baby can move his body, arms and legs in tiny wriggling movements.

8 Weeks Gestation (10 Weeks Pregnant)
Crown–rump length of embryo: 31 – 42 mm/Weight: 2 – 5 g

As your baby's cerebral hemispheres expand, their walls thicken and the fluid-filled lateral ventricles inside become relatively smaller. As development progresses, the hemispheres enlarge forward to form the frontal lobes, upwards and sideways to form the parietal lobes, and then backwards and underneath to form the occipital and temporal lobes. As a result of this great expansion in size, and the concertina-like folding up of the brain, the cerebral hemispheres eventually cover the midbrain and hindbrain and fill 80 per cent of your baby's head. At this stage, the surface of the cerebral hemispheres still look smooth and unwrinkled. They communicate with each other through a bridge of tissue formed from the tip of the neural tube.

The optic nerves that connect the eye and brain start to form from the stalk between each optic vesicle and the brain. The inner ears are completely formed and the external parts of the ear are growing.

The bumps over the back of the head and upper neck are now smoothing over and the head is becoming more erect. The ankles and wrists are formed.

Your baby is now recognizably human – after just 8 weeks of development. The organs have all been laid down and the basic shape of the brain, spinal cord and limbs is formed. Your baby is protected by amniotic fluid and nourished through the umbilical cord, which is now completely formed to connect your baby with his developing placenta.

FETAL STAGE OF DEVELOPMENT

The embryonic phase of development ends after the 8th week. Your baby is now known as a fetus (meaning *young one*) and his growth continues rapidly.

9 Weeks Gestation (11 Weeks Pregnant)
Crown–rump length: 44 – 60 mm/Weight: 8 g

As your baby's cerebral hemispheres expand and thicken, several structures, also (and potentially confusingly) known as nuclei, form inside. These are concentrated areas of nerve cell bodies – grey matter – which act as control centres for different body functions. Other nerve cell bodies concentrate on the outer part of the cerebral hemispheres to form the grey matter where the majority of brain cell connections will form. These nerve cell bodies put out long, fine filaments known as *axons*, which pass down into the underlying layers of the cerebral hemispheres.

Each axon has the daunting task of having to find the right pathway through all the millions of other brain cells and axons surrounding it to reach its correct destination. The growing axon finds its way in the dark by putting out a special feeler – a long tube known as a growth cone. This is equipped with the cellular equivalent of magnets – banks of receptors arrayed on the tube surface that can detect special proteins. Some of these proteins attract the growth cone towards them, while others repel it away.

Collections of nerve cell axons therefore start to run together like cables – all attracted by the same proteins – to connect up important areas of the brain. One particularly large collection of axons running through each cerebral hemisphere is known as the left and right internal capsule respectively.

Axon fibres start to grow through a bridge of tissue connecting each hemisphere. This allows the two halves of the brain to communicate with each other as well as with the rest of the brain. This bridge of tissue will eventually carry fibres that connect the:

- smell centres of the left and right side of the brain to each other (olfactory bulbs and temporal lobes)
- left and right parts of the brain involved in the complex, physical aspects of behaviour governed by emotion and instinct (hippocampus)
- frontal lobes and parietal lobes with each other; this connection, which is the largest and most important, is known as the corpus callosum; as it develops in size, it arches up over the roof of the developing third ventricle.

In front of this bridge of tissue, the optic nerve from each eye meets and exchanges fibre so that some nerve fibres from each eye cross over to the other side of the brain.

The pupils of your baby's eyes are now completely formed and continue to grow. Fingers and toes have formed but are joined by webs of skin. The ovaries or testes are fully formed inside the abdominal cavity, and the external genitals are taking shape, although the baby's sex cannot yet be told by examining these.

By the end of this week, all his essential organs are formed and most of them – except the lungs – are beginning to show signs of function. Your baby is now recognizable as a tiny human, although his head is relatively large and represents almost half his entire length. His limbs also seem relatively short and thin, as few muscles have yet developed. Your baby is now quite actively moving his limbs and flexing his spine.

Fetal growth is now so rapid that the length of your baby will double over the next three weeks.

10 Weeks Gestation (12 Weeks Pregnant)
Crown–rump length: 61 – 64 mm (2½ in)/Weight: 9 – 13 g (⅓ – ½ oz)

Your baby's brain and other organs continue to develop and grow. The first connections between brain cells – known as synapses – start to form. These are the connections that help to wire each brain cell permanently into place within the neural network. From now on, the neurons in your baby's brain start to produce spontaneous, co-ordinated pulses of electrical activity. These send messages from one part of the brain to another and start laying down the neural circuits that are vital for normal functioning of your baby's brain and nervous system. As each human cell only contains around 100,000 genes, there are several orders of magnitude too few to be responsible for the complex evolution of your baby's brain. Genes guide the process – for example by coding for the production of proteins and nerve growth factors that attract or repel moving neurons – but it is the inherent electrical activity of the neurons themselves that is responsible for laying down the complex interconnections that form your baby's neural network. This electrical activity guides the development of your baby's brain, which literally starts to shape itself. The genes that drive this process are now thought to be the same ones that in later life are involved in the processing and storing of new information (learning and memory).

Your baby's nervous system is now mature enough for him to move quite actively within his protective bubble of amniotic fluid, of which there is just over 3 tablespoonfuls (50 ml). You won't be able to feel these movements for another few weeks, however. His eyes are now just about fully formed and he can squint, open his mouth and wriggle his fingers and toes. The pituitary gland at the base of his brain starts to produce hormones, including growth hormone.

Your baby's intestines can now actively absorb glucose – the main fuel required by brain cells. He will also swallow small amounts of amniotic fluid which will be processed by his tiny kidneys and passed out into the amniotic fluid again as urine. This swallowing activity is regulated by his brain and is important for the development of the intestines, as amniotic fluid contains various growth factors. His fingers and toes are fully formed and have started to grow nails.

Your baby's head is now rounder in shape but is still bent forwards. Muscle development continues so that movements become stronger.

11 Weeks Gestation (13 Weeks Pregnant)
Crown–rump length: 65 – 79 mm (2½ – 3 in)/Weight: 14 – 24 g (½ – ⁶⁄₇ oz)

Your baby's face is now more human looking as his eyes start to move closer together and his ears move up from his neck to the

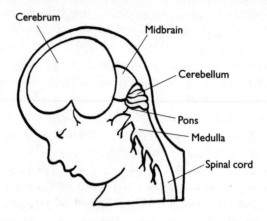

Brain development at 11 weeks

sides of his head. His body is now growing more rapidly in relation to the size of his skull. His head represents one half of the total fetal length and, as the neck is fully formed, can now move freely. By 21 weeks of gestation, his head will represent around a third of total fetal length, and by birth his head will make up around a quarter of his total length.

Your baby's eyelids have just about met and will soon fuse together so the eyes are closed. All his internal organs are continuing to grow. The sex of your baby is now obvious from his external genitals.

12 Weeks Gestation (14 Weeks Pregnant)
Crown–rump length: 80 – 93 mm (3 – 3 ½ in)/Weight 25 – 49 g (1 – 1 ¾ oz)

By 12 weeks after fertilization, your baby is fully formed. The framework for all his organs, muscles, limbs and bones are in the right place but are still tiny and immature. From now on, he will grow in size and all his organs, including his brain, will mature until he is capable of life outside the womb.

Large numbers of primitive neurons (neurocytes) start to move into the cerebral hemispheres which continue to thicken rapidly. The hindbrain has developed two sprout-like growths that will become the cerebellum – the part of the brain which helps to control posture and movement.

His neck has elongated so the shape of his head is more obvious.

His spinal cord has developed so that on the inside are the bodies of the nerve cells (grey matter) and on the outside are all the nerve filaments (axons making up the white matter) that run up and down the cord like wires. Some of these wires connect different parts of the cord, while others pass information to and from the brain and either join or leave the spinal cord at one of the 31 pairs of spinal nerves.

13 Weeks Gestation (15 Weeks Pregnant)
Crown–rump length: 94 – 104 mm (3 ¾ – 4 in)/Weight: 50 – 79 g
(1 ¾ – 2 ¾ oz)

Your baby's brain is still only around the size of a kidney bean. All brain cells originate from the layer of cells that originally lined the central cavity of the neural tube. These cells multiply at the astonishing rate of 250,000 cells per minute and start to move out of the tube into the brain swellings. This process will continue until the seventh month of fetal development. Once the immature neurons have left the neural tube lining, most can no longer divide and multiply after they take up their final positions. This means your baby is born with all the nerve cells he will ever possess. The one exception seems to be the nerve cells in the olfactory nerve running from the smell receptors in the nose to the olfactory bulbs of the brain. These seem capable of being generated and replaced continuously throughout life.

Glial (glue) cells in the developing brain act like scaffolding so that newly divided brain cells (neurons) can climb out of the neural tube, through the white matter, and reach the outer part of the cerebral hemispheres, the grey matter or cortex. The cortex begins to develop in six layers. Somehow, the neurons climbing up the glial cells seem to know which is the right point to jump off and start forming a layer. They are thought to follow chemical signals whose concentrations guide their way. As the framework for one layer is completed, the next wave of neurons climb higher, through the initial layers to form a new layer on top. The way these layers form seems to be vital for ordered thought processes in later life, and to help avoid future problems such as schizophrenia, dyslexia and some types of epilepsy.

His body is now growing faster than his head, so that he looks more in proportion. His muscles are stronger and his movements are becoming more vigorous.

He can now suck his thumb. His eyes are still moving closer together on his face.

14 Weeks Gestation (16 Weeks Pregnant)
Crown–rump length: 105 – 114 mm (4 – 4 ½ in)/Weight: 80 – 99 g (2 ¾ – 3 ½ oz)

By the end of this week, your baby's limbs are fully formed and all his joints can move. Your baby is now waving his arms and legs frequently, and some mothers now feel these movements as little flutters – especially if they have already had a previous pregnancy. First-time mothers may not feel this so-called 'quickening' for another 2 – 4 weeks.

Your baby is now capable of making all the movements a full-term baby can make, such as sucking his thumb, startling in response to loud sounds, making breathing movements from his chest wall, hiccuping and moving his eyes. Every time your baby moves, electrical messages pass up from his muscles to his brain.

These help to stimulate development of his cerebellum, which controls posture and movement, and the motor cortex of his cerebral hemispheres, which are involved in initiating voluntary muscle movements. This stimulation boosts the laying down of new cells, and the connections between those already present.

Your baby starts to develop a covering of fine, downy hair called lanugo. He now also begins to grow eyebrows and eyelashes.

15 Weeks Gestation (17 Weeks Pregnant)
Crown–rump length: 115 – 124 mm (4 ½ – 4 ¾ in)/Weight: 100 – 149 g (3 ½ – 5 ¼ oz)

Neurons are continuing to climb up into the outer layers of your baby's cerebral cortex. Recent research suggests that the way each brain cell becomes specialized to perform a particular function depends on the activity of different genes. These genes become active in the glial cells of some parts of the developing brain. Each gene codes for the production of a particular protein. When one gene activates, for example, it produces a protein that diffuses away from the cells which made it to become less and less concentrated. Brain cells in the regions where this protein is most concentrated develop into cells that process information from the senses (sensory neuron). Brain cells in regions where this protein is less concentrated become specialized to send messages to your muscles (motor neurons), while brain cells in areas where the concentration of this protein is very low develop into cells that sort and relay information between other brain cells (association neurons). Some research suggests your baby is capable of starting to learn (adapt his behaviour in response to a stimulus) from this time onwards.

Your baby is now starting to lay down fat (adipose tissue).

16 Weeks Gestation (18 Weeks Pregnant)
Crown–rump length: 125 – 134 mm (5 – 5¼ in)/Weight: 150 – 199 g (5 ⅓ – 7 oz)

Some of the nerves linking your baby's limb muscles to his nervous system now start to develop a fatty outer coating. This protective sheath forms when special glial cells wrap round the axons, rather like a short length of insulation tape wrapping round and round a section of electrical wire. This coating process is known as myelination, and the protective insulation is called the myelin sheath. It is a vital part of the way the nervous system conducts messages and matures. Once a nerve is coated in its myelin sheath, it can transmit messages from the muscles to the brain more quickly, allowing fast, co-ordinated movements rather than slow, jerky ones. Many mothers have felt their baby move by the end of the 16th week.

17 Weeks Gestation (19 Weeks Pregnant)
Crown–rump length: 135 – 145 mm (5 ⅓ – 5 ¾ in)/Weight: 200 – 259 g (7– 9 oz)

Your baby's brain cells are continuing to multiply at a rate of 50,000 – 100,000 per second and his brain is enlarging rapidly.

By now, your baby's spinal cord has started to form thickenings where complex nerve connections will supply the upper and lower limbs. The spine now begins to grow longer at a faster rate than the spinal cord, so that by the seventh month of development, the spinal cord no longer reaches to the end of the vertebral column, but ends at the same level as your baby's kidneys.

18 Weeks Gestation (20 Weeks Pregnant)
Crown–rump length: 146 – 160 mm (5 ¾ – 6¼ in)/Weight: 260 – 300 g (9 – 10 ½ oz)

Hair begins to appear on your baby's head. He is rapidly growing in length and weight and by now you will usually be able to feel his movements quite obviously. His fingerprints are starting to form as ridges. His hands can grip firmly. Teeth buds start to develop in the jawbones.

19 Weeks Gestation (21 Weeks Pregnant)
Crown–rump length: 161 – 180 mm (5 ¾ – 7 in)/Weight: 301 – 349 g (10 ½ – 12 oz)

Your baby's eyes are still shut, but he can now move his eyes slowly from side to side. His taste buds are well developed and he now starts to drink quite large amounts of amniotic fluid.

20 Weeks Gestation (22 Weeks Pregnant)
Crown–rump length: 181 – 190 mm (7 – 7 ½ in)/Weight: 350 – 440 g (12 – 15 ½ oz)

Over the last 15 weeks, your baby's brain has been expanding at the phenomenal rate of up to 100,000 new brain cells every second and his cerebral hemispheres are becoming larger, with a thicker outer layer (cortex) that develops six layers of cells. By now, most of the axons growing out from the neurons in your baby's brain have arrived at their destination and the basic diagram for the neural network is in place. The cortex will soon start to fold at the surface to accommodate this rapidly increasing number of cells. Some evidence suggests that your baby starts hearing sounds from your environment from this stage onwards.

The cartilage surrounding the inner ear starts to turn to bone now and his ears are almost fully formed and in the right place.

21 Weeks Gestation (23 Weeks Pregnant)
Crown–rump length: 191 – 200 mm (7 ½ – 7 ¾ in)/Weight: 441 – 520 g (15 ½ – 18 ½ oz)

Your baby's heart rate has now dropped to around 140 – 150 beats per minute.

All his organs are maturing and starting to function, except his lungs, which remain immature for several weeks until the small air exchange sacs (alveoli) are completely formed.

22 Weeks Gestation (24 Weeks Pregnant)
Crown–rump length: 201 – 210 mm (7 ¾ – 8 ¼ in)/Weight: 521 – 650 g (18 ½ – 23 oz)

Your baby will now consistently respond to touch and to sound. Your womb is quite a noisy place, what with the:

- rhythmic whooshing sound of blood passing through your internal arteries
- the gentle pulsing noises of blood flowing through the placenta
- the humming noise of blood flowing through your main veins
- the lub-dub sound of your heart beating
- the gurgling noises of your intestines
- the soft swooshing rhythm of air flowing in and out of your lungs.

Your baby can also hear voices and will learn to identify your voice, that of your partner, and any others he hears frequently. A loud noise may make him jump.

You may also be aware of him coughing or having an attack of the hiccups.

23 Weeks Gestation (25 Weeks Pregnant)
Crown–rump length: 211 – 220 mm (8 ¼ – 8 ¾ in)/Weight: 651 – 800 g (23 – 28 oz)

By now, all the layers of the back of your baby's eyes (retina) have developed, including the light-sensitive cells known as rods and cones.

The cells that control conscious thought are starting to develop and your baby becomes more sensitive to sound and movement. He starts to develop a cycle of sleeping and waking. Up until now, he has rarely been still for more than five minutes at a time.

His limbs have developed more muscle but they still look thin, as only a little fat has been laid down. Your baby's organs are now starting to mature and, if he had to be delivered early as a result of preterm labour, he would have a chance (albeit small) of survival in an intensive special care baby unit.

24 Weeks Gestation (26 Weeks Pregnant)
Crown–rump length: 221 – 230 mm (8 ¾ – 9 ¼ in)/Weight: 801 – 950 g (28 – 33 ½ oz)

At around the sixth month of fetal development, some of the long, fine filaments extending from each nerve cell (axons) in the brain start to gain a protective myelin sheath. This myelination process is important as it allows brain impulses to travel faster, enhancing your baby's ability to learn. This is the optimum time to start playing music or graded noises such as the cardiac curriculum to your baby (more of this in Chapter 5). At first, only the axons from concentrated collections of nerve cells in the cerebral hemispheres (basal ganglia) become myelinated. Later, sensory nerve fibres passing up from the spinal cord start to myelinate, but the process is slow. In fact, at birth, only brain cells controlling vital functions such as breathing, heart rate, temperature, reflexes, seeing, hearing and touch are fully myelinated – most of your baby's nerves are still unmyelinated. Myelination will continue after birth in a systematic fashion and is largely complete by the end of your child's second year. Some nerve fibres in the brain and spinal cord are thought to remain unmyelinated until after puberty, however. It is thought that your baby can now experience pain if subjected to invasive medical procedures in the womb, although it is possible that pain perception occurs much earlier.

From this week onwards, the light-sensitive cells in the retina of your baby's eyes start to accumulate more and more long-chain polyunsaturated fatty acids (LCPs). These LCPs are vital for development of sight and visual acuity. Your baby's eyelids, which have been fused since the 11th – 12th week of gestation, now start to separate. Most babies do not have at birth the eye colour they will eventually develop; the colour of their blood vessels can impart a startlingly blue tinge to the eyes. Proper pigmentation of the eyes (green, hazel, brown or, indeed, blue) usually develops a few days or weeks after birth.

By now, the air sacs in your baby's lungs are almost fully formed, but are in a collapsed state and full of fluid. He still needs to make a substance called *surfactant*. This will eventually line his airsacs, reducing their surface tension so his lungs can expand and collapse more easily during breathing.

25 Weeks Gestation (27 Weeks Pregnant)
Crown–rump length: 231 – 240 mm (9 ¼ – 9 ½ in)/Total length: 34 cm (11 ½ in)/Weight: 951 – 1,100 g (33 ½ – 38 oz)

The total length of your baby, from head to foot, can now be easily measured, as well as the crown–rump length (from head to bottom).

The surface of your baby's brain is enlarging but still looks smooth, resembling the kernal of a Brazil nut rather than a walnut at this stage. From 25 weeks of gestation, until the first few months after birth, your baby's brain will rapidly increase in size. This is commonly referred to as the brain growth spurt. This spurt is due to:

- a rapid increase in number of brain cells
- increased development of communication branches (dendrites) from each brain cell body (known as 'arborization', as these outgrowths resemble small trees)
- increased establishment of connections (synapses) between brain cells
- development of a fatty, myelin sheath around the axons of more and more neurons.

These processes all require the laying down of fats, especially essential fatty acids, and maternal diet during this phase of brain development is critical for optimum brain growth and future intellectual potential (more in Chapter 6).

26 Weeks Gestation (28 Weeks Pregnant)
Crown–rump length: 241 – 250 mm (9 ½ – 9 ¾ in)/Total length: 35 cm (12 in)/Weight: 1,101 – 1,249 g (38 – 44 oz)

Your baby is now covered in a fatty, white grease known as vernix. This gives his skin an outer waterproof layer to help protect him from chemicals in the amniotic fluid.

Your baby spends a lot of time asleep, but now starts to develop a pattern of quiet sleep and active sleep that alternates every 20 – 40 minutes throughout the day and night.

His body has grown more than his head during the last few weeks, so his head now looks in better proportion to the rest of him.

27 Weeks Gestation (29 Weeks Pregnant)
Crown–rump length: 251 – 260 mm (9 ¾ – 10 ¼ in)/Total length: 37 cm
(12 ½ in)/Weight: 1,250 – 1,390 g (44 – 49 oz)

The retina at the back of his eyes has now developed its layers of light-sensitive cells that will help your baby see. From now on, the number of connections (synapses) between nerve cells in the part of the brain involved in interpreting visual images from his eyes starts to increase dramatically until around 2 months after birth. Then, between 2 – 4 months after birth, the number of connections will suddenly increase by at least a factor of 10, corresponding with a sudden improvement in your baby's vision around this time.

Your baby's skin becomes less wrinkled as he lays down more fat. He is now starting to get more cramped inside the womb as his length and weight increase.

28 Weeks Gestation (30 Weeks Pregnant)
Crown–rump length: 261 – 270 mm (10 ¼ – 10 ¾ in)/Total length: 38 cm (13 in)/Weight: 1,400 – 1,590 g (49 – 56 oz)

The surface of your baby's brain has now formed shallow grooves (sulci), deeper grooves (fissures) and convolutions (gyri), making it resemble the surface of a walnut. These undulations dramatically increase the surface area of his brain so many more brain cells can be fitted in and connected up. At this stage, the amount of brain tissue is continuing to increase dramatically – by as many as 100,000 brain cells per minute. This rate will tail off as the pruning process begins. Brain growth will continue as more fatty myelin sheaths are laid down.

29 Weeks Gestation (31 Weeks Pregnant)
Crown–rump length: 271 – 280 mm (10 ¾ – 11 in)/Total length: 40 cm (13 ½ in)/Weight: 1,600 – 1,790 (56 – 63 oz)

From now on, excess brain cells that have made the wrong connections, or which have formed networks that do not receive enough information traffic, start to die. This process of programmed cell death (apoptosis) is designed to conserve neural pathways that are useful and prune out those that are unwanted or erroneous. This process continues during the seventh and eighth month of pregnancy and reaches a peak four weeks before your baby is due to be born. Many of the neurons that die are not erroneous, but are deemed superfluous given the amount of stimulation your baby receives in the womb. A programme of prenatal stimulation and environment enrichment can help lay down additional connections between neurons in your baby's cerebral cortex so that they do not degenerate and so that, as a result, your baby is born with extra brain cells, extra communication links (synapses), additional muscle strength and an enhanced ability to learn.

30 Weeks Gestation (32 Weeks Pregnant)
Crown–rump length: 281 – 290 mm (11 – 11 ½ in)/Total length: 42 cm (14 in)/Weight: 1,800 – 1,999 g (63 – 70 oz)

Most babies have now turned upside down so their head is in the right position for birth. Some babies don't turn until the last few weeks of pregnancy, however.

31 Weeks Gestation (33 Weeks Pregnant)
Crown–rump length: 291 – 304 mm (11 ½ – 12 in)/Total length: 43 cm (14 ¼ in)/Weight: 2,000 – 2,249 g (70 – 79 oz)

By the time of birth, your baby's head is already around 2 per cent larger than your birth canal. Your baby's brain is surrounded by a series of flat bones in the skull which are not yet fused. These bones are soft and can slide over one another to overlap so that the skull can mould to pass through the birth canal without damage. Two spaces occur where these bones meet, one at the front and one at the back of the skull. These are known as the anterior and posterior fontanelles.

32 Weeks Gestation (34 Weeks Pregnant)
Crown–rump length: 305 – 318 mm (12 – 12 ½ in)/Total length: 44 cm (14 ½ in)/Weight: 2,250 – 2,499 g (79 – 88 oz)

By now, your baby is perfectly formed and his head is in correct proportion to the rest of his body. Increasing amounts of fat are now being laid down underneath the skin.

Your baby now has four activity patterns: quiet (slow wave) sleep, active (REM or rapid eye movement) sleep, quiet awareness and active awareness. From now onwards, these four patterns are easier to differentiate when fetal activity is monitored.

The placenta has now reached maturity and is approaching its peak efficiency after which it stops growing and starts to age.

33 Weeks Gestation (35 Weeks Pregnant)
Crown–rump length: 319 – 330 mm (12 ½ – 13 in)/Total length: 45 cm (14 ¾ in)/Weight: 2,500 – 2,749 g (88 – 97 oz)

Your baby's arm and leg muscles are now fully linked up to the nervous system so that relatively co-ordinated movements occur. He tends to lie with his arms and legs drawn up and can grip quite strongly with his fingers. If you are playing him music or heart sounds in the womb, he will frequently rock his body in time to the sounds, which helps to increase his muscle strength.

34 Weeks Gestation (36 Weeks Pregnant)
Crown–rump length: 331 – 340 mm (13 – 13 ½ in)/Total length: 46 cm (15 in)/Weight: 2,750 – 2,999 g (97 – 106 oz)

Your baby's brain and nervous system are now fully developed. Reflexes such as sucking are still poor, however.

Your baby is still covered in large amounts of lanugo, but this will slowly disappear before birth.

In baby boys, the testicles have usually descended into the scrotum from the abdomen by now.

35 Weeks Gestation (37 Weeks Pregnant)
Crown–rump length: 341 – 350 mm (13 ½ – 14 in)/Total length: 47 cm (15 ¼ in)/Weight: 3,000 – 3,100 g (106 – 109 oz)

The skin on your baby's face has now lost many of its wrinkles and looks smoother. His eyes now blink automatically and can sense changes in light filtering through your abdominal wall.

The placenta reaches its peak efficiency around now, allowing the maximum transfer of oxygen, glucose and other vital nutrients to your baby. As much as 70 per cent of these nutrients are destined for your baby's brain.

36 Weeks Gestation (38 Weeks Pregnant)
Crown–rump length: 351 – 360 mm (14 – 14 ¼ in)/Total length: 48 cm (15 ½ in)/Weight: 3,101 – 3,250 g (109 – 114 oz)

Your baby's brain contains two to three times more nerve cells than he will have as an adult. During the last 8 weeks in the womb, 40 – 75 per cent of these cells will disappear through the process of programmed cell death (apoptosis) mentioned earlier if they have not been properly wired in and are therefore seen as unnecessary. The number of brain cells will continue to fall at a slower rate throughout childhood and then level off during adulthood.

His fingernails and toenails are now fully grown and reach to the ends of his fingers.

37 Weeks Gestation (39 Weeks Pregnant)
Crown–rump length: 361 – 370 mm (14 ¼ – 14 ½ in)/Total length: 49 cm (15 ¾ in)/Weight: 3,251 – 3,400 g (114 – 120 oz)

Your baby's consciousness and co-ordination are now well established. When he is born, his brain will weigh around 350 g (12 oz) – about 10 per cent of his total body weight. During the first year of life, his brain will triple in weight to 1,000 g (2 lb 3 oz) as new brain connections and the fatty myelin sheath that coats nerve fibres are laid down.

By the time he reaches adulthood, your baby's brain will contain hundreds of millions of cells fewer than he has now, yet will still weigh an average 1.4 kg (3 lb).

38 Weeks Gestation (40 Weeks Pregnant)
Crown–rump length: 371 – 380 mm (14 ½ – 15 in)/Total length: 50 cm (16 in)/Weight: 3.4 kg (7 ½ lb)

By now, the brain cells in the outer part of the cerebral hemisphere have formed into six layers as a result of the incoming and outgoing fibres connecting them with neighbouring nerve cells. Neurons in different areas of your baby's brain start to become specialized (differentiated) so that cells involved in controlling movement, for example, take on a pyramidal shape, while those involved in detecting stimuli from the senses take on a granular appearance.

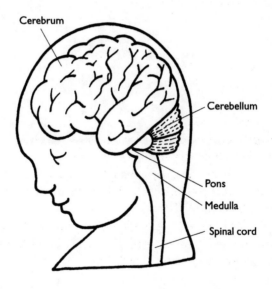

The brain at birth

Lanugo has just about disappeared. Small amounts of body hair may still be present, however; these will soon disappear after birth. Your baby is covered in protective vernix which is especially thick in skin creases such as the armpits and groin.

The hair on his head may vary from a few wisps to hair that is 2 – 4 cm long.

Your baby is now ready to be born. The average pregnancy lasts 266 days (38 weeks) from conception – or 280 days (40 weeks) if counting from the first day of your last period. Only 1 in 20 babies is born on the due date calculated at the beginning of pregnancy, however. A birth date that is up to 2 weeks earlier or 2 weeks later than the calculated date of delivery is considered normal and does not have any bearing on your baby's subsequent intelligence.

2

How Your Baby's Brain Works

Your baby's brain and nervous system contain specialized cells, known as neurons, that can generate and transmit electrical impulses. These become specialized into three broad groups:

1 Motor neurons – which carry signals from the central nervous system to the body to control various actions
2 Sensory neurons – which gather information and carry signals to the brain and spinal cord
3 Association neurons – which act as connectors between different neurons and pass signals between them so information can be sorted, compared and processed.

Each neuron is protected and nourished by supporting cells called glial, or glue cells. These do not carry electrical impulses but act as scaffolding to anchor neurons and also wrap around them, supplying busy neurons with the oxygen and glucose they need to function properly. There are several different types of glial cells, including:

- Microglia (small cells) – that act as scavengers to root out and destroy infection
- Schwann cells – that wrap round the axons of neurons in the brain and spinal cord to form myelin sheaths
- Astrocytes (star-shaped cells) – that control the flow of fluid and nourishment from the bloodstream to individual brain cells.

Each neuron has an expanded, bubble-like area known as the cell body. This contains the cell's control centre (nucleus) which houses a complete set of your baby's genes – half of which have come from you, and half from your baby's father. Each neuron has a number of projections radiating from its cell body, known as axons and dendrites. Dendrites allow a brain cell to communicate with other nerve cells in the close vicinity, while an axon allows the brain cell to communicate with nerve gland or muscle cells further afield.

Axons

Axons are fine filaments that carry electrical impulses away from each neuron cell body – rather like a telephone wire. Researchers are only now beginning to understand how each axon grows in the right direction. They are attracted and repelled by trails of chemicals, following the scaffolding guidelines laid down by structural glial cells to connect up with the right target nerve or muscle cells.

Axons contain a number of long internal filaments that help to strengthen them and maintain their shape. They also contain long tubules that pass from the cell body to the axon tip. The tubules are thought to act as a transport system, carrying nerve chemicals (neurotransmitters) down from the cell body, where they are made, to the junctions at the end of the axons (synapses – see below). The end of each axon divides into several smaller branches known as telodendria. These branches make contact with other nerve cells, or with the membranes of muscle or gland cells.

Dendrites

Dendrites are projections that receive impulses coming into the cell, rather like arrays of antennae. Their name literally means *like a tree*, as they divide to form many different layers of branches. The dendrites develop short knob-like twigs known as dendritic spines where they come into contact with axonal endings to form a connection (synapse). Exciting new research suggests that these spines can grow, change in shape or shrink depending on the amount of stimulation they receive. The basic shape of new, unstimulated dendritic spines is a small ball on a long, narrow stick, similar to a popsickle. This narrow stalk is thought to act like a bottle-neck to slow incoming information from a new, untried source. With repeated stimulation, the spine changes shape to resemble a mushroom with a fatter stalk and a bigger, umbrella-like cap. The cap can be rounded outwards, flattened on top, or cupped to resemble a sink-plunger. These mushroomed spines seem to enhance or speed up transmission of information from the synapse to the dendritic tree and down to the main neuron cell body. The latest theory is that repeated stimulation allows the passage of information to become easier, and that this change in shape, in turn, seems to be linked with learning and memory.

If a mushroomed dendritic spine then falls into disuse, it seems to collapse in on itself and shrink to form a blunt stub.

This enlarging and shrinking of dendritic spines according to how often they are used has now been explained. When communication chemicals are released at a synapse to diffuse across the synaptic cleft to the other side, a nourishing chemical called *human nerve growth factor* is also released. This stimulates enlargement of the dendritic spine and maintains and enlarges the synapse. If the synapse is not stimulated frequently enough, the dendritic spine will wither away due to lack of this growth-stimulating factor. The nerve growth factor also seems to suppress a gene that codes for the production of a powerful, synapse-destroying enzyme. Lack of activity in a neural pathway, and lack of nerve growth factor, means this destroyer gene can switch on so the synapses creating the unused links are pruned out.

Multipolar Neurons

Each neuron can be classified according to the number of filaments radiating from its cell body:

- a *unipolar* neuron has a single long filament (axon) which leaves the cell body and then branches
- a *bipolar* neuron has two separate long filaments (axons) that leave the cell body separately and then branch
- a *multipolar* neuron has a single long axon plus varying numbers of dendrites.

The cells found in the brain are mostly multipolar neurons. Some neurons found in the central nervous system and in the retina of the eye have dendrites but no axons, however.

Over 85 per cent of the neuron cell bodies found in your baby's brain are concentrated in the outer part of his hemispheres – the

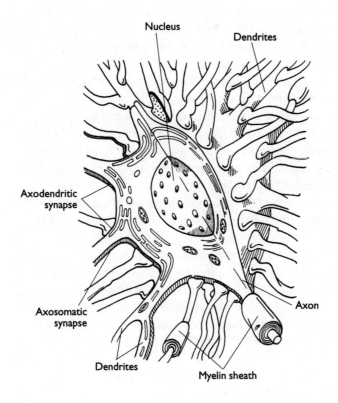

Nucleus

Dendrites

Axodendritic synapse

Axosomatic synapse

Axon

Dendrites

Myelin sheath

Brain development: A. The embryo brain produces many more neurons than necessary, then eliminates the excess. B. The neurons that are left create axons, which in turn produce connecting branches. C. Some connections are stimulated by electrical impulses. Those that are not stimulated waste away. D. After birth, all the new experiences cause a flood of new connections between axons and dendrites. This electrical activity fine-tunes the brain circuitry, establishing which connections will remain and which will be pruned.

so-called grey matter. They also cluster together to form areas of grey matter – the basal ganglia – deeper in his brain. These are involved in controlling complex movement sequences such as walking. As each of these cell bodies is capable of forming at least 20,000 different dendritic branches, the grey matter of the cerebral cortex is filled with literally trillions of synaptic connections. It is these connections that are so vitally important for human intelligence.

Many of the neurons in the brain have axons that are only a millionth of a centimetre long, and which only send messages between one layer of the cortex and another. Others have axons that are at least a metre long and send messages to the spinal cord and other parts of the body.

In some parts of the brain, the terminal branches of one neuron's axons surround the body of the cell it is connecting with like a net (as with the basket cells of the cerebellum and autonomic ganglia). In other places, axons intertwine with the dendrites of neighbouring cells (for example, the climbing fibres of the cerebellum). Axons may also end directly on a dendrite (as with the apical dendrites of the cortical pyramids) or occasionally end directly on the axon of another neuron (axo-axonal endings).

Synapse

Information is passed from one neuron to another at the point where the axon from one cell meets a dendritic spine, or the cell body of another. Transfer of information occurs at a special gap called a synapse. On average, the axon of each brain cell divides to form 1,000 synaptic endings. As the development of dendrites dramatically increases the surface area of a neuron, the vast majority (98 per cent) of synapses in the cerebral cortex are between an axon of one cell and the dendritic spines of another (axodendritic synapses). Most of the remaining 2 per cent of synapses form between the axons of one neuron and the cell

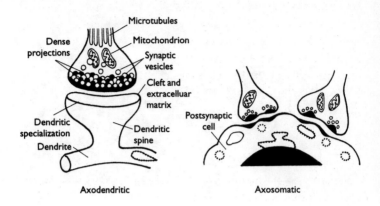

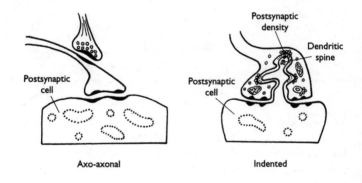

Various kinds of synapses

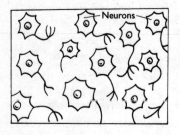

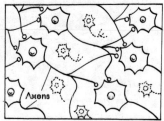

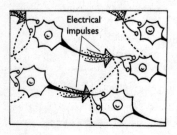

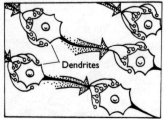

Synapses on a motor neuron

body of another (axosomatic synapses). Some nerve cells in the brain and retina which possess dendrites but no axons are still capable of passing electrical impulses from one cell to another through dendro-dendritic synapses.

Each neuron is covered in so many synaptic knobs from so many different neurons, that it appears to be encrusted with them like a seaside rock covered with limpets. Although the area covered by a single synaptic knob is small, there are so many synapses that often 40 per cent of the membrane covering a neuron's cell body, and 70 per cent of the membrane making up the dendritic tree, is involved in synaptic connections. In the adult forebrain, the ratio of synapses to neurons has been calculated at 40,000 to 1.

At a synapse, an end branch (telodendron) of an axon forms a swelling known as a synaptic knob (sometimes also known as a terminal button). These act as the transmitters of information across the synaptic gap. On the other side of the synapse, the membrane of the second neuron thickens to form a bulb-like swelling that acts as a receiver. On dendrites, these swellings are known as dendritic spines, as mentioned above. The gap between the transmitter and receiver (the synaptic cleft) is minuscule – it has been measured as 30 – 50 nanometres (millionths of a millimetre).

Inside each synaptic knob there are structures known as mitochondria, which produce energy and act rather like batteries to power the transmission of signals across the synaptic gap. The majority of synaptic knobs are also filled with granules containing small packets of communication chemicals known as neurotransmitters.

The membrane on either side of a synapse has special qualities. It contains a long-chain polyunsaturated fatty acid (docosahexaenoic acid, or DHA) which makes it more fluid than the membrane found on other parts of each brain cell. DHA seems to be important for rapid transmission of signals from one neuron to another. DHA levels of brain tissue steadily increase from around 20 weeks gestation as the number of synapses expands. This increase continues after birth in breastfed babies, whose brains have been found to be made up of around 10 per cent DHA by weight. Babies fed formula milks that are not enriched with DHA show a fall in levels to less than 8 per cent by weight. If there is less DHA in the diet, other, less optimal fatty acids have to be incorporated into the synapse membranes, which will slow synaptic function. The amount of dietary DHA incorporated into your baby's brain cells is strongly linked with his intellectual potential (see Chapters 6 and 13).

During life in the womb and for the first 10 years after birth, the number of synapses in your baby's brain increases exponentially to form quadrillions of connections. It is the overproduction of these synapses, followed by selective pruning out of those that are unused and unwanted, that shapes the neural pathways which will dictate your baby's personality, skills and future potentials. The more synapses he starts with, the more ways his brain cells have for exchanging information with other neurons. The more synapses he has, the more likely it is that he can process and respond to new information and the more likely he is to learn and to show gifted intelligence.

How Your Baby's Nerve Cells Generate Electricity

All the cells in your baby's body are bathed in a sea of fluid containing a variety of chemicals and salts. Once dissolved, these separate into particles that carry an electric charge. These particles are known as ions. The two most important chemicals involved in generating electricity in nerve cells are *sodium* and *potassium* ions. These each carry a small positive electric charge that is partially balanced by *chloride* ions, which carry a negative charge.

The membrane surrounding each body cell – including nerve cells – contains microscopic pores through which ions can flow in or out of the cell. Some pores contain a pump that actively moves ions across the cell membrane so they become concentrated on one side or the other. One of the most important membrane pumps is the sodium-potassium pump. This forces sodium ions out of cells by swapping them for potassium ions, which therefore become concentrated inside the cells.

The sodium-potassium pump transports three positively-charged sodium ions out of a cell for every two positively-charged potassium ions it carries in. It is therefore an electrogenic (electricity-producing) pump, as it produces a net movement of positive charge out of each cell.

The movement of positively- and negatively-charged ions means that every cell in your baby's body acts like a mini battery to produce a minute electrical charge. The electrical charge across cell membranes, known as the membrane potential, varies from -9 millivolts (mV) to -100 mV in different tissues. It averages around -70 mV in human nerve cells. Interestingly, the active transport of sodium and potassium ions in and out of cells is one of the main energy-using metabolic processes occurring the body. It accounts for 33 per cent of the energy (in the form of glucose) used by body cells, and 70 per cent of the energy used by nerve and brain cells.

CONCENTRATION OF VARIOUS IONS INSIDE AND OUTSIDE A NERVE CELL

ION	Concentration inside cell	Concentration outside cell
Sodium (Na+)	15 mmol/l	150 mmol/l
Potassium (K+)	150 mmol/l	5.5 mmol/l
Chloride (Cl-)	9 mmol/l	125 mmol/l

Resting membrane potential = -70 mV

The movement of electrically-charged ions is the main way in which nerve cells generate electricity. To produce an electrical impulse, a neuron must first be triggered by a *stimulus*. A stimulus is anything inside or outside the cell that produces an electrical response. Stimuli are varied and may be external (such as pressure, sound, light, smell, taste, temperature) or internal (for example changes in hormone or salt levels).

If the stimulus is large enough, it reaches the neuron's threshold level and triggers a sudden opening of the gate-like pores bridging the nerve cell membrane. In the resting state, the inside of the nerve cell is rather like a charged battery and contains a slight negative charge (-70 mV). Activation of the neuron and opening of the flood gates results in a mass flow of electrically-charged ions in opposite directions, so that the inside of the cell becomes positive and the outside of the cell negative. This condition – known as depolarization – only lasts for a short time before the cell returns to its original resting state. This charge is propagated as a wave of electricity called the nerve impulse. The nerve impulse can sweep along the nerve axon at speeds as fast as 100 metres per second. Nerve fibres that are cold (as, for example, happens to the nerve fibres round a bruise when ice is applied to dull the pain), and those that do not have a myelin sheath, conduct impulses more slowly.

The axons of larger nerve cells are coated in a fatty myelin sheath which helps make electrical transmission faster. The myelin sheath consists of a series of special glial (glue) cells that wrap round the axon rather like beads on a string. This lets the electrical impulse 'jump' along the spaces between the glial cells to speed up the rate of transmission.

When the electrical impulse reaches the synaptic cleft, two things can happen. At a biochemical synapse, the impulse does not jump straight across but is converted into a chemical signal. At an electrical junction, the impulse jumps straight over to produce an electric charge in the target cell. The importance of these two types of synapse is explained in the pages that follow.

BIOCHEMICAL SYNAPSES

At a biochemical synapse, the electrical impulse arrives at the synaptic knob and triggers the release of stored packets of chemicals. The mineral calcium is essential for this release. The nerve chemicals diffuse across the synapse until they reach the special receptors on the membrane on the other side of the junction. These receptors are special proteins that straddle the cell membrane of the next neuron. Neurotransmitters stick to their receptor proteins and force them to change shape. This opens up the pores in the membrane of the next neuron so that electrically-charged ions can flood in or out of the cell. If enough stimulation occurs, and enough pores are opened, the next nerve cell in the chain will depolarize and generate an electric current. In this way, the neurotransmitters pass the impulse on. The neurotransmitters released into the synaptic cleft are quickly taken up again and recycled, or broken down, so the synapse is once more 'armed' and ready to spring into action as soon as it receives an appropriate electric signal.

The delay between an electrical impulse arriving at a synaptic knob, and a response being generated in the target cell, is around 0.5 milliseconds – the time it takes for enough chemicals to diffuse across the synaptic cleft and be detected on the other side. This time is known as the synaptic delay. Transmission of a signal through a particular pathway therefore becomes slower as more and more synapses are involved.

The speed of transmission of messages across a synapse seems to be linked with the amount of DHA incorporated into the membrane. DHA is a very fluid fatty acid and may let the protein gates in the synaptic membrane open and close more easily. This may explain why the concentration of DHA and the speed of synaptic transmission seem to be closely linked with intelligence.

ELECTRICAL SYNAPSES

At a few synapses, there is a low-resistance bridge between the two neurons that lets an electric message pass straight across, from one nerve cell to the next, with barely any delay. Some synapses are capable of passing messages across both chemically and electrically, so there is an initial, rapid transmission of a direct electric signal, followed up with a slower, chemical signal. These are known as conjoint synapses.

ONE-WAY CONDUCTION

The vast majority of synapses in the brain are biochemical synapses. Although the biochemical transmission of messages from one neuron to another is slower than pure electrical transmission, it is a vital process in the human brain. Chemical synapses ensure that electrical messages only pass in one direction from one cell to another. This is because neurotransmitters are only stored at one side of the synaptic cleft. An electrical impulse arriving at the opposite side of the synapse just peters out and is not passed on, as there are few – if any – chemicals on that side to be released. This valve-like function is essential, as axons are quite happy to pass electrical impulses in either direction. This would produce information chaos and even short-outs if this were allowed to happen in the brain. The message can only be passed on when the electrical impulse arrives at the synaptic knob, on the side where chemicals are stored.

Information Pathways

There are a hundred billion nerve cells in your baby's brain, each of which diverges to form an average of 1,000 connections with other neurons, and which in turn has between 1,000 and 40,000 other neurons converging on it. The number of possible paths an electrical impulse can take through your baby's brain is astronomically large and measured in trillions of trillions.

Different synaptic knobs on a particular neuron may contain different neurotransmitters. The same electrical impulse travelling down a single axon may therefore trigger the release of two or even three different chemicals to transmit different messages to different target neurons. The same message from the same neuron can therefore have different meanings and trigger different reactions in different parts of your baby's brain.

As each neuron receives lots of different messages from lots of different neurons at any one time, these will interact. For example, messages from one particular neuron may make it less receptive to messages from another neuron (during sleep or extreme relaxation, for example, the brain is less likely to respond to noise). In contrast, some types of messages may make a neuron over-sensitive to signals from other nerve cells (during a state of extreme arousal such as fear, for example). Essentially, messages are of two main types: react or don't react. Each neuron balances these messages and, if enough 'react' messages are received from enough neurons, an electric charge will be generated in the target neuron. This charge will then race down the nerve cell axon to be transmitted across to the next neurons in the information net.

If only a few messages are passed to a particular neuron – not enough to trigger an electric current – it will remain in a partially excited state, ready to fire if enough additional messages are received. If it is not activated frequently enough to pass messages on – that is, if it is in a circuit that does not seem to be needed very much – a neuron may suffer from programmed cell death and die. This is particularly likely to happen during the eighth month of pregnancy – before your baby is born – if the environment is not enriched with stimuli.

Brain Waves

Millions of nerve impulses are passed from neuron to neuron in the brain per second. This produces an electrical field that can be measured by a special brain wave machine (electroencephalograph) to produce a recording known as an electro-encephalogram (EEG).

This shows different wave patterns depending on the activity level of the brain. There are four main patterns of brain wave:

1 Alpha waves – which occur during waking periods when the eyes are closed
2 Beta waves – which occur frequently in infants, but are associated with concentration in adults
3 Theta waves – which occur frequently in children, but in adults are usually associated with meditation and creative thought
4 Delta waves – which occur during deep sleep.

How Your Baby's Brain Grows

During fetal development, your baby's brain produces at least twice as many brain cells as he needs. The excess cells are only loosely wired in with a few dendrites and synaptic connections to other brain cells. If they do not make a certain minimum number of connections with other brain cells, and do not receive enough nourishing nerve growth factor as a result of the synapses that have been made, these dendrites and synaptic connections are programmed to eventually wither and die. At least 40 per cent – and sometimes as many as 75 per cent – of these early brain neurons are lost during prenatal development. This pruning process starts around the seventh month and reaches its peak during the eighth month of pregnancy. By stimulating your baby in the womb, more neural pathways are hard-wired in to expand the range of possibilities for future development. After he is born, the number of synapses in his brain will again explode exponentially to form quadrillions of new synaptic connections. This process will continue up until puberty. Selective pruning will then once again dominate as your child's brain undergoes its last stage of shaping as he matures into adulthood.

Your baby is born with the maximum number of brain cells he will ever own. Yet at birth, his brain only weighs around 350 g.

During the first year of life, his brain will almost treble in weight to up to 1,000 g. By the time he reaches adulthood, his brain will contain hundreds of millions of cells fewer than he has at birth, yet will still weigh an average of 1.5 kg. The number of nerve cells present have halved since birth, yet the brain has quadrupled in weight. How can this be?

As each neuron develops a new connection with another nerve cell, it triggers the appearance of tiny bumps on the cell's surface from which a fine, dendritic extension develops rather like a TV aerial. Dendrites act to increase the volume and surface area of each cell so that it has a larger 'landing site' for connecting up with axonal endings (telodendria) from other nerve cells. The more connections a neuron receives, the more dendrites it grows in response. In other words, the more information the neuron senses is out there, the more antennae it puts out to receive it. The neuron is literally making itself more receptive to information from other parts of the brain. By putting out 'feelers' in this way, each neuron cell body becomes increasingly connected to the neural net, which therefore expands at a rapid – almost exponential – rate. At the same time, the dendrites are putting out more thorny spines which, with increased stimulation, expand from the thin popsickle shape to the thick, mushroom shape as described previously. It is this increasing number of branches and spines that fill most of the grey matter and contribute to the increase in volume and thickness of the brain. In fact, as the cerebral cortex expands in size with continued stimulation and learning experiences, the cell bodies in the cortex are pushed further and further apart by their proliferating dendrites. This widening continues until around age 1 year, then selective pruning starts to remove unwanted and under-used synaptic connections as those in active circuits continue to grow and become stronger. This dismantling of unused circuits doesn't seem to occur to any great extent until puberty, however, but increases in rate from the age of around 10 years.

Another major contributor to brain weight are the glial cells and myelin sheaths. As the brain becomes more active, the glial cells get larger and wrap themselves around the growing neurons to supply them with nourishment. The fatty myelin sheaths surrounding the axons of some brain cells form when glial cells multiply in number and wrap themselves around an axon like concentric bands of insulating tape. By the time of birth, only the nerve cells controlling vital functions such as breathing, heart rate, temperature, reflexes, seeing, hearing and touch have started to myelinate. Nerve cells in the cerebellum are not fully myelinated until the age of 2. As nerve tracts gain their fatty sheaths and electrical transmission becomes faster, so your baby acquires new skills such as reaching for objects, standing, crawling, walking, running and hand skills. The parts of the brain involved in learning (hippocampus, cerebral hemispheres) and the part of the brain involved in controlling the sleep-wake cycle (reticular activating system) will not have matured and myelinated until your child has reached puberty. As a result, the human ability to learn, remember, think, interpret and plan all continue to mature until adulthood.

The tripling in brain weight during the first year of life is a growth rate unique to humans. This is essential to the survival of our species. Your baby has to be born at a stage of development when he is not so helpless he cannot survive, but his brain is still small enough to be delivered through your pelvis. By the time of birth, your baby's head is already around 2 per cent larger than your birth canal, and will only fit through because his skull bones are designed to overlap each other, allowing the shape of the head to mould. If the brain were much larger, enough to support intelligent behaviour, normal delivery would become impossible. It is thought that Neanderthal man became extinct due to his over-large head interfering with childbirth. Cro-Magnon man, on the other hand, with his smaller head, continued to multiply and gave rise to *Homo sapiens* – modern man.

The Synaptic Blueprint

A fascinating question that is attracting a lot of attention is how and why neurons in your baby's developing brain find the right target neurons and make the right synaptic connections. A number of different factors are involved. The most important of these seem to be distinctive chemical attractants, which guide neurons from one part of the brain to the neurons they need to shake hands with in another area. In this way, an axon may glide like a snake past the neurons it is *not* interested in to strike at the target it needs. The axon may make inappropriate connections at times, but somehow these are recognized and disappear. Similarly, a neuron that is only hooked up to a few other neurons, and which does not attract much electrical or chemical traffic, will wither and die away. Eventually, only the correct connections, and those that are needed to deal with the level of stimulation received, will survive through to birth (and even fewer will remain by adulthood). Researchers now partly understand how this wiring pattern is sorted out.

By around the 20th week of gestation in the womb, the axons of most brain cells have arrived at their general destination and started making connections. Neurons fire off spontaneous electrical impulses around once every minute. If enough cells connected to a particular target neuron fire enough impulses (together with their nerve growth factor), the target cell reaches its stimulus threshold and also fires, sending the electrical message forwards. At the same time, however, the target cell releases a flood of proteins known as *trophic factors*. These factors feed back to the neurons which have just stimulated the neuron, but there is an extra, rather clever layer of complexity. Only the neurons that have just fired an impulse at the target cell are receptive to these trophic factors, which encourages them to make additional connections to the same target cell, and to strengthen those that are already present. Cells that are activated together are therefore wired up together, so that related pathways are strengthened together. As a result, other neurons connected to the target cell through different, less active pathways, get crowded out, as do the dud connections leading nowhere. Lack of feedback in the form of trophic chemicals – as well as lack of nerve growth factor from the neurons one connection back – cause unwanted connections to degenerate. This same process continues after birth, but instead of spontaneous electrical activity driving the process forwards, it is the stimuli your baby receives from his enriched environment.

Long-term changes in the shape of the dendritic spines, and the way a synapse fires, result from the pattern of activity the neuron experiences. Conduction of messages at a particular synapse is strengthened or weakened on the basis of past experience. This in turn leads to thickening of the cerebral cortex and seems to represent the basis for learning and memory. By stimulating your baby's brain in the womb, by providing the right nutrients, and by avoiding dietary and lifestyle toxins, you can help to maximize the number of brain cells with which your baby is born. Most importantly, you can help to maximize the number of synaptic connections that are present in your developing baby's cerebral cortex, and strengthen them. These are undeniably the bases for optimum intelligence.

HOW DENDRITES SEEM TO BE LINKED WITH INTELLIGENCE

The fact that dendrites are named after a tree's structure is very apt. An oak, for example, has a thick trunk that divides into two or three major branches, which in turn split into thinner branches before dividing further into yet smaller branches. Eventually, the oak tree grows to produce thousands of small twigs, each of which can be traced back to the main trunk through a complex pathway of branching divisions.

In the same way, a single dendrite on a neuron cell body keeps dividing to form successive levels of branches. As each dendrite grows longer and longer, it is more likely to split or branch. Eventually it will produce six, and sometimes up to seven or eight successive layers of branching points. These branches are an important part of the concept of intelligence. They also help to explain how your child's genes and stimulation from his environment interact to help increase his level of intelligence.

The first, second and third level of branching are known as lower-order branchings. These are thought to be determined by his genes. The fourth, fifth, sixth and sometimes seventh or eighth levels of branching are known as higher order-branchings. Some of the important higher-order branchings are determined by his genes – those that are essential for survival, for example. Others that are involved in intelligence seem to be mainly determined by stimulation and interaction with his environment, especially in the womb and during the first few years of life. (See page 249).

NERVES AND MUSCLES

Many axons from the brain send nerve signals to muscle cells which help to control their movement. As axons from a number of brain cells make their way towards a muscle, they are attracted to each other by a protein secreted by a particular gene. This encourages them to run together to form a bundle of nerve fibres. Once an axon reaches a muscle cell and connects up with it, it spontaneously starts to fire electrical signals. This electrical activity switches off the gene that produces the attractant protein, so the axon's fibres can spread out and connect up with different muscle cells in the same area. This maximizes the number of connections between the axons in a nerve and the muscle cells in a muscle, so a strong muscular contraction occurs when a nerve transmits the right signal. Even more astounding is the finding that blocking this particular gene boosts expression of another, related gene, involved in long-term memory. Once a nerve hooks up with a muscle, the brain starts to memorize how this particular muscle is used so that complex actions like blinking, reaching for a ball, walking, holding a pen – even driving a car or flying a plane – can be performed literally without thinking.

A special synaptic connection forms between the synaptic knob at the end of an axon and a muscle cell. This connection is known as a neuromuscular junction. An electrical impulse arriving at the neuromuscular junction is converted into a chemical signal, as occurs at most synapses between two nerve cells. When the chemical signal diffuses across the neuromuscular synaptic cleft, it triggers contraction of the connecting muscle fibre.

In between muscle contractions, there seems to be some continued, low level of communication between the nerve and muscle cell. If a muscle loses its nerve connections, for example, it starts to shrink and waste away. It is thought that the nerve cell provides a regular infusion of a muscle growth factor that keeps the muscle cell healthy. Interestingly, when a baby experiences a prenatal enrichment programme, his muscle development also seems to benefit. Stimulated babies are born with well-developed, well-defined muscles and are incredibly strong. They develop good head control unusually early and often learn to crawl, walk and run earlier than expected (see Chapter 5). This suggests that prenatal stimulation enhances not just the synaptic connections between brain nerve cells, but also the synaptic connections between nerve and muscle cells. Perhaps increased activity in the motor cortex of the brain, which initiates muscle movement, increases the amount of muscle growth factor the nerve cells feed to the muscle cells they communicate with. Another factor is that your unborn baby sways in time with the rhythm of music and other sounds he hears, which also exercises and strengthens his muscles.

Brain Structure

By the time your baby is born, his brain has a similar construction to your own. His brain is divided into several different departments that each run a different part of the body. There are three main regions: the cerebrum, the cerebellum, and the brain stem.

THE CEREBRUM

The cerebrum is the largest part of his brain and accounts for around 85 per cent of brain volume and weight. The cerebrum is divided into two halves, the right and left cerebral hemispheres. These are arranged in intricate folds (gyri), small grooves (sulci) and deeper grooves (fissures) that increase the total surface area. The outer part of the hemispheres (cortex) contains brain cells arranged into six layers. In adults, the cortex measures from 2 – 6 mm. This is where the brain interprets all the information it receives. Beneath the cortex is a layer made up of the axons travelling down from their neuronal cell bodies in the cortex. When these axons eventually become myelinated, they take on a white appearance and this brain tissue will be referred to as white matter. The neuronal cell bodies, which remain unmyelinated, look grey and are therefore referred to as grey matter. Embedded in the white matter are concentrations of grey neuronal cell bodies referred to as nuclei or ganglia. As mentioned previously, large tracts of nerve axons link the different parts of each hemisphere to each other and to other regions of the brain.

The cerebral cortex is responsible for interpreting sensations, initiating movement and for the processes involved in thinking, speaking, writing, singing, calculating, creating, planning and organizing.

The cerebral hemispheres communicate with each other and the rest of the body through bundles of nerve fibres that cross from one side of the body to the other. The left side of the brain controls the right side of the body and vice versa. Nine out of 10 babies will show a preference for using their right hand for actions involving careful co-ordination. The remaining 10 per cent of babies are either left-handed, or able to use both the left and right hand equally well (ambidextrous). Handedness is controlled by the cerebral cortex. In most right-handed people, the left hemisphere is dominant and controls logic and speech, while the right hemisphere produces imaginative and creative thoughts. In left-handed people, this pattern of function seems to be reversed. Handedness does not seem to have any consistent link with intelligence, although some research suggests that left-handed people have an increased tendency to a certain amount of awkwardness when performing certain tasks.

Each cerebral hemisphere is divided into a number of lobes:

☺ the frontal lobes
☺ the temporal lobes
☺ the parietal lobes
☺ the occipital lobes.

Each lobe is divided into different regions that have their own important functions. Some regions receive information from sense organs and receptors and are involved in interpreting sensations such as those produced by sound and light waves. These are known as *sensory areas*. Other parts of the brain control the

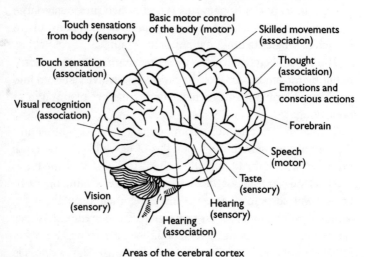

Areas of the cerebral cortex

movement of voluntary muscles such as when walking or running. These are known as *motor areas*.

Sensory Areas

Sensory parts of the cerebrum receive information from the sense organs and other receptors throughout the body. They sort and analyse information in different areas so it can be understood.

Motor Areas

Motor areas control the body's skeletal muscles involved in voluntary movements. The axons from cells in each motor area run together to form a motor nerve, which then crosses the body to control the opposite side. Nerve cells on the left part of the brain therefore control movement in the right-hand side of the body.

Association Areas

Association areas are where the interpretations from the sensory areas are analysed and where instructions from motor areas are fine-tuned. They are involved in thought and comprehension and make us fully conscious and aware. Association areas allow us to analyse experiences and interpret them in a logical and artistic way. In right-handed people, association areas in the left hemisphere are involved in logic and comprehension, while those on the right deal with the perception of shape and feelings.

Thalamus

The thalamus is a small cluster of grey matter deep inside each cerebral hemisphere. It acts as a relay centre that sorts, interprets and directs sensory nerve signals from the sense organs to the sensory areas of the cortex. Surrounding the thalamus is the limbic system.

The Limbic System

In evolutionary terms, the limbic system is one of the oldest parts of the brain. It influences unconscious, instinctive behaviour related to survival as well as mood and emotions. Many of these instincts become modified by learned moral, social and cultural traditions. The limbic system is closely linked to detection of smell, which is why some smells can trigger strong memories and emotions. One part of the limbic system, the hippocampus, is involved with learning, recognition of new experiences, and memory – especially of physical, three-dimensional relationships.

The Hypothalamus

The hypothalamus is situated between the thalamus and pituitary gland. The hypothalamus regulates body temperature, food intake, water and salt balance, blood flow, sleep-wake cycles and the secretion of some hormones. It is also responsible for generating some 'primitive' emotions such as anger and fear.

THE CEREBELLUM

The cerebellum is the second largest part of the brain and is found towards the rear at the base of the brain behind the brainstem and under the occipital lobes of the cerebral hemispheres. It is divided into two, tightly folded halves that are made up of many myelinated nerve fibres. The cerebellum has a distinctive, leaf-like pattern in cross-section which is sometimes described as the tree of life. It is responsible for co-ordinating muscle movements, maintaining balance and for helping some learning processes.

THE BRAIN STEM

The third main part of the brain, the brain stem, connects the brain to the spinal cord. It contains centres that are vital for regulating survival functions such as breathing, heart rate, blood pressure, digestion, posture and reflex actions such as swallowing and vomiting. It contains the reticular activating system that helps to maintain consciousness. It also helps to control movements of the tongue and vocal cords involved in speech. All sensations from your baby's body below his neck will have to pass through his brain stem before being relayed on their journey to higher centres in the brain.

THE MENINGES

The entire brain and spinal cord are protected by three membranes, the meninges (dura mater, arachnoid layer, pia mater) that contain blood vessels and secrete shock-absorbing cerebrospinal fluid.

How Your Baby's Brain Communicates with the Rest of His Body

The brain communicates with the rest of the body through special cranial nerves in the head and through the spinal cord.

CRANIAL NERVES

There are 12 pairs of cranial nerves (numbered I – XII) which carry motor signals to muscles in the head and neck region, and carry sensory information back to the brain. Some cranial nerves are involved in sight, hearing, balance smell or taste sensation. Others control facial expressions. The cranial nerves that leave the head pass into the body through holes in the base of the skull.

Cranial nerve pair	No.	Function
Olfactory Nerves	I	Carry information from smell receptors in the nose to the olfactory centre of the brain

Optic Nerves	II	Carry information from light receptors in the retina of the eye to the visual centres of the brain
Occulomotor Nerves	III	Control some voluntary movements of the eye muscles and eyelids and focus the pupil and lens
Trochlear Nerves	IV	Control some voluntary movements of the eye muscles
Trigeminal Nerves	V	Each trigeminal nerve has three branches, the ophthalmic, maxillary and mandibular, that supply sensation to parts of the face and control chewing muscles
Abducent Nerves	VI	Control some voluntary movements of the eye muscles
Facial Nerves	VII	Carry information from taste buds to the brain, control salivation and tear production, and control muscles used in facial expressions

Vestibulocochlear Nerves	VIII	Carry information about hearing and balance from sense organs in the ear to the brain
Glossopharyngeal Nerves	IX	Control some muscles used in swallowing, and carry some information relating to taste, touch and temperature sensation in the mouth
Vagus Nerves	X	Regulate many automatic functions such as heart rate, breathing and production of stomach acid; also involved in speech; carry some information relating to taste, touch and temperature sensation in the mouth
Spinal Accessory Nerves	XI	Control voluntary muscles that move the head and neck; also involved in speech
Hypoglossal Nerves	XII	Control some muscles used in swallowing

SPINAL CORD

Your baby's brain is connected to the spinal cord by a thick bundle of nerve fibres that emerge through a hole in the base of the skull (*foramen magnum*). Like the brain, the spinal cord is protected by three membranes (meninges) and cerebrospinal fluid and it also has a bony protection in the shape of the spinal vertebrae.

The spinal cord is made up of an internal area of grey matter which contains nerve cell bodies, and an outer coat of white matter containing myelinated axons. In cross-section, the grey matter forms a shape similar to two butterfly wings joined by a narrow bridge. Each wing is made up of three triangular areas known as horns. The rear, or dorsal horn, contains nerve cells that process incoming sensory information from the body. The front, or ventral horn, contains nerve cells that send messages to voluntary muscles and help to control movement. Between these two horns is a small, lateral or side horn, containing cells that send automatic, 'housekeeping' messages to parts of the body outside our voluntary control, such as the glands, blood vessels, and the heart and intestines.

Sensory fibres from the rear of the cord join motor fibres from the front to form 31 pairs of spinal nerves (8 pairs connected at the level of the neck, 12 pairs in the chest, 5 in the lower back, 5 at the sacrum and 1 at the tail bone).

Your baby's brain communicates with the body below his head through nerve fibres that pass through the spinal cord and spinal nerves. A few of the cranial nerves also enter the neck and chest so the brain is in closer contact with vital functions such as the heart rate.

THE PERIPHERAL NERVOUS SYSTEM

The central nervous system (brain and spinal cord) connects with the peripheral nervous system, which forms a network throughout the rest of the body. Fibres from many different nerve cells run together in cables to form nerve trunks which branch into smaller and smaller nerves.

The peripheral nervous system has three main divisions:

1 Autonomic nerves – which carry information from the central nervous system to organs, glands and blood vessels. This controls involuntary actions such as contraction of the intestines, regulation of heartbeat, blood pressure and body temperature,

and secretion of some enzymes and hormones. The autonomic nervous system is further divided into the sympathetic and parasympathetic systems, which produce opposite effects (for example dilation or contraction of a blood vessel). The sympathetic system tends to prepare the body for stress, while the parasympathetic system maintains or restores energy, helping to keep the body in a stable condition.

2 Motor nerves – which send instructions from the central nervous system to skeletal muscles and control voluntary movements.

3 Sensory nervous system – which passes information from the body and sense receptors back to the central nervous system so that the brain can monitor the body's internal and external environment.

How Your Baby Learns to See

The outer part of your baby's cerebral cortex is thrown into wrinkles so it resembles the kernal of a giant walnut. The cell bodies of the neurons of the cortex are arranged into six layers which run parallel to the surface of the brain, following the up and down contours. In the part of the brain involved in sight – the visual cortex – there are also columns of cells running perpendicular to these layers, like chimney stacks, each of which receives information from either the right or left eye.

The back of the eye contains two sorts of light-sensitive cell:

1 rods – which detect dim light, but only register in black or white

2 cones – which detect coloured light and give colour vision in bright light.

Your baby is born with around 6 million cones and 120 million rods in each eye, each of which contains light-sensitive pigments.

When light stimulates these cells, they send signals to the cortex which are interpreted as either dim light, or bright, coloured light. This is thought to occur in the fourth layer of the visual cortex. The light messages are then transmitted upwards to the fifth and sixth layers of the cortex. Here, the patterns of light signals are interpreted according to the pattern in which they stimulated the rods and cones. Put simply, light reflecting from a series of black-and-white stripes will land on the back of the eye and stimulate a pattern of rods and cones that represents a series of black-and-white stripes. The messages from these specific cells arrive at the outer layers of the visual cortex and in turn switch on neurons that are programmed to respond only to stripes. Yet other neurons will only respond to signals representing specific angles – such as 45 degrees, 60 degrees, 90 degrees, or to specific shapes such as circles, squares or triangles. Others will only respond to straight lines, curves or zig-zags. An extra layer of complexity is added by the fact that information from both eyes is compared and interpreted by another part of the brain to generate a three-dimensional image of what your baby has seen. These neurons mature at different rates, so that during the first year of life your baby starts off seeing simple black-and-white shapes before recognizing more complex patterns and colours (see Chapter 12 on how to stimulate your newborn baby during play).

How Your Baby Learns to Hear

The senses of hearing and balance both involve the inner ears, and rely on stimulation of special receptors called hair cells. Sound is created by waves of pressure causing the air to vibrate. These sound waves are caught by the outer ear and funnelled in through the ear canal to the ear drum (tympanic membrane), which starts to vibrate in sympathy. These vibrations trigger a chain of movement through three tiny, hinged bones in the middle ear, which amplify the sound and channel it to the inner ear.

The inner ear (labyrinth) is made up of the cochlea – a snail-like structure that detects sound – and three fluid-filled semicircular canals that detect movement. In the cochlea, different tones stimulate different sound receptor cells. These send messages to the part of the brain concerned with detecting sound – the auditory cortex. Here, it seems that individual neurons are stimulated by different types of sound: soft whispers, loud bangs, high pitches, low pitches, long notes, short notes, individual musical tones or repetitive clicks, for example. The pattern in which the neurons are stimulated is then interpreted by a different part of the brain so they are perceived as voices, music and other sounds. Your baby can learn to distinguish over 1,500 musical tones, and hear sounds ranging from 10 – 140 decibels (dB) in loudness.

Taste

Your taste buds are located on small bumps on the surface of your tongue. These have a central pore filled with saliva into which tiny sensory hairs dip to detect dissolved chemicals. Different regions of your tongue are sensitive to each of the four different tastes: sweet (tip of the tongue), bitter (back), sour (edges of tongue at the back) and salty (sides of tongue at the front). All tastes are made up of a combination of these four basic flavours plus stimulation of pain receptors (such as chilli peppers) and overall sensations produced by consistency, texture and temperature and the smell of the food.

Your sense of taste was most developed at birth as you had taste buds all over the inside of your mouth and cheeks as well as on the tongue. With increasing age, taste sensation deteriorates as your number of taste buds falls. This explains why older people cannot sometimes tell if a food has been salted enough, and prefer stronger tastes such as crystallized ginger.

Touch

Your skin contains a number of nerve endings that can detect light touch, sustained pressure, cold, warmth or pain. Some sense receptors are bare nerve endings, while others have a complicated structure. The healing power of touch has been used for thousands of years in therapies such as massage or laying on of hands.

Smell

Every day, you breathe over 23,000 times, bringing up to 10,000 different aromas towards the smell receptors at the top of your nose. Tiny hair-like nerve endings detect dissolved aromatic substances. Sniffing helps to draw airborne particles up towards the receptors to detect faint smells.

The part of your brain involved in smell perception is close to the area dealing with memory and emotions. Smell, therefore, evokes powerful emotional responses. Your sense of smell was strongest at birth – a three-day-old baby can even recognize the smell of his own mother's milk. By the age of 20, your sense of smell is only 82 per cent as good as when you were born. By the age of 60, it has fallen to 38 per cent and by 80, it is only 28 per cent as sensitive as at birth. Sense of smell is more acute in women than men – and is strongest around the time of ovulation.

- The sense of smell can detect an average of 4,000 different odours – some people can detect 10,000 different smells.
- The human nose is more sensitive than laboratory equipment (such as gas-liquid chromatography and mass spectrometry) designed to analyse odours.
- The brain quickly becomes used to smells and stops detecting them (that is, the smell no longer triggers a conscious response).
- Not being able to smell is called *anosmia*.

3

What Your Baby Can Sense in the Womb

Until recently, the awareness and learning potential of a baby in the womb was underestimated and largely ignored in the Western world. Eastern philosophies were rather more advanced, giving a newborn baby an age of one, rather than nought, to acknowledge that birth is just a milestone on the continuum of human development.

The human brain defines us as individuals more than in any other species. It is such a highly complex organ that it needs a long period of development and maturation both in the womb and during childhood before it reaches its full potential.

While developing in the womb, your baby soon possesses every sense an adult has, although these are immature. The newborn baby is capable of seeing, hearing, smelling, tasting and feeling gentle touch, pressure and pain, and is capable of quite complex patterns of behaviour. It is illogical to assume these abilities are suddenly triggered at birth and were absent while the fetus was immersed in the womb. Research has now confirmed that your baby starts to move, feel, smell, taste and sense touch and pain before birth. With these senses, your baby learns to relate to his environment and starts to enjoy his surroundings as his consciousness forms. He senses and can respond to a variety of stimuli. It is only recently that Western researchers have accepted that unborn babies can feel pain, however.

What your baby can hear, see and feel at different stages of development in the womb has fascinated many researchers. His mind starts life as a blank canvas on which all learned experiences in the womb will have a lasting effect. His brain slowly becomes alert and he acquires the capacity to learn. It is now clear that the quality and quantity of stimulation your baby receives in the womb has an enormous, long-lasting effect on his future potential – physical, intellectual and emotional.

Your baby's sense receptors which detect light, sound, taste, smell, temperature and pressure are all modified nerve cells that have grown out from his nervous system.

Awareness

Exactly when your baby becomes aware of his surroundings is unknown. The first synapses – connections between brain cells – form during the 10th week after conception (12th week of pregnancy), but awareness probably does not start until around the 20th week of development. It may occur earlier, however.

Night and Day

Your baby is aware of light and dark and the changing patterns of day and night. Studies show that your baby's heart rate varies in a predictable way over a 24-hour period. His heart rate and blood pressure are lowest around 4 in the morning – just like yours – and rise again just before waking to reach a natural peak mid-morning. During the last 3 months of pregnancy, your baby regularly exercises the muscles he will need after birth – including those involved in breathing. He spends around half his time breathing, and for some reason, these episodes of breathing are most usual during the early morning hours, 1 – 7 a.m. These breathing movements are thought to be important for stimulating and laying down the correct pathways for breathing in the respiratory centres of the brainstem. This learning process is vital to ensure the breathing mechanism is mature, and in place, immediately after birth.

His biorhythms can be affected by jet lag when travelling across time zones, and when clocks leap forward in spring or fall back in autumn. Some of these patterns depend on your own hormone levels and how they affect him, but some depend on his own developing hormone system as well.

Sound

The way your baby's brain responds to sound and the way his auditory pathways are laid down evolves throughout fetal life. There is no doubt that the sounds heard in the womb are essential to help your baby's auditory cortex develop and mature.

His ears are fully formed by around the 20th week of development and your baby's brain will start to show electrical responses to sounds heard outside the womb before 24 weeks of development. The ear is fully functional and can start to pick up sound as noise at around 30 weeks after conception. Before this, however, he can still hear, but is thought to detect sounds as vibrations rather than noise. Studies show, for example, that babies born very prematurely, before 30 weeks gestation, react differently to rhythmical sounds than those born at full term. Full-term babies quickly become calm on hearing a metronome beat 144 times per minute, while preterm babies do not. This suggests that a baby may be aware of his own heart rate (around 140 beats per minute), as a metronome beating at 72 beats per minute (the average maternal heart rate) seems to be less calming.

When he develops awareness of sound, your baby hears a veritable symphony from your own body – the non-stop lub-dub of your heartbeat, the hum of blood circulating in your veins, the whoosh, whoosh whoosh of blood pumping through your arteries and placenta, the gurglings from your intestines as you digest your food, and the soft, background, sea-like noises of air flowing in and out of your lungs.

As far back as 1960, it was first suggested that your baby becomes strongly attached to, or *imprints* on these sounds, especially that of your heartbeat. Tapes have since become available of heartbeat sounds and 'womb music' to help calm a crying baby after birth. The imprinting theory is now unfashionable, however.

As well as your own special sounds, your baby is very aware of the noises occurring in your environment. These filter through to him, muffled by your abdominal wall, womb muscle and the fluid surrounding him. Deep, low-frequency sounds reach him better than high-pitched ones – he can therefore detect male voices better than female ones. He also learns to recognize the individual patterns of speech that different people use. As the male voice he is likely to hear most often is usually that of his father, your baby will recognize his daddy's voice as soon as he is born. It is rather worrying to think that if you continue working up until term however, your baby may be more familiar with the voice of your male boss!

He will still recognize your voice better than that of anyone else, however. This is partly because he hears your voice most, as he is always with you, but mostly because your body tissues are such a good conductor of vibration and sound. When you hear your own voice on a tape-recording, it sounds totally different to how you usually hear yourself speak. This is because you are used to hearing your voice modified by sound waves passing through your tissues to your middle and inner ears. In the same way, your baby hears your voice when you speak, conducted to him both through your body tissues and through the air surrounding you. Your voice will be one of the first things your baby is aware of when he comes out of the twilight world of the preconsciousness to reach awareness. Your baby will therefore find your voice one of the most soothing and comforting sounds as he senses you all around him. His heart rate will often slow in the womb when you start to speak. This effect also continues after birth. Studies involving newborn babies under 24 hours old showed they could recognize their own mother's voice, and that their heart rate slowed on hearing it. Other voices made their heart rate go up.

If your baby hears a particular sound again and again while he is in the womb, he will eventually ignore it. When a baby is observed during ultrasound examination, he can be seen to move in response to the first time he hears a sound. If the sound is repeated regularly every 30 seconds, however, he stops moving in response after he has heard the sound four or five times. This is known as sound adaptation. In one study, babies of mothers who had diabetes, but had excellent control of their sugar levels, were tested at 28, 32 and 36 weeks gestation. When exposed to sounds and observed on ultrasound scans, their babies seemed to take longer to adapt to a repeated stimulus than babies of mothers who did not have diabetes. Blood glucose monitoring suggested there was a link between fluctuating levels of glucose and the length of time it took for a baby to adjust to a stimulus. It may be that maternal diabetes and fluctuating glucose levels impair nerve function, which adds another reason to the many why mothers with gestational diabetes should maintain tight control of their sugar levels throughout pregnancy.

One of the most fascinating findings is that your baby learns to recognize stories and music he hears in the womb. Researchers have found your baby's heart rate will slow when he hears a story that has been read to him regularly, twice a day, during the last few weeks of development. If you have read the story to him, then when the same story is read by a strange woman whose voice he has not heard before, his heart rate will still slow in response. If the new woman reads a different, unfamiliar story, however, his heart rate remains unchanged or goes up. This suggests that your baby can recognize the sounds and rhythms associated with a particular story he has heard many times before. It shows he is capable of both listening and learning in the womb.

Babies whose mothers played classical music to them (from 20 weeks development) for 10 minutes, twice a day, were compared with babies who did not hear classical music in the womb. Babies who were musically stimulated seemed to develop more quickly, started talking up to 6 months earlier, and had improved intellectual development. Most significantly of all, they were able to memorize musical phrases with little effort and sing them back note-perfect before the age of 2 years. Many also enjoyed making up songs on the piano and went on to become accomplished musicians. The object of playing music to your baby in the womb is not to create a musical genius, however. The aim of prenatal musical stimulation is to help your baby reach his fullest potential by boosting the number of brain cells and brain cell connections he is born with. This will give him the best possible start in life, and the best chance of developing a whole range of skills, of which an enjoyment of music is but one part.

One consequence of allowing your baby to become used to a familiar tune is that it will help to soothe him. After he is born, crooning the same song will often act as a trigger, helping him settle and sleep. Perception of sound continues to develop and mature, right up until birth, and continues to develop during the first 4 years of life.

Sight

By the 10th week of development, your baby has a well-formed eye, but the connections to the brain and the formation of the visual cortex are not yet present. He therefore cannot see at this stage. Once light starts to stimulate the receptors in the back of the eye and send messages to the brain, these will modify the way his visual cortex is laid down. This process starts in the womb.

Your baby sees everything inside your womb in shades of black, grey and white. This is partly because light is dim, so it is mainly the rod cells in his eyes that are working, and partly because the colour vision of his cones is not thought to develop until at least 2 months after birth. He can recognize the difference between light and dark, day and night, and can see the outline of his hands, knees and umbilical cord when they pass in front of his eyes.

If a torch is held against the mother's abdomen during ultrasound examination and flashed on, the baby will be seen to turn his head towards the light. If the flash is repeated every 30 seconds he will ignore it after he has seen it four or five times, however. This is known as light adaptation.

Touch

During the first half of pregnancy, your baby has plenty of space inside the womb. As your body moves, he will sway within the fluid. Around this time, the amount of amniotic fluid present is no longer enough to allow him to float fully in his allotted room. Some parts of your baby will press against some part of your womb, so he becomes aware of a gentle pressure around him. Soon, he will start to kick out or touch the parts of you he senses around him.

Throughout pregnancy, especially in the last 3 months, your womb contracts regularly for several minutes at a time. These tightenings – known as Braxton Hicks contractions – squeeze your baby and are thought to be an important stimulus for his developing senses and brain, as well as helping to tone your uterine muscle in preparation for labour. When your uterus contracts, it acts as a trigger for the baby to stop breathing – because momentarily, blood flow to the placenta will be reduced and oxygen levels will fall slightly. At the same time, the contraction changes the brain wave pattern your baby is producing so, for example, if he is in REM sleep (see below), it seems to wake him up or stimulate him to enter slow-wave sleep.

When you stroke or pat your abdomen, he will sense the stimulus and may quiet down and become alert. He may respond by kicking or reaching out to where he senses the change in pressure, and if you touch him when he kicks, he may kick again in response. Some babies will seem to play a game and follow you in a circle around your tummy, kicking or patting as you move your hand from quadrant to quadrant.

It seems that your baby may be able recognize who is touching him through your abdomen by the pattern of pressure and movements he feels. When a baby is observed during an ultrasound examination, he seems to recognize his father's touch and will move towards it. When an obstetrician places his or her hands on the same areas, with the same pressure, the baby suddenly stops responding as if he realizes he is in communication with a stranger.

Your baby also starts to become aware of himself, and will suck his thumb – perhaps enjoying the sensation and comfort this creates. He will also play with his fingers, touch the top of his head and grip the umbilical cord as it sways in the water around him.

Temperature

Your baby is aware of the warmth inside your womb. Even though he does not experience cold before birth, his body is still programmed to respond to this potentially life-threatening situation after birth and he will shiver, develop goose pimples and scream.

Taste

Your baby is floating in warm amniotic fluid, which he drinks regularly. Its flavour will vary according to your diet – garlic, in particular, and aromatic curry spices, can be detected. The processes that flavour your amniotic fluid with dietary factors are similar to those that flavour your breastmilk and the secretions of oil glands around your nipple. It is thought that by tasting your amniotic fluid, your baby will recognize the taste of your milk – assuming your diet does not change drastically between the time of birth and your milk letting down. Some researchers have noted, for example, that Indian women used to eating highly spiced foods may have difficulty initiating breastfeeding if they remain in hospital and eat a very different diet than they are used to.

SMELL

The parts of your baby's brain involved in detection of smell are among the most primitive in an evolutionary sense. At birth, your baby must be able to recognize the taste and smell of breastmilk, and to know it is a life-giving essential food, even though he has not tasted or smelled it in the womb. This recognition is deeply ingrained and based on pheromones – chemical attractants – secreted by the modified sweat glands (Montgomery's tubercles) that swell and become more prominent around the nipple during pregnancy. Taste and smell are closely linked, and it is known that garlic in the amniotic fluid and in your baby's bloodstream can stimulate both the taste and smell receptor areas in the brain.

Sleep and Wakefulness

After around 32 weeks of development in the womb, your baby has developed four activity patterns: active sleep, quiet sleep, active awareness and quiet awareness. The brain wave patterns show that active sleep is similar to rapid eye movement or REM sleep, in which the eyes are constantly on the move and the brain is extremely active. Quiet sleep is equivalent to slow-wave (or non-REM) sleep, in which the eyes are relatively still.

Up until around 32 weeks of development, your baby spends a lot of time in a state resembling REM or active sleep. After 32 weeks, he starts to spend more time in the awareness states, until by the time he is born, he is awake for around 8 hours out of every 24.

Interestingly, REM sleep is when children and adults dream. Does this mean your baby is dreaming too? No one really knows.

Awareness of Your Activities

When you make love, your baby is probably aware as well. When you are aroused, your pulse and blood pressure go up, and your baby will be aware of these changes. During orgasm your womb may contract, and he will sense this – as well as your complete relaxation and calm afterwards.

The Importance of Stimulating the Senses in the Womb

As already discussed, during fetal development your baby's brain produces at least twice as many brain cells as he needs. The excess cells are only loosely wired in. If they do not make a certain minimum number of connections with other brain cells, they will eventually wither and die just before your baby is born. At least 40 per cent – and sometimes as many as 75 per cent – of brain neurons are lost during prenatal development, most during the eighth month of pregnancy.

You can help to minimize this loss by:

- providing a stimulating womb environment for your baby
- eating a healthy diet providing adequate levels of vitamins, minerals and essential fatty acids
- having regular rest periods to improve the circulation of oxygenated blood to your baby
- avoiding excess exposure to toxins, including alcohol, cigarettes and environmental pollutants.

4
What Is Intelligence?

The brain, rather than the heart, is where your baby will learn to feel emotions such as love, anger and fear. It is also where he will start to think, decide, initiate and control his actions. Billions of nerve impulses – both chemical and electrical signals – will flash through his brain per second. His brain has to learn to apply some semblance of order to them. The brain is often compared to a computer, but it is much more powerful than that. While it can channel information to the right biological 'filing cabinet' for interpretation, storage and retrieval, the brain is also capable of creativity and original thought – something no man-made computer has yet achieved. Combined together, all the abilities your baby's brain possess will help to determine his intelligence.

There is much argument over the exact definition of intelligence. Most researchers agree it represents a potential rather then a fully-developed ability, and that, as well as being shaped by an inherited, genetic component, it is shaped by experience and learning. Interestingly, over the last 30 years the average IQ score of 5-year-old children in the UK seems to have increased by as much as 8 points. In the US, studies since 1932 suggest that the average IQ of preschool children has increased by around 3.5 points per decade.

Brain Structure and Intelligence

As discussed in Chapter 2, the dendrites arising from your baby's brain cells resemble the forking branches of trees. An oak, for example, has a thick trunk that divides into two or three major branches, which in turn split into thinner branches before dividing further into yet smaller branches. Eventually, the oak tree grows to produce thousands of small twigs each of which can be traced back to the main trunk through a complex pathway of branching divisions. In the same way, a single dendrite on a neuron cell body keeps dividing to form successive levels of branches. As each dendrite grows longer and longer, it is more likely to split or branch. Eventually it will produce six, and sometimes up to seven or eight successive layers of branching points. These branches are an important part of the concept of intelligence. They also help to explain how your child's genes and stimulation from his environment may interact to help increase his level of intelligence.

The lower-order branchings (first, second and third level) are thought to be determined by your genes.

Some of the important higher-order branchings (fourth, fifth, sixth and sometimes seventh or eighth levels) – those that are essential for survival, for example – are also determined by the genes, while those that are involved in intelligence seem partly to be determined by stimulation and interaction with the environment, especially in the womb and during the first few years of life.

On another level, the number of brain cells your baby is born with increases his potential intelligence, as he literally has more counters to play with. By providing prenatal stimulation and supplying optimum amounts of vitamins, minerals and polyunsaturated essential fatty acids (especially DHA) to your baby in the womb, you are:

🐸increasing the number of brain cells he is born with
🐸increasing the number and size of the connections (synapses) between his brain cells
🐸speeding transmission of information across synapses from one brain cell to another.

An enriched environment that continues throughout childhood will ensure more and more synaptic connections are laid down in more and more pathways. At the same time, the progressive branchings of the dendrite trees increases the 'reach' of each cell and its potential for more and more connections with more and more cells that are further afield. This underlying brain architecture and the connections between his brain cells are thought to be biological building-blocks of intelligence which allow learning to occur.

Stimulation and an enriched environment can undoubtedly boost your child's intelligence. Einstein left his brain to science, and was found to have a greater density of neurons and synapses in a part of the brain called the prefrontal cortex.

What Is Intelligence?

Intelligence is an abstract potential made up of the capacity to learn and adapt. Its physical basis depends on the number, arrangement and interconnections of the brain cells your baby is born with, while its development depends on the experiences and sensations that help him learn. Some scientists believe intelligence is made up of three factors:

1 speed of thought
2 ability to learn
3 ability to solve problems.

By this simplistic definition, the home computer on your desk is also an intelligent member of your household!

Others argue that intelligence consists of seven specific skills:

1 understanding the meaning of words
2 fluency with words
3 working with numbers
4 visualizing things in space
5 memory
6 speed of perception
7 reasoning ability.

Assuming it is programmed with the right software, your home computer can probably do all of these things, too.

Perhaps coming closer is the identification of the following seven intelligences:

1 linguistic
2 mathematical-logical
3 musical
4 visual-spatial
5 physical
6 social
7 introspective.

The last two intelligences on this list are starting to sound a bit less like your home computer and a bit more like a human being.

What are the special qualities that will allow your developing super baby to become intelligent? To try to explain this, other researchers have further divided intelligence into 120 specific abilities in an attempt to get the definition right.

These abilities are divided into three groups: logical processes, the kinds of information processed, and the results of these processings. This led to increased research exploring the relationships between creative and analytical thought.

There is no doubt that environment has a major influence on the way intelligence develops. Similar babies will develop different abilities depending on their level of nutrition, education, interaction between family members and the expectations placed on them. In the outbacks of Brazil, for example, I came across a 5-year-old child who was severely stunted in size and development as a result of being left alone in her cot all day and night while her parents went out to work. The impoverished child could not walk or talk and her mental development was severely compromised due to lack of environmental stimulation. Given a different start in life, her level of intelligence would have been vastly greater.

INTELLIGENCE TESTS

The widespread use of intelligence tests has unfortunately led to the idea that intelligence is a single, measurable quality. At present, however, there is no known method for assessing absolute inborn intelligence. One day we may have a simple scan test that can link the volume and number of brain cells your baby is born with, the density of his synaptic connections, their speed of transmission plus the complexity of his dendritic branchings to come up with an accurate assessment of his future intellectual potential.

Current intelligence tests are designed to provide an estimate of a person's mental abilities by assessing his or her skills in a number of different areas such as mathematical ability, logical reasoning, vocabulary, general knowledge, comprehension, perceptual ability, pattern recognition and the understanding of relationships between different concepts or objects.

Intelligence tests have caused a lot of controversy about what kinds of mental abilities constitute intelligence, and whether the intelligence quotient (IQ) gives a true representation of these abilities. Traditional intelligence tests do favour the affluent from certain cultural backgrounds, and discriminate against less privileged racial, ethnic and social groups. Non-cultural tests have therefore been devised to measure the intelligence of preschool children more fairly.

Intelligence Quotient (IQ)

The intelligence quotient (IQ) is based on an average score of 100. Intelligence tests were originally scored on the basis of mental age in relation to chronological age, as intelligence increases with maturity. IQ was therefore obtained by dividing mental age (say for example 12) by the chronological age (say 10) and multiplying by 100 to obtain the result (120).

The concept of mental age is rarely used now, however, and IQ is based on statistics. Tests are designed so that three-quarters of results fall within the range of 80 and 120. An IQ of less than 65 indicates that a person is in the bottom 1 per cent for his or her age group. An IQ above 135 indicates an IQ in the top 1 per cent for a person's age group. Exceptionally gifted children will have an IQ above 140.

Most psychologists now believe that IQ represents only part of intelligence and that intelligence is but one factor in overall mental prowess. Nevertheless, tests to assess intelligence and IQ are widely available and used. They give a useful, ballpark assessment of ability and are the best estimates we have at present.

Intelligence is not a static factor, however. It is a fluid, malleable entity that can be shaped according to the information and stimulation an individual receives. This is similar in concept to a brand new home computer that proudly boasts a 1-gigabyte hard disc and 64 kilobytes of RAM (random access memory). It can't do anything with them unless you give it information by downloading software and programming information in the form of data. Your baby's brain is born with many software programmes in place (his instincts, reflex behaviours and biological control mechanisms). What he now needs is environmental data or stimuli.

Heredity and Intelligence

The relative importance of heredity versus environment in producing optimum intelligence is hotly debated. There is no doubt that some aspects of intelligence are inherited – perhaps due to the convolutions and degree of folding of the cortex, levels of branchings of particular dendritic trees, or the speed and nature of chemical reactions occurring at particular synapses.

Some recent evidence suggests that the inherited component of intelligence is largely linked with the speed of transmission of signals from one brain cell to another across the synaptic cleft. The home environment and level of stimulation a baby receives also play a vital role, however.

Memory

Some intelligence tests merely assess the ability to recall stored memories. While a good memory is usually part of a high IQ, this is not necessarily so – some people can recall amazing lists of facts due to a so-called photographic memory. They may not be able to use the recalled facts in an intelligent way, however.

Memories are the brain's storehouse of information. There are three main types of memory:

1 Sensory memory – which briefly stores facts and experiences for a split second
2 Short-term memory – which stores facts for around 5 minutes
3 Long-term memory – which can store facts for as long as your baby's lifetime.

Sensory memories can be retained and registered as short-term memories. Without repetition, short-term memory only lasts for around 30 seconds. If the information is important enough, a short-term memory can be converted into a long-term one by studying and repeating it. If the memory can be linked with another remembered fact, a visual image or even a smell, these triggers will make it easier to store and retrieve it.

The ease with which long-term memories can be recalled at a later date depends on how well they were encoded. If a memory is poorly stored it may remain elusive and frustratingly 'on the tip of your tongue'.

Long-term memory can be divided into:

☺Habit memory, for example learned skills such as holding a feeding bottle by the handles, placing a spoon in the mouth and riding a pedal bike

☺Recognition memory, for example storage of general knowledge (names of objects, shapes and colours, for example) and personal experiences (such as 'garlic tastes nice', 'radiators are hot').

These two forms of long-term memory are thought to be processed in different parts of the brain.

HOW MEMORY IS STORED
Researchers are still unsure exactly how memories are stored in your baby's brain. Most believe that new connections (synapses) are laid down between brain neurons, and that new protein molecules are made which store some information. It is possible

that spare genetic material – DNA not being used to hold the genetic code – is involved, or that electrical circuits play a part.

Different types of memory are stored in different parts of the brain. How to write or ride a bicycle is stored in areas involved in muscle actions, for example, while memories of music are stored in parts of the brain involved in hearing. One part of the brain in particular – the hippocampus – seems to be important in processing and storing long-term information.

Continued mental activity seems to be important to maintain intelligence. New research suggests that dementia and Alzheimer's disease are three times more common after the age of 55 in people who have not studied for a higher academic qualification. The old adage 'use it or lose it' could apply to your brain, too. Previous studies suggest that IQ peaks at the age of 26, then remains constant until at least the age of 40. Reasoning powers can continue to improve with experience, but number-crunching potential falls off with lack of practice. People in an intellectually demanding job seem to have a later drop in IQ than those in a job involving little brain power.

5

How to Stimulate Your Baby in the Womb

A prenatal stimulation programme has many advocates – and a decreasing number of detractors. It is important to state straight away that the aim of prenatal enrichment is not to breed a race of super-beings. The aim is to allow your baby to achieve his full genetic and intellectual potential by giving him the best possible start in life, the best possible environment for his brain to develop, and to increase his chance of acquiring several desirable character traits.

Taking part in a prenatal enrichment programme has many beneficial spin-offs:

- by interacting with your baby several times a day, it helps form a special bond that will bring you closer to your child once he is born
- by following a careful diet enriched with vital nutrients needed for brain growth you will be improving the health of both yourself and your baby
- by understanding the importance of giving your baby the best possible start in life you are more likely to succeed in breast-feeding for at least the first 4 to 6 vital months
- by stimulating your baby's brain in the womb, you are helping to increase the neural pathways linking each brain cell into his neural net
- by stimulating your baby's brain in the womb, you boost the number of brain cells your baby is born with, and the number of connections they make with neighbouring cells
- the dietary changes you make may reduce his risk of dyslexia, attention deficit hyperactivity disorder, schizophrenia and some forms of epilepsy
- you are likely to boost his intelligence.

These different factors will help your baby function at his highest possible level.

By boosting your child's brain development in the womb, he will be on the road to achieving his full potential. He will be sensitive, good-natured, content, compassionate, alert, and as bright as his genes and environment allow. A programme of proper nutrition, DHA enrichment, vitamins and minerals, pre-natal stimulation and the benefits of breastfeeding is surely worth undertaking for any child.

Stimulation and Your Baby's Brain

Your baby's brain is literally shaped by the stimuli and nutrients received from his environment. While this process starts at conception, many parents only start their child's learning programme from the time he is born. It is now widely felt that it is more beneficial to begin one stage earlier – while your baby's brain is still developing in the womb. By enriching his prenatal environment with additional stimuli, you can encourage the growth and development of his brain cells (neurons) so they develop more complex 'communication antennae' (dendron trees), more 'satellite dishes' (dendritic spines) and stronger synaptic connections.

Researchers now know that regular stimulation of a particular neural pathway triggers the release of neurotransmitters and special nerve growth factors that pass messages from one brain cell to another. This process helps to 'hard wire' increased numbers of brain cells into your baby's neural net. His enriched environment means he will develop a thickened cerebral cortex and fewer brain cells will be lost as a result of programmed cell death in the few weeks before he is born.

Unstimulated Brain

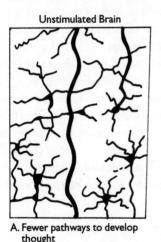

Stimulated Brain

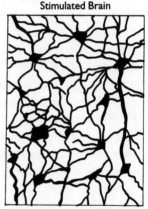

A. Fewer pathways to develop thought

A. Unstimulated brain.

B. A rich network of pathways to facilitate learning

B. Stimulated brain.

By communicating with your baby in the womb through talking, touching, playing music or singing to him, you will increase his awareness and level of perception. This process is fun and will help you and your family bond closely with the baby you will soon welcome into your home.

Every mother enjoys some form of communication with her baby before birth. A prelearning programme will help fathers and siblings establish an affectionate relationship with their baby, too. Prenatal communication also helps change your expectations and the way you relate to your baby once he is born. You will probably feel closer to him, and find there is a closer, more empathic link between you. While you can buy devices to help you stimulate your baby in the womb, it is possible to do something similar with no more equipment than is found in the average home.

HOW DO WE KNOW THE FETUS CAN LEARN IN THE WOMB?

The process of learning can be said to have occurred when your baby is exposed to a particular stimulus in the womb and his behaviour changes, or adapts, so it is different to that of a baby who was not exposed to the same stimulus.

A number of observations have shown that babies can learn to recognize sounds they hear in the womb. As mentioned in Chapter 3, research shows that your baby's brain will show electrical responses to sounds heard outside the womb by around 20 – 24 weeks of development. Before this time, he can still detect sounds but probably hears them as 'vibrations' before his ears and brain are fully connected. Other research suggests your baby can start to learn from as early as 15 weeks after conception.

Voices

Your baby hears your own voice through both the airwaves around him, and as sound vibrations carried through the tissues of your body. He learns to recognize the tone, pitch and speech patterns that are unique to you, and will instantly identify your voice after birth. Recordings made inside the womb show that your voice is heard very distinctly and is only slightly muffled. This probably plays an important part in allowing your baby to become 'imprinted' on you before birth. This helps him recognize you after he is born and helps him bond with you.

Deep male voices pass through your abdominal wall to reach him more easily than the sound of female voices, and he will learn to recognize those male voices he hears most frequently. He will still prefer the sound of his mother, however, whose presence surrounds him for every moment of life before birth. If a newborn baby hears his mother whisper in one ear, and his father whisper in the other, he will usually turn towards his mother's voice – he recognizes your pattern of speech even though whispering removes the tones and pitch. Similarly, if he hears his father whisper in one ear, and an unknown male whisper in the other, he will turn towards his father 4 times out of 5.

Researchers have invented a device that allows newborn babies to choose which sounds they hear through a set of headphones depending on whether they suck a teat quickly or slowly. They found that newborn babies will suck faster in order to hear their own mother's voice in preference to that of a stranger. They prefer hearing their mother's voice muffled, as it would have sounded in the womb, and to hear their mother speak in her native tongue rather than a foreign language in which her speech patterns and sounds are entirely different. In the same way, researchers found that newborn babies prefer to hear their mother's heartbeat – which they have learned to recognize in the womb – rather than their father's voice. These effects can be shown immediately after birth, before the baby has even heard any voices outside the womb.

Similarly, when newborn babies using the equipment described above were given the option of hearing a story their mother had read them while in the womb (twice a day from 34 weeks pregnancy), or a different story, they invariably indicated (by sucking faster on the teat) that they wanted to hear the story they knew rather than a new one. This is not very different from older children, who usually prefer a favourite, familiar bedtime story to one they have not heard before.

Music

A professor of psychology took note when a new mother said her baby seemed to respond to the catchy theme tune of a popular soap opera which she had watched regularly throughout her pregnancy. He assessed the babies of a group of new mothers who had also watched the programme during their pregnancy and compared them with a group of mothers who had not watched the programme. Two to four days after birth, he played the theme tune to all the babies and noticed their behaviour. Those who had heard the tune during life in the womb responded by stopping moving, their heart rate slowed and they became quiet and alert. Those who had not heard the tune previously showed no change in their behaviour when the music was played. Clearly the babies who had heard the tune prenatally had learned to recognize it.

Babies can learn to recognize several different pieces of music that are played to them regularly prenatally. They will also show a preference for one tune over another, just as adults do in later life.

This recognition is present even at 37 weeks gestation, as ultrasound studies show that the baby of a mother who watches a TV programme regularly will respond to its theme tune by increasing his movements when it is played. New research suggests your baby can start to learn and respond to sounds as early as 22 weeks – almost exactly as soon as his ears and brain have become properly wired up. New ways of visualizing the baby in the womb – 3D ultrasound for example – may show that the fetus is capable of learning and changing his responses to various stimuli even earlier than this. Remember, though, that if your baby hears a particular sound again and again while he is in the womb, he will eventually ignore it.

Taste/Smell

A study was performed in which newborn babies were placed in a crib to which a cotton pad was affixed on either side. The pad on the left had been placed inside the bra of the baby's mother for 3 hours and was impregnated with her odour, while that on the right contained the smell of another new mother. Each baby showed a strong preference for his own mother's smell and turned towards that pad, suggesting they had learned to recognize their own mother's smell in the womb.

A similar study was performed to see if a baby could learn another smell in the womb. Garlic is known to enter body secretions, including the amniotic fluid and the baby's bloodstream. One group of mothers agreed to stop eating garlic in the last 3 weeks of pregnancy, while a similar group ate garlic regularly until an average of 6 days before delivery. This 'wash-out' period ensured that none of the mothers in the garlic-eating group smelled of garlic at childbirth. The newborn babies were then placed in a crib and given the choice of smelling a pad impregnated with garlic or an unscented but moist pad. The babies born to mothers who had eaten garlic during the last month of pregnancy spent almost three times as long sniffing the garlic pads – 55 per cent of the time compared with only 20 per cent of the time for babies whose mothers had not eaten garlic. This suggests that newborn babies initially dislike the pungent scent of garlic unless they have been exposed to it in the recent past and can remember it so it seems familiar.

Dyslexia

Researchers have noticed that babies receiving prenatal stimulation seem less likely to develop dyslexia. Dyslexic children seem to respond differently to stimuli such as sudden noises, reacting with a fetal 'startle' reflex movement that usually disappears soon after birth in those who do not have dyslexia. This retention of a fetal reflex may result from understimulation in the womb. It may also be linked with deficiency of dietary essential fatty acids (see Chapter 6).

The Cardiac Curriculum

Using rhythms that resembled the mother's own heartbeat to stimulate the baby in the womb was the idea of Dr Brent Logan, director of the PreNatal Institute in Oregon. This idea was based on the earlier work of an American psychologist, Lee Salk, who noted in the 1960s that mothers naturally hold their young against their left side after birth. Out of 287 new mothers, 78 per cent of left-handed mothers and 83 per cent of right-handed mothers subconsciously held their baby on their left side, against their heart. This did not seem to have anything to do with which hand was dominant. Studies of classical painting and sculptures of mother and child also revealed that in 80 per cent of cases, the baby was held against the mother's left side – within hearing distance of her heart. In comparison, when people were observed carrying inanimate packages, there was no clear preference – 50 per cent held them on the left, and 50 per cent on their right.

Follow-up studies in which newborn babies were played heartbeat sounds continuously for 4 days showed that those hearing the tape cried less, slept better and put on more weight than those not exposed to the sounds. The babies seemed to be 'imprinted' on the sound of a heartbeat – a sound they had lived with throughout their developing awareness in the womb.

More advanced imaging techniques have allowed babies to be observed in the womb while listening to BabyPlus, a unit similar in size to a personal cassette player that can be strapped on by a pregnant mother and that plays rhythmic sounds to her baby. Babies in the womb have been observed to use particular sucking patterns that show they recognize the sound, are relaxed and seem to enjoy the pleasure that stimulation gives. They often rock rhythmically from side to side when BabyPlus is on, which may contribute to their good neck, back and muscle tone. Stimulation of neural pathways also helps to strengthen the connection between nerve and muscle cells, providing stimulation and nerve growth factors that boost muscle development.

While BabyPlus sounds monotonous to the adult ear, its rhythm and subtle sequential changes are beneficial for your baby's developing brain. It starts pulsing at around one cycle per second (1 hertz), similar to the rhythm of newborn babies' brain wave pattern (slow-wave 1–2 hertz) and to the rhythm of your own heartbeat. By the time the sounds reach him, they sound very similar to your own blood as it surges past the womb in your arteries. As the BabyPlus stimulus speeds up week by week, your baby compares and contrasts it with the constant background noises in his surroundings (your breathing, heartbeat, placental blood flow, venous blood flow, etc.) and recognizes that the rhythm has changed. As the sounds speed up, his brain has to process the sounds he hears more quickly in order to compare them with your own heart rate. This stimulates neural pathways and means he starts building up a memory bank for different rhythms. This is why repetitive, rhythmic sounds seem to be best at stimulating your baby's developing brain.

Prenatal stimulation means more brain cells are present, with more connections between them, so the activity in your baby's brain is more advanced. Pilot studies confirm that infants receiving prenatal stimulation show significantly more mature brain wave patterns on EEG recordings at birth, compared with unstimulated babies.

WHAT IS THE BABYPLUS UNIT LIKE?
The BabyPlus unit measures 11.5 cm × 7.5 cm × 2.5 cm. It uses 4 AA batteries and has an adjustable strap that attaches it around your expanding waist. There is also a clip to attach the unit to the waistband of your clothes if you prefer. The unit is powered by 16 small buttons on the front. From 24 – 40 weeks pregnancy, the unit is designed to be used twice a day for 30–60 minutes at a time.

How Do You Use It?
Just strap it on and press the button number corresponding to the number of weeks you have used it, as follows:

Duration of Pregnancy	BabyPlus programme
24	1
25	2
26	3
27	4
28	5
29	6
30	7
31	8
32	9
33	10
34	11
35	12
36	13
37	14
38	15
39	16
40	16

If your baby goes past his due dates, you can keep on with programme number 16, or go backwards, giving your baby a chance to go back over earlier material.

If you start BabyPlus later than 24 weeks, calculate how many days remain before your estimated date of delivery and divide the figure by 16. This gives you the number of days you should use each of the 16 numbered programmes. If you obtain a fraction when dividing the number of days by 16, round up or down to the nearest whole number. For example:

You start using BabyPlus when you have 84 days of pregnancy remaining. Divide by 16 to get the number 5.25, which you round down to 5. Start using BabyPlus twice a day, starting with programme 1, then every 5 days (instead of the usual 7 days) move on to the next programme in the sequence.

Loudness

The sounds made by the BabyPlus unit may seem loud, but by the time they reach your baby they are muted by 30 – 35 decibels as a result of passing through your abdominal wall and womb tissues. Once the sounds reach your baby, the loudness is enough for him to take notice but not enough to startle or annoy him. In fact, the sound of your blood rushing through the placenta is heard quite loudly in the womb – measured at up to 95 decibels – this is as loud as a passing train! BabyPlus is designed to reach your baby at a loudness level of 35 decibels.

PLAYING MUSIC TO YOUR BABY

You can also play your baby music in the womb using a personal cassette player. This became popular in the 1980s and mothers and researchers alike reported benefits in babies' performances, with improved understanding, social behaviour, creativity and strength. In the womb, babies also seem to synchronize their limb movements to the music they hear, almost as if they are jigging along. These limb movement changes last for many minutes. Some parents choose classical music, some pop music and others folk music, depending on personal preferences. It is important not to play music that is too complex, however. A simple, repetitive beat seems to work best. The music also needs to be repeated regularly so your baby learns to recognize it. This will happen automatically if a mother regularly watches or listens to a favourite television or radio programme with its distinctive theme tune.

Some research suggests that music is too random to provide optimal prenatal stimulation, and that the cardiac curriculum sounds work better. Music is still beneficial, however. Recent research among 3-year-olds who were stimulated with singing and musical training showed they achieved higher marks in standard intelligence tests; similar benefits may occur in the womb – especially with regard to spatial awareness and numerical aptitude.

A prenatal stimulation trial in Russia involving babies who were either stimulated for an hour morning and evening for 15 weeks with BabyPlus, stimulated with music, or unstimulated, showed the following results:

Observed Feature	Form of Prenatal Stimulation		
	BabyPlus	Recorded Music	No prenatal stimulation
Relaxed body at birth	75%	57.2%	44.5%
Hands open at birth	66.7%	57.2%	33.4%
Eyes open at birth	91.7%	71.4%	85.7%
Facial stares at birth	66.6%	57.2%	55.5%
First infant speech (babbling)	1.5 wks	3 wks	4 wks
First response to maternal voice	5 wks	7 wks	9 wks
First playing	4 mths	5 mths	4.7 mths
First gesture	2.5 mths	8.5 mths	later
First verbal request	8.8 mths	9 mths	later
First points to named body parts	10 mths	12 mths	later

The trial is continuing and has now enrolled over 2,000 subjects.

Parents who have used BabyPlus are extremely enthusiastic about the results. They report that their children:

☺ are relaxed, calm and contented
☺ are alert and responsive
☺ have good head control at birth
☺ have a strong back
☺ have an incredibly strong grip
☺ seem to have heightened senses
☺ have excellent memory and concentration skills
☺ have long attention spans
☺ focus on your face surprisingly early and can hold your gaze
☺ seem very knowing and aware
☺ seem empathic and bond closely with family members
☺ reach their developmental milestones earlier than expected

- have remarkable language acquisition skills
- are sharing and sociable, engaging and responsive
- are articulate and communicative
- are sensitive to moods, situations and their surroundings
- are less fearful of new situations
- have enhanced creativity
- are more likely to have a high intelligence measured in the 125–150 range (average for the population is 100).

Should We Stimulate the Fetus in the Womb?

Research suggests that fetal brain development can be stimulated while in the womb. These studies are still ongoing, and as a result some doctors urge caution. It is undeniable, however, that babies given a sensible stimulatory boost in the womb are born with a number of desirable traits as above. No adverse effects have yet been reported.

It is important not to stress your baby, however. Try not to startle him, and don't bombard him with constant stimulation for hours at a time. Babies need their quiet periods, too. Limit your prenatal play-school sessions to no more than 1 hour in the morning and 1 hour in the evening – at the same time each day if possible, so you set up a routine. This will help you remember to do it, and also seems to encourage anticipation in the baby. Many mothers have reported that their baby starts to kick and 'complain' if his BabyPlus session is late, for example.

CAN PRENATAL STIMULATION HAVE ANY HARMFUL EFFECTS?

There is no evidence that prenatal stimulation is harmful in any way. Many women worry that if their baby is born with a larger brain, there is an increased risk of problems at delivery or of a Caesarean section. In fact, the opposite seems to be true – prenatal sound stimulation seems to lead to shorter, less painful labours, lower numbers of Caesarean sections and non-traumatic births. When born, babies are more likely to have a relaxed body, open eyes, unclenched fists and remarkable physical strength.

By the time of birth, your baby's head will normally be slightly larger than the size of the birth canal anyway. During birth, the skull is squeezed so the flat skull bones overlap each other slightly, allowing your baby's head to mould to the size of the birth canal. Most women who have used a programme of prenatal stimulation have delivered their baby vaginally in the normal way.

Interestingly, research suggests that babies born by Caesarean are more intelligent overall than babies born by vaginal delivery, however. It may be that brain size has something to do with this. A modern Caesarean section with epidural pain relief is now very safe and perhaps even desirable. A recent survey among doctors working as obstetricians and gynaecologists found that 31 per cent of female obstetricians and 17 per cent of male gynaecologists would prefer to have their own baby delivered by Caesarean section. This intervention is therefore not always one to be feared (see Chapter 11).

How to Enrich Your Baby's Prenatal Environment

You can start from around 15 to 20 weeks gestation (17 to 22 weeks pregnancy). Aim to stimulate your baby for no more than 2 hours per day in total.

USING VOICE

☙ Speak regularly to your unborn baby, stroking or patting your tummy in a particular way to attract his attention before you do so, for example pat three times regularly on both sides so he gets to know when he is being addressed.

☙ Tell him a favourite story once a day.

🐸 Introduce new stories throughout your pregnancy and tell them regularly, in addition to the familiar story he is hearing every day.

🐸 Get family members to greet your baby as well as you – for example when your partner comes home from work in the evening, or a child arrives home from school.

🐸 When talking to family members, tell your baby who they are so he has the chance to associate voices with names.

🐸 If you have already chosen possible names for your child, use these when addressing your baby so he or she starts to recognize them.

🐸 Some researchers suggest using a speaking tube (for example the inside section of a kitchen roll) against the abdomen when talking to your baby so sounds are transmitted in a more focused way. A fetal 'phone' which does something similar is also available in some countries.

🐸 If you know any foreign phrases, or someone who speaks a second language, expose your unborn baby to these sounds so he gets to recognize the different sounds – alternatively, play him language-learning tapes.

🐸 Sing to your baby, especially repetitive songs and chants.

🐸 Sing along to your favourite music on the radio.

USING MUSIC

🐸 Play music to your baby – choose a simple tune that you like and play it once a day.

🐸 Introduce other simple tunes to your baby and play them regularly.

🐸 If you have a musical instrument, or even just a cheap, toy keyboard, play musical scales to your baby so he learns to recognize different notes and their relationship to each other.

🐸 Attach a personal cassette recorder to your clothing or a belt around your waist and play your baby music – choose rhythmical, repetitive sounds or chants, or perhaps a tape of yourself or other family members singing or chanting.

USING TOUCH

There is some evidence that very premature babies show strong negative reactions to tactile stimulation, compared with positive responses to sound. Conversely, some studies suggest that older premature babies love having a gentle massage, in that they then put on weight faster and thrive better. It has been found, for example, that premature babies who are rocked, rubbed and stroked for 15 minutes, four times a day, develop improved co-ordination and ability to learn as they get older.

If you want to stimulate your baby with touch, do so sparingly for only short periods of a few minutes twice a day early on in your pregnancy. During the last 6 weeks of pregnancy you can massage your baby for slightly longer – up to 15 minutes – and more frequently – up to four times a day. Some things you can try include:

🐣 patting your tummy gently using a regular rhythm
🐣 regularly and rhythmically stroking your baby while you are talking to him
🐣 rocking your own body to and fro gently, while supporting your abdomen in your arms – or sitting in a rocking chair.

USING LIGHT

There is some evidence that very premature babies show strong negative reactions to visual stimulation, compared with positive responses to sound. Therefore, if you want to stimulate your baby with touch and light, do so sparingly, only a few times a day. When unborn babies are observed using ultrasound while a light is flashing on and off, they seem interested and respond at first, then ignore the stimulus after the fourth or fifth flash. Some things you can try include:

🐣 holding a torch against your tummy and flashing it on and off slowly, no more than 3 or 4 times

☺holding a torch against your tummy and flashing it on and off a few times when telling a particular story, singing a particular song or listening to a particular piece of music.

USING BABYPLUS

Strap on the unit for 30–60 minutes twice a day, morning and evening, ideally starting from around 24 weeks.

Keep a diary of the music you play, the stories you read and the voices your baby hears to see if your baby seems to calm down, become alert or show other signs of recognition when he hears them after birth.

Case Histories

Many of the following names have been changed for reasons of confidentiality.

Amanda and Eva

'I had an excellent pregnancy and took folic acid and a multinu-trient supplement from 8 months prior to conception. While pregnant, I took a vitamin and mineral supplement, evening primrose oil, fish oils and, for the last 2 months, raspberry leaf tablets.

'From the 18th week of pregnancy, I noticed the baby responded to touch and moved around a great deal, allowing us to establish a good relationship with our baby.

'I started BabyPlus at 20 weeks, using it 1 hour per day in the late afternoon. I noticed that the baby used to kick more if I missed the time.

'I had a remarkably painless labour (which I attribute to the yoga and raspberry leaf tablets). I finally needed a Caesarean as the waters became stained with meconium (fecal material from the baby's intestines).

'Eva was born with an unusually large umbilical cord that took 2 weeks to drop off. Straight away, we noticed she had excellent head control, a strong back, and seemed very alert. She recognized my voice straight away and turned to me immediately. At birth, it was noticed that Eva had noisy breathing, thought to be due to a floppy larynx. As a result she was kept in the neonatal ward for observation until given the all-clear by an ENT surgeon. Eva remained calm throughout, however, and this trait has continued. Eva only cries if she has wind or a dirty nappy.

'She took to breastfeeding straight away, is unusually alert and is good with other people. She genuinely smiled within 3 days of birth. She really looks at faces, mobiles and lights and is very inquisitive and strong. A real delight!'

Susannah and Max
'We are thrilled with our decision to use BabyPlus and feel it has made a great contribution to our son Max's development.

'At birth, he was incredibly alert with eyes opening after a few minutes to calmly survey the world around him. There was no hint of crying and his open palms signalled his relaxed state of mind.

'Our family were amazed at his concentration and hand-eye co-ordination from an early stage. He smiled in his sleep at 5 days, and smiled at us at 3 weeks. First held his head up for several seconds at 1 week. At 3–4 weeks he was swiping at the plastic animals on his multi-gym and at 5 weeks could hold a rattle and put it into his mouth. He started babbling repetitively at 6 weeks.

'Max is a strong baby, with health visitors commenting on his unusual back strength and his ability to bear weight. He could sit unaided at 3 months old.

'Max is a happy, contented baby full of laughter, fun and mischief. He seldom cries and communicates with a wide repertoire of sounds. He is very affectionate and loving, sociable and quick on the uptake. He is very mature for his age and always on the go, showing interest in his surroundings and examining objects carefully.

'Many people have commented on his physical strength, cheerful nature and maturity.'

Sally and Samuel

'I followed a prenatal enrichment programme by taking folic acid, vitamins and minerals, evening primrose and fish oils. In the last 2 months of pregnancy I also took raspberry leaf tablets recommended by a midwife. From 20 weeks I used BabyPlus and also played music to my baby in the womb. We stroked the baby through my tummy regularly, told stories and sang nursery rhymes.

'The baby had several scans as he seemed to be growing faster than expected. My dates seemed to be 6 weeks out at first, then 8 weeks as the baby continued to grow quickly. His head was at the upper end of the normal range and I was given the option of trial of labour, or a Caesarean section. Without any hesitation, I opted for the Caesarean! Samuel was born quietly, eyes open and squinting into the bright operating theatre lights. He did not cry, and held his father's gaze as if to say 'So that's what you look like.' His musculature was well defined and the paediatrician commented that he did not seem like a newborn baby with his strong back and uncurled limbs. The umbilical cord was so thick the clip only just snapped on.

'He was a very affectionate baby from the start, with many people commenting on how "cuddly" he was. He hardly ever cries – less than 30 minutes per day, and usually only when he has wind. He smiled within 5 days and was fascinated with his stim-mobile, black-and-white patterns and drawings of faces. He slept in the same room as us for the first year. Our bedroom ceiling has dark brown wooden beams forming a striking arched pattern with the ivory paint in-between. Samuel spent a lot of his waking hours in the room following the bold patterns with his eyes. He seemed to remember the nursery rhymes he heard in the womb and was quickly soothed to sleep with them.

'He was very aware of his hands from birth and constantly held them together, rubbing one over the other. He lifted his head off the floor by 3 weeks of age, rolled over at 3 months, sat up in his high-chair to be fed at 4 months, crawled by the age of 8 months and was running from one end of the front room to the other by the age of 1 year. By the age of 1 year he had also established his own complex method of communication with us using noises and hand movements. He has a wonderful sense of humour and loves making people laugh by standing on one leg, sticking his tummy out or mimicking your own movements. He particularly likes wagging his finger at you and saying "no" when you do something silly.

'He loves listening to music and will jig and dance as soon as he hears a tune. His head measurements are still on the upper limit of normal. We can't help comparing our little boy to other children and realizing that there is no doubt that he seems bright. He needs constant stimulation, but we are glad we decided to follow a prenatal programme and to continue breastfeeds twice a day from weaning until 9 months. The most astonishing event was when one of his slippers went missing when he was 12 months old. We couldn't find it and didn't think to ask Samuel until 3 days later. Without thinking, I said "Where's your slipper, Samuel?" He went straight to a small drawer, opened it and pulled the missing slipper out. Quite a feat of memory after all that time.'

Susan and Nicky

'I started using BabyPlus from 18 weeks, as I'd read that babies become conscious of external sounds at this time. Within weeks, I was aware of stronger movements when I used BabyPlus and soon the baby began reminding me when it was time for her session.

'At birth her eyes were open, her hands relaxed and neck tone excellent. She let out a piercing scream once she was taken away from me to the next room, but settled as soon as she was brought back and put to the breast. She seemed to recognize my voice quickly, but more surprisingly seemed to recognize her dad's voice within 10 hours of birth. She smiled in her crib at 2 days old. Everyone comments on how relaxed and content she seems. She wakes up smiling and happy, not fretful. At 8 weeks she reached for toys and at 12 weeks rolled from her back to her stomach unaided. She was crawling by 13 weeks. She sat in her high chair at 5 months absorbed by things going on around her, and looked more like a 9-month-old. At 8 months, she had such good finger control she could pick up a single "Hundred & Thousand" rather than the more usual fistful – a skill not usually expected until over 1 year old. She took her first unaided steps at 9 months. Her memory is astounding and she can remember where she put a discarded toy if you ask her to fetch it. She slept through the night from 8 weeks of age.'

Hannah and Tracy

'Tracy's eyes were open at birth. She had excellent neck tone and could lift her head almost immediately from birth. She let out a small cry at birth but was then perfectly calm. She seemed to recognize my voice and her dad's immediately. The paediatrician was impressed with her strength and head control. All healthcare professionals have stated that she seems very advanced for her age, as if she is several months older than she is. She is very alert and curious, as well as calm and sociable. She consistently smiled at 2–3 weeks whenever she was spoken to. She started babbling at 4–5 weeks.

'She needs constant stimulation and we marvel at her maturity, social skills and relaxed temperament. She has slept through the night from 6 weeks old. She is incredibly strong, smiles a lot and is a real thinker.'

Maisie and Stacey

'I ate a healthy, varied diet, took a vitamin supplement and continued with outdoor activities. I started using BabyPlus at 23 weeks pregnancy. I was a little concerned at first as the thumping sounds seemed so loud and repetitive. The baby kicked and moved while I was using it and we hoped she wasn't trying to get away. After a while, however, we noticed that she seemed to complain and kick even more if her BabyPlus time was late. Stacey was born using acupuncture for pain relief, after less than 4 hours in the labour suite. Her eyes were open at birth, hands relaxed and she did not cry. She took to breastfeeding straight away. Her back seemed very strong and she was sitting unaided by 5 months. She has slept through the night for 12 hours since the age of 5 months. Her curiosity and interest in everything are noticeable, as is her contented nature. We are so glad we followed a prenatal enrichment programme.'

Charlene and Harry
'We used a prenatal enrichment programme and played classical music, sound tapes and Irish folk music to the baby throughout my pregnancy. He reacted to the same music when we played it to him after his birth by rolling flat on his back and promptly going to sleep. The doctors were impressed!'

Katie and Lewis
'We used music tapes and a speaking tube to stimulate Lewis in the womb. My husband spoke Italian to him. I was sceptical to start with. We do have a very alert baby however, and he definitely reacts when Italian is spoken.'

Linda and Lucy
'I started playing the BabyPlus tapes for up to 1.5 hours a day from 24 weeks until Lucy was born, 11 days early. She became quite responsive and seemed to know when the tape was next due. She is by no means a genius child, but is unusually perceptive, sensitive and articulate.

'She spoke in full sentences and was very fluent by the age of 2. At 3, she would say how "extremely difficult" things were to do and understood concepts such as "larger than", "smaller than" or "same as". She controls pencils with a steady grip and drew complex pictures from an early age, which she would proceed to name. When she was just 4 years old she could pick out a recognized tune at a toy keyboard, and loves listening to music. At the age of 4 she could also remember a holiday we had taken a year earlier and describe things she had seen that we had not even realized she had noticed. She is very secure, confident, inquisitive, content and needs constant stimulation.'

6
Eating for a Super Baby

It is important to follow a healthy diet not only during pregnancy, but in the preconceptual period when you are only thinking about having a baby. This ensures that enough vital building-blocks such as vitamins, minerals and essential fatty acids are available right from the start of the development of your baby's brain. It is now accepted that taking folic acid can reduce the risk of a neural tube defect by as much as 75 per cent, for example. Other nutrients such as B_{12} and the trace minerals can reduce this risk even further. They can also help to ensure your baby's early 'blueprint' is laid down in such a way that his future risk of coronary heart disease, high blood pressure and diabetes in later life are minimized. A healthy diet before pregnancy also ensures you have enough nutritional reserves to supply your baby, even if you suffer from morning sickness. Similarly, a good diet is vital after your baby is born, when you are breastfeeding – and perhaps building up reserves for another pregnancy in the not-too-distant future.

World-wide, there is a strong link between poor maternal nutrition and low birthweight babies. Babies born at optimum birthweights (3.5 – 4.5 kg/7¾ – 10 lb) have the lowest risk of developmental disorders such as those of the brain, spinal cord and nervous system. Unfortunately, as many as 50,000 babies with a low birthweight are born in England and Wales each year. These babies have a higher risk of physical or mental handicap, with up to 8 per cent suffering severe disorders such as:

- cerebral palsy
- mental retardation
- faulty development of the lungs
- blindness
- deafness
- epilepsy.

Studies show a significant relationship between the size of a baby at birth and maternal diet at or around the time of conception. These first few weeks of gestation are a time of rapid division of cells. The central nervous system (brain and spinal cord) are often fully developed before the pregnancy is even recognized. Babies of teenage mothers are particularly at risk. Studies show their diets are low in iron, calcium, vitamin A and riboflavin, particularly if they're trying to lose weight. Low birthweight is also linked to smoking and excessive alcohol intake (see Chapter 9).

A healthy diet is even more important when you have a multiple pregnancy, as you have to nourish two or more infants rather than one. This becomes even more vital when twins are identical and share the same placenta, rather than each having a placenta of their own. Over the last few years it has been realized that twins sharing a single placenta are more at risk of poor nutrition due to placental insufficiency, and therefore have five to ten times the chance of brain damage or death.

Interesting research, conducted over 20 years, also suggests that poor maternal diet during pregnancy may increase the rate of criminal behaviour linked with impaired prenatal brain function. This is thought to lead to character traits associated with delinquency such as:

- irritability
- impulsive behaviour
- seeking immediate gratification
- short attention span
- language difficulties
- poor reasoning ability
- poor memory skills
- unfocused thinking
- poor concentration
- exaggerated responses to minor frustrations
- lower intelligence.

Some of these traits can be identified from the age of 3.

Diet and Brain Development

While you are pregnant, over half of the nutrients you eat are used by your growing baby – one of many reasons why pregnant women feel tired even during the early months while their baby is still quite tiny.

One of the main energy-using metabolic processes in your baby's body is the active transport of salts in and out of cells in preparation for cell division. In your baby's central nervous system alone, new brain cells (neurons) are produced at a rate of 250,000 per minute. Although new brain cells are being formed throughout your baby's body at an even greater rate than this, three quarters of your baby's total energy needs at birth result from the workings of his brain and peripheral nervous system.

Poor nutrition will result in an undernourished, under-sized baby who is small for dates. If growth in the womb is seriously reduced, this is known as intrauterine growth retardation.

Your baby can cope with small reductions in nutrients and oxygen for short periods of time by diverting supplies of glucose and oxygen to the brain and away from his other body cells. This ability is partly due to a small hole in your baby's heart during fetal development. This is designed to let oxygenated blood, arriving in the right side of his heart directly from the placenta, cross straight over into the left side of the heart and up towards the brain. (This hole usually closes over at birth so that blood from the right side of the heart is sent to the lungs instead, to pick up oxygen once your baby is separated from the placenta.)

Although this process protects the brain, it does divert blood and nutrients away from his other vital organs, however. Therefore, if nutrition remains poor for a significant amount of time, your baby's other organs, such as the liver and pancreas, tend to be smaller than normal. Researchers now suspect this is the reason why babies who are malnourished in the womb are more likely to develop abnormal cholesterol levels and diabetes in later life. The smaller liver means your offspring is unable to handle cholesterol so well, leading to a higher risk of hardening and furring up of the arteries (atherosclerosis), high blood pressure, coronary heart disease and stroke in the future. Similarly a small pancreas impairs glucose metabolism and increases his future risk of diabetes.

Studies have shown, for example, that men born with a large placenta and the highest placental weight/birthweight ratio were at the greatest risk of developing hypertension (high blood pressure) in later life. Babies with placentas weighing less than 700 g (1¼ lb) have a lower risk of hypertension in later life.

The development of your baby's brain requires very different nutritional building-blocks than those of the rest of his body. His muscles and tissues have the greatest need for protein, his bones need minerals, while his brain and nervous system have the most need for fats – especially essential fatty acids. For optimal brain growth, you therefore need to provide your baby with enough of the right sorts of dietary fats during pregnancy.

When it comes to brain potential, dietary essential fatty acids are equally as important as vitamins, minerals and energy supply – both during pregnancy and in the first year of life after birth. When your baby is born, his brain weighs around 350 g (12 oz) – 10 per cent of his total body weight. Sixty per cent of the weight of your baby's brain is made up of fats, with 20 per cent of brain weight composed of long-chain polyunsaturated fatty acids (LCPs). It is therefore vital that your diet provides enough fats of the right sort for healthy fetal brain cells. Unfortunately, 8 out of 10 pregnant women are deficient in the all-important essential fatty acids.

Essential Fatty Acids

Essential fatty acids (EFAs) belong to a group of oils known as long-chain polyunsaturated fatty acids (LCPs). While your body can make small amounts of the EFAs from other dietary fats, they are often in short supply – especially during pregnancy. You therefore need to get adequate amounts from your food, which is why they are labelled 'essential'. There are two main essential fatty acids:

- linolenic acid (of which one type is gamma-linolenic acid, found in evening primrose oil)
- linoleic acid.

Once in your body, these two EFAs act as building-blocks to make cell membranes, sex hormones, and hormone-like chemicals (prostaglandins) found in all your body tissues. EFAs can also be converted into two other types of LCPs that are especially important during pregnancy. These are:

☙ arachidonic acid (AA), which you make from linoleic acid
☙ docosahexaenoic acid (DHA), which you make from linolenic acid.

If EFAs are in short supply – as they are in 8 out of 10 pregnant women – both you and your baby will be deficient in LCPs as well. In addition, your baby's metabolism is not mature enough to start performing these conversions on his own until at least 4 months after birth. He is therefore dependent on obtaining them from breastmilk or enriched formulas, otherwise he will remain deficient during his early development when his visual acuity and brain cells desperately need them.

Essential fatty acids are needed for healthy cell membranes, nerves and hormone balance. They are especially important for the structure and development of your baby's brain, and make up 20 per cent of brain weight (your baby's dendritic trees and synapses are especially rich in LCPs). EFAs are also converted into hormone-like chemicals (prostaglandins) that help to ensure the healthy development of your baby, reduce the risk of premature delivery, protect against high blood pressure during pregnancy and soften your cervix to trigger childbirth when the time is right. Studies suggest that male babies have a higher need for EFAs than females.

DEFICIENCY OF EFAs IS COMMON DURING PREGNANCY

Research in many countries, including the UK, US and the Netherlands, shows that even in normal pregnancy, a mother's EFA status is marginal, with low EFA levels that tend to fall lower with each successive pregnancy. EFA deficiency is especially likely with multiple pregnancies when the needs of two or more babies must be met rather than one.

Lack of essential fatty acids is common. The World Health Organization recently warned that the growing trend towards following a low-fat diet means many pregnant women do not get all the essential fatty acids they need. A healthy adult woman needs around 6 – 10 g EFAs per day. During pregnancy and breastfeeding, these needs are increased to an average of 14 g EFAs per day, or approximately 4,000 g per pregnancy. This is equivalent to 10 litres of soy oil over the course of her pregnancy!

As pregnancy requires such high levels of EFAs, and as intakes are generally low, maternal essential fatty acid status declines throughout pregnancy and breastfeeding. Stores are not readily replenished – as the diet still remains poor in EFAs – so that with each subsequent pregnancy, essential fatty acid deficiency becomes increasingly marked.

If your diet is lacking in EFAs, your metabolism can make do with the next best fatty acids available, but this is not ideal. Every cell in your body – and that of your growing baby – is surrounded by a fatty envelope known as the cell membrane. When your diet is rich in EFAs, your cell membranes contain a higher percentage of LCPs and are flexible, healthy and youthful. If your diet is poor in EFAs, your cell membranes include more of other types of fat which tend to make them more rigid and prone to dryness, itching and premature ageing. The EFA content is important for the way receptors and communication channels embedded in the cell membrane work.

It is an interesting observation that first babies are often more intelligent than their younger siblings. It is interesting to speculate that lack of EFAs – especially DHA – may be an important factor in this. Recent research in the Netherlands involving 244 women who were pregnant for the first to seventh time has shown that maternal blood levels of DHA are significantly lower in women who have previously given birth compared to those pregnant with their first child. Blood samples from the umbilical artery and vein also showed significantly higher DHA levels in first children compared with later ones. Birth order was found to play a significant role in determining how much DHA was available to the developing baby. Further research is needed to see what effect this has on the intellectual potential for children born second or later in a family. Certainly women planning a second or subsequent pregnancy are well advised to take essential fatty acid supplements to protect themselves and their baby from the potential effects of deficiency.

YOUR BABY'S BRAIN AND LCPs

The two LCPs, arachidonic acid (AA) and docosahexaenoic acid (DHA), are vital for the development of normal brain and eye function, especially during the last 3 months of pregnancy. They are so important to your baby's growing brain that the placenta extracts them from your own blood and concentrates them in your baby's circulation, so his levels of AA and DHA are twice as high as your own.

DHA is transported to your baby's central nervous system and incorporated into brain cell membranes. It makes up 10 – 15 per cent of the weight of your baby's cerebral cortex. It is found mainly in the areas of membrane occurring in the synaptic connections between brain cells. DHA is also concentrated in the light-sensitive cells at the back of your baby's eyes, where it makes up 50 per cent of the weight of each retina. It is not found in high concentrations in any other body tissues, with the exception of spermatozoa in the male testicles after puberty. It is present in each cell, however, in the membrane of the tiny structures (mitochondria) that act as cell batteries and provide energy.

DHA and AA are long-chain, polyunsaturated fatty acids. This means there are lots of gaps in the structure of the molecule where hydrogen atoms are missing. These gaps make the fats more flexible and fluid, and seem to allow signals to pass more easily from one brain cell to another. Because of DHA's structure, it keeps synaptic membranes in a more fluid state so that the membrane receptors can function more easily. DHA also seems to have a beneficial effect on neurotransmitter activity – perhaps it allows communication chemicals to be released into the synaptic cleft more quickly.

A synapse rich in DHA allows maximum speed of transmission of a signal from one brain cell to another. When DHA is in short supply, other long-chain fatty acids are incorporated into the synaptic membrane and, as a result, speed of transmission is slowed. High levels of DHA allow optimal brain function. Deficiency of DHA interferes with brain function.

Adequate levels of DHA and AA are vital for optimum development of your baby's growing brain and eyes. In fact, the size of his brain, and his head circumference, are linked to his blood levels of DHA and the development of these levels during the first year of his life. By the age of nine months after birth, babies fed on mother's milk (which is rich in LCPs) or formula enriched with DHA have much more advanced eyesight with significantly better visual acuity compared with those receiving formula that does not contain DHA.

AA is important for making strong, flexible, elastic blood vessel walls that reduce the risk of bleeding into the brain, especially in premature infants (see Chapter 10).

Developmental Problems Due to Lack of LCPs

If EFAs are in short supply, they are replaced with less optimal long-chain fatty acids so that the electrical transmission of signals between brain cells is impaired. Babies whose brains contain low levels of LCPs have significantly impaired brain development and lower intelligence.

It is now believed that a low-fat diet providing too few EFAs during pregnancy may be linked with an increased risk of the offspring developing dyslexia.

Dyslexia is a condition in which there is a considerable discrepancy between intellectual ability and written language skills. There is:

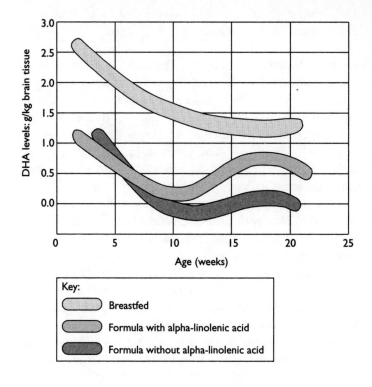

Diet and DHA in newborns

☺ an unexpected failure in learning to read and write

☺ an unusual anatomical symmetry in language areas of the brain, which are more normally larger in the dominant cerebral hemisphere (the left side in right-handed individuals)

☺ microscopic differences in the way cells are organized during development in the language areas of the brain

☺ difficulty in processing rapid changes in visual stimulation (such as flickers, motion)

☺ impaired night vision (dark adaptation)

☺ poor peripheral vision

difficulty in processing rapid changes in the sounds involved in speech.

It is now thought that dyslexia is a brain development disorder linked with deficiency of certain essential fatty acids in the womb. This leads to mild abnormalities in the membranes of synapses in the fetal brain, which are less fluid than normal and which transmit information more slowly. This may help to explain why dyslexia is more common in males, who have a higher requirement for EFAs than females. DHA is particularly important for visual perception; research is under way to see if giving fish oil supplements (a rich source of AA and DHA) to pregnant women with a family history of dyslexia can help to prevent the condition in the early stages of their baby's development. Recent studies have confirmed that fatty acid metabolism is abnormal in people with dyslexia, with increased turn-over of two lipids – phosphethanolamine and phosphocholine. This may be a genetic difference which is made worse by lack of dietary EFAs, and improved by a diet rich in EFAs. Some research also suggests that dyslexia results from under-stimulation of the fetus in the womb, which allows the primitive fetal reflex behaviour to sudden noise (the startle reflex) to persist (see Chapter 5).

There is also direct evidence that lack of EFAs and other metabolic abnormalities involving the way EFAs are handled in the brain may lead to attention deficit hyperactivity disorder, autism and schizophrenia, all of which are associated with dyslexia. One in three people with schizophrenia, for example, has abnormally low levels of AA and DHA. This occurs in those with a form of the disease known as neural development schizophrenia, in which symptoms come on at a young age, and is associated with a decline in reasoning and ordered thought. Lack of dietary EFAs may not be the root cause of these conditions, but may trigger it in those predisposed to them through other genetic or environmental factors. It is also possible that these conditions are linked with poor ability to absorb EFAs from the intestines, or problems with the way EFAs are handled once they reach the brain. Most evidence suggests the problem is dietary, however, with higher rates of schizophrenia in children conceived during times of starvation, in those with a poor diet and in those who were not breastfed.

From around 4 – 6 months after birth, babies have a metabolism that is mature enough to start making small amounts of DHA from other dietary essential fatty acids, assuming these are available. Babies born with very low levels of DHA due to an enzyme defect that stops them making DHA (adreno-leukodystrophy) can sadly become 'floppy' (have low muscle tone due to abnormal nerve supply), blind and mentally retarded, and will fail to survive if the condition is not recognized. Giving supplements of DHA has proved very successful in protecting eyesight and preventing death.

Many children with hyperactivity or attention deficit disorder are now also thought to have a deficiency of essential fatty acids, either because they cannot absorb dietary EFAs normally from their intestines, because their EFA requirements are higher than normal, or because their body cannot handle EFAs properly. Boys are more commonly affected than girls, and this fits in with the observation that males in general have higher requirements of EFAs than females.

Lack of EFAs has also been linked with an increased risk of allergies such as eczema, asthma and hayfever in later life, and may also be linked with cradle cap – a scaly scalp condition – in newborn infants.

Deficiency of EFAs is made worse by lack of zinc, which is needed for the chemical reactions that convert EFAs to hormone-like substances known as prostaglandins which are involved in regulating inflammatory conditions (such as eczema and asthma) in the body.

Lack of AA causes small blood vessels in a baby's brain to be less elastic and more fragile. This may increase the risk of a bleed into the brain (intracranial haemorrhage), especially in premature infants.

HOW LACK OF EFAs CAN AFFECT YOU

If you are lacking in the EFAs, your baby will obtain a lot of the AA and DHA he needs from your body's richest store – your own brain. This may account for the slight shrinkage (2 – 3 per cent) in maternal brain size seen in some pregnant women, and cause the poor concentration, poor memory, forgetfulness and vagueness that many women experience during the last few months of pregnancy. By boosting your dietary intake of EFAs, AA and DHA throughout pregnancy, you can help to optimize development of your baby's brain and eyes.

Pregnancy is a time of rapid production of new cell membranes and itchy skin is common, especially towards the end of pregnancy. Increasing your intake of EFAs will help make your skin feel softer and smoother within a few weeks. Anecdotal evidence also suggests that obtaining more EFAs during pregnancy may help to prevent stretch marks.

NB If you develop severe itching during pregnancy, you should always seek medical advice.

Lack of essential fatty acids can cause symptoms including:

- thirst
- urinary frequency
- dry, rough, pimply skin
- itchy skin
- dry hair
- dandruff
- brittle nails
- lowered immunity with frequent infections.

How to Get EFAs from Your Diet

The levels of essential fatty acids found in your blood during pregnancy, and the concentrations found in breastmilk during lactation, vary depending on the amount of essential fatty acids you get in your food. Average DHA concentrations in the breast-milk of British mothers is 0.2 per cent for example, six times lower than that of North American Inuit women (1.2 per cent) who eat plenty of fish. Oily fish (such as mackerel, herring, salmon, trout, sardines, pilchards) are the richest dietary source of EFAs, containing 10 to 100 times more DHA than non-marine food sources such as nuts, seeds, wholegrains and dark green, leafy vegetables. The amount of DHA reaching the babies of pregnant vegan women is lower than that in fish- and meat-eating women.

- Docosahexaenoic acid (DHA) is found in fish oils.
- Arachidonic acid (AA) is found in many foods such as seafood, meat, dairy products, eggs.
- Linoleic acid, from which the body makes AA, is found in sunflower seeds, almonds, corn, sesame seeds, safflower oil and extra virgin olive oil.
- Linolenic acid, from which the body makes DHA, is found in evening primrose oil, starflower (borage) seed oil and black-currant seed oil.
- Both linoleic and linolenic acids are found in rich quantities in walnuts, pumpkin seeds, soybeans, linseed oil, rapeseed oil and flax oil.

Unless you eat around 30 g of nuts or seeds per day and 300 g of oily fish per week, however, your diet is likely to be deficient in these vital building-blocks. For the average person, this means increasing their fish intake by a factor of 10! Some research suggests the balance of EFAs in rapeseed oil may be better for brain development than that in olive, safflower or sunflower seed oils, so it may be worth switching to rapeseed oil for cooking.

You can help maximize your baby's full brain potential by increasing your dietary intake of foods rich in essential fatty acids, and by taking a sensible level of supplements.

Do I Need an EFA Supplement?

Not everyone wants to make drastic changes to their diet, especially during pregnancy, and in any case, not everyone likes eating fish. Some doctors advise against taking standard omega-3 fish oil supplements (designed for healthy heart and joints) during pregnancy as these contain a fatty acid (EPA) that prolongs bleeding time and may therefore increase blood loss during delivery. Omega-3 fish oils do have other benefits during pregnancy however (such as boosting fetal growth) but it is best to only take these under medical advice. You should also avoid cod liver oil during pregnancy because of its high vitamin A content. New EFA supplements are now designed for safe use during pregnancy however. These contain gamma-linolenic acid, DHA and AA (for example, Efanatal) or DHA alone (for example Neuromins derived from microalgae in the US) and have no EPA content. These can be taken when planning a pregnancy, while expecting and when breast feeding.

By improving your intake of EFAs through dietary changes, or by taking supplements, you can:

☺improve the development of your baby's eyes and brain
☺improve your baby's visual acuity
☺reduce your risk of pregnancy-associated high blood pressure (pre-eclampsia)
☺reduce your risk of a preterm delivery
☺reduce your risk of a low birthweight baby
☺reduce fluid retention during pregnancy (oedema)
☺reduce your risk of poor concentration and forgetfulness towards the end of pregnancy
☺reduce your risk of dry, itchy skin problems
☺possibly reduce your risk of stretch marks
☺possibly increase the intelligence of your baby through improved brain development.

During pregnancy, you are laying down over 5 kg (10 lb) fat that will provide one-third of the energy cost of milk production during the first 100 days after delivery. The composition of fats in these stores will depend on your dietary intake. By eating the right sorts of fats – especially essential fatty acids – you will be laying down EFA reserves to help top up the amount of EFAs present in your breastmilk. In other words, any excess you eat over and above your baby's immediate needs during pregnancy will not be wasted. A significant proportion can be stored and mobilized later, while breastfeeding, to continue the supply needed for eye and brain development during the first 4 – 6 months of your baby's life after birth.

Garlic

Garlic is a popular culinary plant that also has powerful medicinal effects. It has been shown to:

- lower a raised blood pressure enough to reduce the risk of a stroke by up to 40 per cent
- lower harmful levels of LDL-cholesterol by 12 per cent, and lower raised triglyceride (another blood fat linked with furring up of the arteries) levels by 13 per cent
- reduce the risk of coronary heart disease by up to 25 per cent
- dilate small arteries (arterioles) by an average of 4.2 per cent, and small veins (venules) by 5.9 per cent – which improves circulation by as much as 48 per cent
- decrease the risk of blood clots by increasing clot breakdown (fibrinolysis), decreasing blood stickiness (plasma viscosity) and decreasing blood cell clumping (platelet aggregation).

While all these effects are beneficial in later life, they have also recently been shown to be beneficial in pregnancy. Taking garlic powder tablets during pregnancy can reduce the risk of pregnancy-associated high blood pressure (pre-eclampsia) and improve circulation through the placenta so that the growth retardation associated with pre-eclampsia is less problematic. Garlic has also been shown to boost placental production of factors that stimulate fetal growth. Intriguingly, garlic in the blood-stream stimulates nasal smell and taste receptors – babies in the womb have been shown to be able to detect garlic (see Chapter 5). By eating garlic you can help to stimulate your baby's senses, improve blood flow through the placenta, boost fetal growth and reduce your risk of pre-eclampsia.

Metabolism and Weight Gain During Pregnancy

Pregnancy is a time of great change in your metabolism, which is partly regulated by your hormones, including the pregnancy hormone progesterone. Some of the changes that occur include:

🐢the amount of blood in your circulation increases by as much as a third
🐢the way your body handles protein becomes more efficient
🐢your breast tissues change in preparation for milk production
🐢your need for many vitamins and minerals increases
🐢your intestines become more efficient so you absorb a higher percentage of nutrients such as calcium and iron from your diet
🐢your body's temperature regulating mechanism may change, so one moment you feel hot and sweaty and the next cold and clammy. These changes are most common during high summer and deep winter. They seem to be worse at night and during the last 10 weeks of pregnancy.

Everyone's metabolism is different, and the way pregnancy affects you will be different from the way it affects your best friend and sometimes even the way it affected your mother or sister. It all depends on the particular genes you have inherited.

Some women find their basic metabolic rate increases during pregnancy so they feel constantly hungry. Others find their basic metabolic rate goes down and they gain weight easily without eating very much more than usual.

Whether your metabolism goes up or down, it will become more efficient so you waste less energy as heat. You will also naturally tend to slow down and become less physically active as your pregnancy progresses. This means that more of the energy you consume is available for conversion into fat stores as reserves for breastfeeding when your baby is born.

Your Energy Needs During Pregnancy

Overall, you need around an extra 70,000 kcals energy over the nine months of pregnancy compared to a similar period when you were not pregnant. This is equivalent to 280 extra kcal per day for 250 days, not counting the first month of pregnancy. This doesn't mean you need to eat an extra 240 kcals per day, however. The UK Department of Health recommends that pregnant women only need to eat an extra 200 kcals per day, and only during the last 3 months of pregnancy. The extra energy requirements are met by the fact that your metabolism becomes more efficient – so every calorie you eat counts rather than being wasted – and by the fact that you naturally tend to become less physically active as pregnancy progresses. Women who were underweight at the beginning of pregnancy and those who do not reduce their levels of activity may need more.

The average weight gain during 40 weeks pregnancy is around 12.5 kg (27–28 lb):

Increase in Weight (g/oz) at Various Stages of Pregnancy

	10 weeks	20 weeks	30 weeks	40 weeks
Your baby	5/¼	300/10½	1,500/53	3,300/116
Placenta	20/¾	170/6	430/15	650/23
Amniotic fluid	30/1	250/9	600/21	800/28
Uterus	135/5	585/20	810/28½	900/32
Breasts	35/1¼	180/6¼	360/12½	400/14
Extra blood	100/3½	600/21	1,300/46	1,200/42
Extra fat/fluid	325/11½	1,915/67½	3,500/123	5,200/183
Total Weight Gain	650/23	4,000/141	8,500/300	12,500/423

One study looking at more than 21,000 deliveries found the average weight gain for normal weight women was 14.5 kg (32 lb). One in 100 (1 per cent of) normal weight women were found to put on no weight at all during pregnancy, but their baby did not tend to grow as well as expected. Ideally, normal weight women need to gain between 11.5 kg (25 lb) and 16 kg (35 lb) for best fetal growth.

In the same study, the researchers looked at women who were obese – more than 20 per cent heavier than they should be. Their average weight was 103.5 kg (228 lb) before they became pregnant. The researchers found that 11 per cent of these obese women gained no weight during pregnancy but, surprisingly, this was also found to be unhealthy for their developing babies. They needed to gain between 7 kg (9 lb) and 11.5 kg (25 lb) during pregnancy for optimum fetal growth – even though they were very overweight to start with.

Women who are underweight should try to gain between 12.5 kg (27 lb) and 18 kg (40 lb) during pregnancy.

The extra fat laid down during pregnancy is deposited in places designed to give you the greatest reserves with the least bother. You may notice that you put on weight in unusual places, such as between your shoulders, on your upper back and around your knees as well as on your hips and thighs. This acts as an energy store for when you start breastfeeding. The common places for fat stores to increase include your:

- thighs
- hips
- around the shoulder blades
- breasts
- abdomen
- upper arms
- knees.

Weight gain during pregnancy is vital for the health of both you and your baby, and is something you should feel comfortable about. Do *not* try to lose weight during pregnancy. This may result in a baby with a reduced birthweight, which may lead to developmental disadvantages in later life.

As long as you follow healthy eating guidelines, try not to worry if you feel hungry all the time.

- Eat a good, healthy, varied diet.
- Listen to your metabolism and eat according to your appetite.
- If you are hungry, have a healthy snack – aim to eat 3 meals and 3 snacks per day during the last 6 months of pregnancy.
- Take a vitamin and mineral supplement especially formulated for pregnancy.
- Eat plenty of oily fish or take a supplement such as Efanatol.
- Eat nuts and seeds for fatty acids, and consider taking an evening primrose oil supplement.
- Drink plenty of fluids.
- Take plenty of rest.

A Healthy Diet During Pregnancy

During pregnancy, follow a balanced, varied, wholefood diet containing:

☺ unrefined, complex carbohydrates (such as wholemeal bread, brown rice, wholegrain cereals, wholewheat pasta, baked potatoes) which are an important source of energy, vitamins, minerals and fibre. They are slowly digested and do not cause large fluctuations in blood sugar levels, as can occur from eating simple carbohydrates (such as sugars). Aim to obtain at least half your daily energy intake in the form of unrefined complex carbohydrates. Five to six slices of wholemeal bread per day will help to meet your energy requirements.

☺ fresh fruit and vegetables – which provide minerals, vitamins and fibre. Aim to eat at least 5 servings per day (a glass of unsweetened orange juice with breakfast, large salad with lunch, 2 pieces of fruit during the day plus 2 vegetables with your evening meal equals 6 servings). Buy produce as fresh as possible and use quickly. Wash and, where practical, peel all fruit, salads and vegetables (especially carrots and apples) before eating as the potentially harmful effects of pesticides and fertilizers are not yet fully understood. Eat them raw or lightly cooked – without additional salt. Where possible, steam for a very short time only. If boiling, bring water to the boil before adding the vegetables, as the boiling water helps to destroy enzymes that break down vitamins such as vitamin C. Re-use vegetable water for sauces, gravies and soups.

☺ protein-rich foods (such as lean meat, fish, pulses, eggs, milk, cheese, cereals, nuts and seeds). US recommendations (1989) suggest that protein requirements increase during pregnancy from the normal 50 g to 60 g per day. UK dietary reference values are slightly lower at 45 g per day for non-pregnant women, 51 g per day during pregnancy, 56 g per day during the first 4 months of breastfeeding and 53 g per day for breastfeeding from 4 months onwards. Most women in the Western world already obtain more than 60 g protein per day. Vegetarians can substitute pulses, grains, cereals, nuts and seeds for fish and meat. Avoid liver and liver products, however, due to the risk of vitamin A toxicity.

- calcium-rich foods (such as milk, pasteurized yoghurt, pasteurized cheese, green vegetables, oranges, bread). Calcium is the only mineral whose requirement doubles during pregnancy. It is essential for the development of fetal bones. If calcium is in short supply, it will be leached from your bones and teeth.
- foods rich in essential fatty acids – such as oily fish, nuts and seeds. These are vital for your baby's growing brain and nervous system.
- cut back on your intake of table salt (sodium chloride) by avoiding obviously salty foods, checking labels of pre-bought foods (75 per cent of dietary table salt is hidden in processed foods) and avoiding adding it during cooking or at the table
- avoid highly processed foods jumping with additives
- eat red meat 3 times per week or less, rather than the more usual once or twice per day – eat more fish in its place
- use olive or rapeseed oil during cooking and do not re-use oils (which contain higher amounts of harmful trans-fatty acids)
- when hungry, snack on healthy foods such as fruit, toast, bread, plain biscuits, malt loaf, yoghurt or fromage frais rather than sweet cakes, sweet biscuits, crisps and pastries
- keep your intake of sweets, chocolates and sugary, fizzy drinks to a minimum
- avoid alcohol as much as possible (see Chapter 9)
- avoid foods that are an infection hazard (see Chapter 9) such as:
  - ripened soft cheeses such as Brie, Camembert, Cambozola
  - blue-veined cheeses such as Stilton, Roquefort, Blue Shropshire, Blue Brie, Dolcelatte
  - goat or sheep cheeses such as fetta, Chèvre
  - any unpasteurized soft and cream cheese

- any under-cooked (raw, rare or pink) meat
- raw eggs or any that are not fully hard-boiled
- cook-chill meals and ready-to-eat poultry unless thoroughly re-heated
- all types of paté
- ready-prepared coleslaw and salads
- unwrapped foods that are not re-heated thoroughly (such as sausage rolls)
- unpasteurized milk or dairy products
- shellfish
- all foods past their 'best by' date
- rolls or sandwiches containing any of the above
- soft whipped ice cream from ice-cream machines.

Keep your kitchen clean and dry, with fridge temperatures below 5°C (41°F) and freezer below -18°C (0°F). Wash hands thoroughly before preparing foods. Store raw meat at the bottom of the fridge, covered, and keep it separate from cooked foods. Defrost frozen produce thoroughly before cooking. Cook foods thoroughly, and throw away any that are past their use-by dates. Finally, keep pets out of the kitchen at all times.

Effects of Poor Nutrition at Different Stages of Pregnancy

Poor nutrition occurring only in the first 3 months of pregnancy leads to:

- reduced birthweight
- proportionately small body
- reduced head circumference
- less than optimum brain development and reduced intelligence
- reduced weight of child at 1 year after delivery
- increased risk of high blood pressure in later life
- increased risk of death from haemorrhagic (bleeding) stroke in later life.

Poor nutrition occurring only during the 3rd – 6th months of pregnancy leads to:

- reduced birthweight
- an unusually thin baby
- reduced head circumference
- less than optimum brain development and reduced intelligence
- increased risk of high blood pressure and diabetes in later life
- increased risk of death from coronary heart disease in later life.

Poor nutrition occurring only during the last 3 months of pregnancy leads to:

- body that seems small in proportion to head size
- reduced head circumference
- less than optimum brain development and reduced intelligence
- reduced weight at 1 year of age
- increased risk of high blood pressure, abnormal cholesterol levels and blood clots in later life
- increased risk of death from coronary heart disease or thrombotic (blood clot) stroke in later life.

7

Vitamins and Minerals for a Super Baby

Vitamins

Vitamins are dietary substances that are essential in tiny amounts for a healthy metabolism. Most cannot be synthesized in your body (or not in sufficient quantity) and must therefore come from your food. During pregnancy, and the preconceptual care period, your need for certain vitamins increases.

To give you an idea of how much of each vitamin your diet provides, the following table shows the average intake of each vitamin for British women aged between 16 and 64 years. Against this is given the Recommended Daily Amount (RDA) of each nutrient during pregnancy.

Vitamins	RDA* in pregnancy	Average Intakes
Vitamin A (retinol)	800 mcg	1,058 mcg
Betacarotene	6 mg**	2.1 mg
Vitamin B_1 (thiamin)	1.4 mg	1.2 mg
Vitamin B_2 (riboflavin)	1.6 mg	1.6 mg
Vitamin B_3 (niacin)	18 mg	28.5 mg
Vitamin B_5 (pantothenic acid)	6 mg	4.5 mg
Vitamin B_6 (pyridoxine)	2 mg	1.6 mg
Vitamin B_{12} (cyanocobalamin)	1.5 mcg	5.2 mcg
Folic acid	400 mcg***	213 mcg
Biotin	0.15 mg	28.3 mcg
Vitamin C	60 mg	62 mg
Vitamin D	5 mcg	2.5 mcg
Vitamin E	10 mg	7.2 mg

* New European Community (EC) RDA for adults, which in most cases is greater than the former Reference Nutrient Intake (RNI) for pregnant women. The RNIs for B_{12} and folic acid during pregnancy are quoted, as these are greater than the standard EC RDA for these nutrients for adults.

** There is no RNI for betacarotene; the 6 mg quoted above is the US National Cancer Institute's suggested daily allowance.

*** Women who have previously had a child with a neural tube defect need 5 mg (5,000 mcg) folic acid during the preconceptual care period and up until at least the 12th week of pregnancy.

At first glance, it would appear that most women are obtaining enough of most vitamins except thiamin, pantothenic acid, folic acid, vitamin D and betacarotene. An average is only an average, however. Fifty per cent of women are getting less than the average intakes shown. For example, although the average vitamin C intake is 62 mg per day, the observed intake range is wide, with some women only obtaining 14 mg per day.

Food surveys show that a large proportion of the population is at risk of gross deficiency of vitamins B_1, B_2, B_5, B_6, C, D and E.

At present, the only supplement universally recommended during pregnancy and the preconceptual care period is folic acid to reduce the incidence of fetal neural tube defects. Research suggests, however, that vitamin B_{12} will further reduce the risk of neural tube defects, and that a multivitamin supplement halves the risk of congenital developmental defects in general. The offspring of women who take supplements containing vitamins A (betacarotene), C, E and the B vitamins seem to have a lower risk of developing a future brain tumour. Further research is needed to find out exactly which vitamins and minerals are needed during pregnancy for optimum brain development and optimum growth. Children who receive an adequate intake of vitamins and minerals develop a 4 – 5 point IQ advantage, and seem able to process more information in less time. It is possible that the same beneficial effects on brain function may occur with improved micronutrition in the womb.

It is important not to exceed the recommended doses of any dietary nutrient unless specifically advised to do so by your doctor. Some vitamins and minerals can be harmful in excess.

VITAMIN A (RETINOL)
Vitamin A is a fat-soluble vitamin found only in animal products.

Why You Need It During Pregnancy
Vitamin A helps to control the growth and development of your baby by binding to special receptors inside cells and regulating the way genes are read and coded for the production of enzymes and other proteins. A large number of genes are sensitive to vitamin A and, if it is lacking, fetal growth slows down.

Vitamin A is also needed for healthy cell membranes, including those of the neurons in your baby's brain. It is best known for its role in vision, however. In your baby's eye, vitamin A is converted into the pigment known as visual purple (rhodopsin). When this pigment is exposed to light it changes and interacts with the back of the eye to trigger messages that are relayed to the brain. The first sign of vitamin A deficiency is sensitivity to green light. This is followed by difficulty adapting to dim light (night blindness).

Vitamin A also has an important role as an antioxidant. It forms part of the antioxidant mechanism that is vital for protecting the brain from damage due to exposure to the metabolic chemicals and free radicals (see page 176) produced during the rapid developmental process in the womb. It may provide some protection against cerebral palsy.

Excess intakes of vitamin A are toxic. Intakes of more than 10,000 IU (3,000 mcg, which is more than three times the recommended daily intake for adults) increases the risk of a developmental abnormality affecting the head, brain or spinal cord by a factor of 5. The most harmful time to take excess vitamin A seems to be the first 7 weeks of pregnancy. It is best to avoid supplements containing vitamin A unless prescribed by a doctor as a result of your own low levels of the vitamin. You should also avoid cod liver oil supplements, liver and liver products during pregnancy. The safest way to take vitamin A is as betacarotene (see below).

Women with low levels of vitamin A during the last 3 months of pregnancy also have low levels in their breastmilk. Their babies continue to be deficient in vitamin A during early life after birth, too. This increases their risk of respiratory tract infections, diarrhoea and febrile illness – even though the babies are breast-fed and would be expected to gain protection from maternal antibodies. Lack of vitamin A is increased by iron deficiency, as iron seems to boost vitamin A levels in blood and breastmilk, although it is not yet certain whether iron boosts absorption of vitamin A or interacts with it in another way.

How Much You Need
The UK reference nutrient intake (RNI) for vitamin A is 700 mcg per day. World Health Organization (WHO) recommendations

are significantly higher, at 800 mcg vitamin A daily for adult women and 1,000 mcg per day during pregnancy. Most pregnant women in the Western world already have a vitamin A intake greater than this. Vitamin A deficiency is a common and serious problem in underdeveloped countries, however.

Good Dietary Sources
☺animal and fish liver (avoid during pregnancy – see below)
☺kidneys
☺eggs
☺milk
☺cheese
☺yoghurt
☺butter
☺oily fish
☺meat
☺margarine – which is fortified by law to contain as much vitamin A as that found in butter

Vitamin A is easily destroyed by exposure to light.

Potential Problems
Excess vitamin A is toxic and linked with an increased risk of congenital birth defects such as abnormalities of the kidneys, urogenital tract, and brain. Although liver and liver products are rich in vitamin A, these should be avoided during pregnancy to prevent vitamin A toxicity. You should not take supplements containing high doses of vitamin A during pregnancy unless they are specifically advised by your doctor. The safest way to ensure an adequate supply of vitamin A is to obtain plenty of the pro-vitamin, betacarotene.

BETACAROTENE
Betacarotene is a water-soluble pigment found in yellow-orange and dark green plants. It consists of two molecules of vitamin A

joined together. Nutritionally, 6 mcg betacarotene is equivalent to around 1 mcg of preformed Vitamin A (retinol). On average, around half of ingested betacarotene is converted into vitamin A in the cells lining the small intestine and in the liver.

Why You Need It During Pregnancy
See above for vitamin A. Also acts as a powerful antioxidant (see page 000).

How Much You Need
The US National Cancer Institute (NCI) suggest a minimum of 6 mg per day to reduce the risk of cancer.

Good Dietary Sources

dark green leafy vegetables and yellow-orange fruits, such as:
☺ carrots
☺ sweet potatoes
☺ spinach
☺ broccoli
☺ parsley
☺ watercress
☺ spring greens
☺ cantaloupe melons
☺ apricots
☺ peaches
☺ mango
☺ red and yellow peppers
☺ tomatoes
☺ sweet corn

Betacarotene is destroyed by heat and overcooking.

Potential Problems

Excess betacarotene can cause orange pigmentation of the skin. This is not harmful and fades once intakes are reduced.

VITAMIN B₁ – THIAMIN

Thiamin is a water-soluble B group vitamin that cannot be stored in the body in large amounts. Stores are usually only enough to last one month.

Why You Need It During Pregnancy

Vitamin B_1 plays an important role in metabolism and in the way nerves and muscle cells – including those in the heart – conduct messages to each other, through the release of a common synapse chemical (neurotransmitter), acetylcholine. It is also needed for the production of energy from glucose, for making red blood cells and for the synthesis of some amino acids. It is therefore essential for fetal growth and the normal development of your baby's brain and nervous system. If a mother's diet is lacking in thiamin, her baby has a higher risk of low birthweight.

How Much You Need

The EC RDA for adults is 1.4 mg daily. The UK recommendation is 0.8 mg per day for women, with an additional 0.1 mg during the last 3 months of pregnancy (0.9 mg). World-wide, thiamin deficiency is common, as body stores are usually only enough for one month. Those most at risk of thiamin deficiency are women on weight-loss diets and those drinking large amounts of coffee or tea, which destroy thiamin.

Good Dietary Sources

- brewer's yeast and yeast extracts
- brown rice
- wheat germ and wheat bran
- wholegrain bread and cereals
- oatmeal and oatflakes

- soya flour
- pasta
- meat
- seafood
- pulses
- nuts

Thiamin is easily lost by food processing, as by chopping, mincing, liquidizing, canning and preserving. Boiling reduces the thiamin content of foods by half as it is so water soluble. It is also destroyed by high temperatures and adding baking powder. Toasting bread can rob it of almost a third of its thiamin content.

High intakes of coffee, tea or alcohol can destroy thiamin and lead to deficiency, especially if you are also stressed, as stress reactions quickly use up available thiamin stores.

VITAMIN B_2 – RIBOFLAVIN
Riboflavin is a water-soluble B group vitamin that cannot be stored in the body in large amounts.

Why You Need It During Pregnancy
Riboflavin is essential for many metabolic reactions, including the production of energy and the way your body handles proteins, fats and carbohydrate. It also acts as an antioxidant. Riboflavin is also important for maintaining a healthy immune system, in the production of antibodies, and for keeping skin, hair and mucous membranes healthy. When breastfeeding, up to 15 per cent of your B_2 intake enters your breastmilk; this level increases to 30 per cent as your baby grows and breastmilk changes in composition. This suggests that B_2 is very important for infant growth and development.

How Much You Need
The US recommendation for pregnant women and nursing mothers is 2 – 2.5 mg per day. The EC RDA for adults is 1.6 mg,

while the UK RNI for riboflavin is 1.4 mg per day during pregnancy and 1.6 mg during lactation.

Good Dietary Sources
☺yeast extract
☺liver
☺wheat germ and bran
☺wholegrain cereals
☺milk
☺cheese
☺yoghurt
☺eggs
☺green leafy vegetables
☺beans

Milk is a rich source of riboflavin but is best obtained from cartons rather than bottles. This is because sunlight destroys milk riboflavin quickly.

VITAMIN B$_3$ – NIACIN

Niacin is a water-soluble B group vitamin that cannot be stored in the body to any great extent. Niacin exists in several forms (such as nicotinic acid and nicotinamide) and can be made in the body from the essential amino acid, tryptophan.

Why You Need It During Pregnancy

Niacin plays an important role in metabolism and enzyme function. It is essential for releasing energy from muscle sugar stores (glycogen), for processing fatty acids released from body fat stores, and for the way rapidly dividing cells use oxygen (cell respiration). It works together with thiamin and riboflavin for these tasks, and also works on its own to maintain healthy skin, nerves and intestines. It is important for brain cell function and for maintaining intellectual prowess.

Niacin also joins forces with the mineral, chromium, to form the Glucose Tolerance Factor (GTF). This is essential for the inter-action of insulin with its cell receptors to control glucose uptake by cells. Lack of chromium or niacin is associated with impaired glucose tolerance, which may lead to diabetes in pregnancy.

How Much You Need
The US National Research Council recommends an adult daily intake of 13 – 19 mg per day. In the UK, 13 mg per day is sug-gested for both pregnant and non-pregnant women, with an additional 2 mg per day during lactation. The EC RDA is 18 mg for adults.

Good Dietary Sources
🐮yeast extract
🐮wheat bran
🐮nuts
🐮meat
🐮oily fish
🐮poultry
🐮wholemeal bread
🐮cheese
🐮dried fruit
🐮brown rice
🐮eggs
🐮milk
🐮wholegrains

Potential Problems
Excess niacin can cause facial flushing (which reverts to normal if intake is reduced).

VITAMIN B$_5$ – PANTOTHENIC ACID
Pantothenic acid is a water-soluble B group vitamin that cannot be stored in the body to any great extent.

Why You Need It During Pregnancy
Vitamin B_5 is involved in the metabolism of proteins, fat and carbohydrates. It is also necessary for making glucose, fatty acids and adrenal gland hormones, and for maintaining a healthy nervous system.

How Much You Need
The EC RDA for adults is 6 mg per day. There is no UK RNI.

Good Dietary Sources
🐤yeast extract
🐤nuts
🐤wheatgerm and bran
🐤eggs
🐤poultry and meat (especially offal)
🐤wholegrains
🐤wholemeal bread
🐤beans and vegetables

B_5 is easily destroyed by food processing – even deep freezing.

VITAMIN B_6 – PYRIDOXINE
Natural vitamin B_6 is really a group of six compounds that are converted to the active form – pyridoxine – in the body.

Why You Need It During Pregnancy
Vitamin B_6 is needed for the proper functioning of over 60 enzymes. It is involved in the synthesis of nucleic acids, amino acids and proteins, and for metabolizing body stores of carbohydrate (glycogen) and essential fatty acids. It is especially important during the rapid cell division that occurs in every fetal tissue – especially the brain. Vitamin B_6 is also needed for the synthesis of some brain chemicals (neurotransmitters) which pass messages from one brain cell to another and pass impulses down nerve endings. It helps to regulate the function of sex hormones.

B_6 is sometimes called the 'immune booster' as it is needed by cells that produce antibodies and fight infection (lymphocytes).

How Much You Need
The US and EC RDAs for vitamin B_6 are 2 mg for adults, while the UK reference nutrient intake is lower at 1.2 mg per day for both non-pregnant and pregnant women. In general, the more protein you eat, the more vitamin B_6 you need.

Good Dietary Sources
🐸yeast extract
🐸wholegrain cereals
🐸liver
🐸soya products
🐸bananas
🐸walnuts
🐸meat
🐸oily fish
🐸brown rice
🐸green leafy vegetables
🐸avocado
🐸egg yolk
🐸royal jelly

Vitamin B_6 is destroyed by cooking and by exposure to light.

Potential Problems
Some researchers have linked large doses of vitamin B_6 during pregnancy with possible congenital limb abnormalities.

Very high intakes of vitamin B_6 (several hundreds of mg per day) taken over several weeks or months may produce symptoms of nerve damage (tingling, burning, shooting pains, pins and needles, clumsiness, numbness, even partial paralysis), depression, headache, tiredness, bloatedness and irritability. High doses should be avoided in pregnancy.

VITAMIN B$_{12}$ – COBALAMIN

Vitamin B$_{12}$ is a water-soluble vitamin found in animal sources. No plants are known to consistently contain vitamin B$_{12}$, with the exception of some blue-green algae. Yeast cultures are rich in vitamin B$_{12}$. Vitamin B$_{12}$ supplements made by genetically modified bacterial fermentation are also available. The liver usually has enough vitamin B$_{12}$ stores to last several years. Prolonged deficiency leads to symptoms of pernicious anaemia that creep up slowly.

Why You Need It During Pregnancy

Vitamin B$_{12}$ is needed, together with folic acid, for copying chromosomes when cells divide. It is therefore very important for rapidly dividing cells, including neurons in the brain and spinal cord. Lack of either B$_{12}$ or folic acid leads to the production of abnormal cells that are too large and, as this affects the production of red blood cells, leads to anaemia. Neural tube defects of the developing brain and spinal cord (see page 147) are five times more common in babies whose mother had low blood levels of vitamin B$_{12}$, whether or not folic acid levels are low. Vitamin B$_{12}$ is also needed for the formation of healthy nerve sheaths (myelin) and the transmission of electrical signals down nerve axons.

Dietary vitamin B$_{12}$ is absorbed in the lower part of the small intestine, but only if a carrier protein, intrinsic factor, is present. Intrinsic factor is made in the stomach and vitamin B$_{12}$ deficiency (pernicious anaemia) sometimes develops because of lack of intrinsic factor or disease of the small intestine. Supplementation must then be given through regular injections. If deficiency is not corrected, nerves in the spinal cord can be damaged, leading to a rare condition known as sub-acute combined degeneration of the cord.

Lack of vitamin B$_{12}$ in the mother's diet can cause severe delay in myelination of her baby's brain, spinal cord and peripheral nerves. This results in a shrunken brain and mental retardation, which is to some extent reversible with supplementation. New research also suggests that up to 20 per cent of autistic children may be deficient in vitamin B_{12}, and that treatment may help to prevent further nerve degeneration.

How Much You Need
The EC RDA and UK RNI for vitamin B_{12} is 1.5 mcg per day. No additional supplements are yet suggested during pregnancy, although an extra 0.5 mcg per day is needed while breastfeeding. In view of the fact that neural tube defects do still occur in women taking folic acid supplements, it seems sensible to increase B_{12} intake during pregnancy. Some countries recommend an adult intake of 3 mcg per day.

Good Dietary Sources
☺liver
☺kidney
☺oily fish – especially sardines
☺red meat
☺white fish
☺eggs
☺milk
☺yoghurt
☺cheese

Vegetarian mothers-to-be need to pay special attention to their dietary intake of vitamin B_{12}.

Potential Problems
Vitamin B_{12} deficiency can be masked by taking folate supplements, so B_{12} is usually given along with folic acid where clinically indicated.

FOLIC ACID

Folic acid (also known as folate) is a B group vitamin. It was named after the Latin word for leaf, *folia*, as it was first discovered in spinach and is mainly found in green leafy vegetables. The body stores very little folic acid – it is probably the most widespread vitamin deficiency in developed countries.

Why You Need It During Pregnancy

Folate is needed for a wide number of body functions, including the:

- healthy production of new cells
- metabolism of sugars and proteins
- maintenance of healthy nerves.

When a cell divides in two, its genes are copied so that each daughter cell contains a full set of genetic material. Folic acid is essential for this process, so that if your levels of the vitamin are low, cells that are dividing become larger than normal and are more likely to contain abnormal chromosomes. As pregnancy is a time of rapid growth and division of cells, good supplies of folic acid are vital. In fact, folic acid is the only vitamin you need twice as much of during pregnancy than at any other time. Like vitamin B_{12}, it is especially needed by cells that are dividing rapidly, such as those in your baby's developing central nervous system.

Lack of folic acid during the first few weeks of pregnancy can trigger a type of congenital abnormality known as a neural tube defect. This is when your baby's central nervous system (spinal cord and brain) starts developing – around 3 weeks after the egg has been fertilized (see page 4):

- first, a long thickening forms where your baby's spine will eventually develop
- the edges of this thickening grow upwards to form a U-shaped groove

the walls of the groove start to fold over and fuse to form a
tube which will develop into the baby's brain and spinal cord
groups of cells then grow in and around the tube which will
eventually form the protective back bones (vertebrae).

If folic acid is in short supply, the cells forming the neural tube
cannot grow and divide properly. The neural tube does not fuse
fully along its length, so a gap is left at the top or bottom of the
spine. This is known as a neural tube defect, examples of which
include:

spina bifida – literally meaning split spine – a distressing condition in which one or more of the bones in the back (vertebrae) fail to develop properly so the spinal cord and nerves are
damaged due to lack of bony protection. Sometimes the
membranes surrounding the spinal cord and even the spinal
cord itself may be abnormal, too.
some cases of hydrocephalus (a build-up of cerebrospinal
fluid in the skull due to faulty development of drainage channels) – but probably only those cases associated with spina
bifida.
anencephaly – a rare condition in which most of the brain and
the top of the skull fail to form.

Other birth defects which have been linked with lack of folic acid
include cleft palate, hare lip and abnormalities of the limbs,
heart, lungs and skeleton.

Sadly, at least two babies are conceived with a neural tube
defect every day. If a man or woman has had one previous child
suffering from a neural tube defect, or if either parent is affected
him- or herself, the risk of having a baby with a neural tube
defect is 10 times greater than normal. If a man or woman has
had two affected children, the risk of a third baby with a neural
tube defect is 20 times greater. It is reassuring to know that taking a folic acid supplement can reduce these risks by 75 per cent.

There is still some way to go before all women who are planning a baby or who are pregnant increase their intake of folic acid. A recent survey by the UK Health Education Authority showed that only 27 per cent of women were spontaneously aware of the importance of folic acid during pregnancy, although this was better than the 9 per cent who were aware the previous year.

Folic acid supplements may also help to protect against pre-eclampsia, which was recently found to be linked with high levels of the amino acid, homocysteine. Around one in 10 people inherits higher than normal blood levels of homocysteine. This can damage artery linings (including those in the placenta) and more than triples the risk of a heart attack in later life. One in 160,000 people has extremely high levels, with 30 times the risk of premature heart disease. Folic acid supplements (400 – 650 mcg per day) can lower homocysteine levels to reduce the risk of pre-eclampsia in affected women (and, if continued after pregnancy, supplements also reduce their long-term risk of a heart attack). Folic acid supplements during pregnancy may decrease the risk of the offspring developing a brain tumour during childhood by over 60 per cent.

How Much You Need

If you are planning a baby, you should increase your intake of folic acid in three ways, by:

1 choosing foods which have been fortified with folic acid (including many breakfast cereals and some breads)
2 eating more folate-rich foods such as green leafy vegetables
3 taking a daily dietary supplement of 400 mcg folic acid daily.

Ideally, you should start boosting your intake at least 3 months before trying for a baby, or certainly from the time you stop using contraception. Supplements should continue for at least the first 12 weeks of pregnancy and preferably throughout the whole 9 months. After the first 3 months, you can drop down to taking 200 mcg folic acid if you wish.

If you have previously conceived a child with a neural tube defect, you should take a supplement containing at least 10 times more folic acid. Supplements containing 5 mg folic acid are available on prescription for this purpose.

Research suggests that after having a baby, it takes more than 6 months for a mother to return to her pre-pregnancy folic acid levels.

Good Dietary Sources

Folic acid is such an important vitamin for health that more and more foods are being fortified with it to boost everyone's intake. These are now also easier to spot, thanks to the UK Health Education Authority's new 'flash' scheme which leading manufacturers are adding to their packaging. Look out for flashes saying:

contains folic acid – on foods that can provide at least one-sixth of your daily requirement
with extra folic acid – on foods enriched to provide at least half your daily requirements.

When planning a pregnancy, you should aim to eat foods rich in folic acid as well as taking folic acid supplements.

Folic acid is mainly found in green leafy vegetables and fortified foods.

Good Sources of Folic Acid for Pregnant Women
- fortified foods such as cereals and breads
- green leafy vegetables such as spinach, broccoli, Brussels sprouts, kale, spring greens
- green beans, cooked black-eyed beans and baked beans
- cauliflower
- potatoes
- wholemeal or granary-style bread

🐮yeast extract
🐮soya products
🐮kidney
🐮dairy products
🐮citrus fruit
🐮eggs
🐮yoghurt

Don't boil your vegetables for too long. Eat them crisp – or even raw – as prolonged boiling destroys much of the folic acid present in the green leaves. Folic acid is also destroyed by prolonged contact with light and air, but can be protected by the antioxidant, vitamin C (as by squeezing lemon juice over your vegetables).

Potential Problems

There is no evidence that taking folic acid supplements in the amounts recommended for pregnancy are harmful.

If you have epilepsy, and are taking drugs to stop your fits, you should seek medical advice before trying for a baby. Some anti-convulsant drugs work by interfering with the way your body handles folic acid, so supplements can affect your treatment. It is best to seek specialist advice about which anti-epilepsy drugs are safe to take during pregnancy, and what level of folic acid supplementation you need.

BIOTIN

Biotin is a water-soluble vitamin.

Why You Need It During Pregnancy

Biotin is a co-factor of several enzymes involved in the synthesis of fatty acids and of certain chemicals which are the building-blocks for genetic material (purine nucleotides). It is therefore essential for the healthy division of fetal cells, including those in your baby's central nervous system. Biotin is also needed in the metabolism of some amino acids (protein) and for making glucose, which is the main energy source for your baby's brain cells. Biotin concentrations in human breastmilk are 15 times higher than those in the mother's bloodstream, suggesting that biotin is very important for the growth and development of your baby.

How Much You Need
The US recommended daily amount for biotin is 300 mcg per day. The EC RDA for adults is 150 mcg (0.15 mg).

Good Dietary Sources
⏥liver
⏥kidney
⏥yeast extract
⏥nuts
⏥wholegrain foods
⏥wholemeal bread
⏥egg yolk
⏥oily fish, especially sardines
⏥rice

Biotin is also synthesized by bacteria in your intestines. Deficiency is rare except in people who eat large amounts of raw egg white (not recommended during pregnancy because of the risk of Salmonella). Raw egg white contains a protein called avidin which binds to biotin in the intestines and prevents its absorption.

Potential Problems
Lack of biotin has been linked with severe cradle-cap in newborn babies.

VITAMIN C (ASCORBIC ACID)
Vitamin C is a water-soluble vitamin.

Why You Need It During Pregnancy

Vitamin C is essential for the synthesis of collagen – a major structural protein that is found in just about every tissue in your growing baby. It is necessary for proper growth and repair of tissues and for healthy skin, bones and teeth. It is also involved in the metabolism of some hormones. One of its most important roles is as an antioxidant. It forms part of the antioxidant mechanism that is vital for protecting the brain from damage due to exposure to the metabolic chemicals and free radicals (see page 175) produced during the rapid developmental process in the womb. It may provide some protection against cerebral palsy. Your baby's vitamin C levels are 10 per cent higher than your own, suggesting that it is important for fetal growth and development.

Lack of vitamin C is linked with an increased risk of premature rupture of membranes and preterm labour. This results from poor-quality collagen which breaks down more easily. Vitamin C supplements during pregnancy may decrease the risk of the offspring developing a brain tumour during childhood by over 50 per cent.

How Much You Need

The US and EC RDA is 60 mg per day for adults. Much higher doses of several grams per day are safe and considered by many to be advisable for optimum health. As vitamin C is needed for the production of all your baby's tissues, and as you need more antioxidants during pregnancy, a dose of 500 – 1,000 mg per day is reasonable.

Good Dietary Sources

- blackcurrants
- guavas
- kiwi fruit
- citrus fruit
- mangoes

🙂green peppers
🙂strawberries
🙂green sprouting vegetables such as broccoli, sprouts, watercress, parsley
🙂potatoes

Vitamin C is one of the most unstable vitamins; up to two-thirds is lost by processing, prolonged cooking and storage. For example, the vitamin C content of fruit juice is lost after 2 weeks' storage. It is easily destroyed by cooking and exposure to light. As vitamin C is water soluble, it is lost from vegetables if boiled – some can be reclaimed by using the water to make sauces, gravy, etc. Better still, vegetables should be steamed or boiled with minimal water.

Potential Problems
Lack of vitamin C causes scurvy. Until recently, this was a relatively rare disease in the Western world, but is now becoming more common – especially in teenage mothers who follow a poor diet with little fresh fruit or vegetables.

VITAMIN D
Vitamin D is a vitamin that also acts as a hormone (calcitriol). It can be synthesized in the body by the action of sunlight on a cholesterol-like molecule in the skin. Blood levels of vitamin D are therefore naturally higher in the summer and lower in winter. People living in high altitudes, who cover up their skin in sunlight, or who stay indoors all day are not exposed to enough sunlight to meet their vitamin D needs. They must then rely on getting vitamin D from their diet.

Why You Need It During Pregnancy
Vitamin D is needed to absorb dietary calcium and phosphate from your intestines. It stimulates synthesis of a calcium-transport protein in the lining of your small intestines. Vitamin D is

therefore essential for the growth and maintenance of bones and teeth during pregnancy. Lack of vitamin D causes poor fetal bone development, especially an abnormally formed skull. This can lead to brain abnormalities and future learning difficulties.

How Much You Need
The EC RDA for vitamin D is 10 mcg per day.

Good Dietary Sources
🐟 oily fish – sardine, herring, mackerel, salmon, trout
🐟 fish liver oils
🐟 fortified margarine
🐟 liver
🐟 eggs
🐟 fortified milk
🐟 butter

Vegetarian mothers-to-be need to pay special attention to their dietary intake of vitamin D.

Potential Problems
If vitamin D is lacking during childhood, deformed bones (rickets) result. In adults, weakened, softened bones (osteomalacia) develop.

Excess vitamin D (above 250 mg per day) is toxic, but this only occurs through too much oral intake – not through exposure to sun, where synthesis is self-limiting. Symptoms of excess include high blood levels of calcium, with symptoms of thirst, anorexia, excess urine production and kidney stones.

VITAMIN E
Vitamin E is a fat-soluble vitamin that acts as a powerful antioxidant.

Why You Need It During Pregnancy

As an antioxidant, vitamin E is important for protecting body fat stores and fatty cell membranes from damage – including the essential fatty acids that make up 20 per cent of the weight of your baby's developing brain. It strengthens muscle fibres and may help to prevent miscarriage and make labour easier. Vitamin E is easily transported across the placenta, but premature infants are often born without adequate vitamin E reserves. As a result, their red blood cell membranes are unusually fragile, leading to a haemolytic anaemia and neonatal jaundice.

Severe vitamin E deficiency during pregnancy causes fetal weakness and poor development of the heart, brain, lung and kidneys. Developmental difficulties usually follow. It forms part of the antioxidant mechanism that is vital for protecting the brain from damage due to exposure to the metabolic chemicals and free radicals (see page 175) produced during the rapid developmental process in the womb. It may provide some protection against cerebral palsy. High doses of vitamin E are known to reduce the severity of eye damage (retrolental fibroplasia) due to oxygen treatment in very premature babies.

In general, the more polyunsaturated fats a person eats, the more vitamin E she needs, as polyunsaturated fats are prone to rapid oxidation and rancidity. Vitamin E also boosts immunity and improves skin suppleness and healing.

Vitamin E given at a dose of 300 mg per day seems to reduce the risk of complications associated with uterine fibroids during pregnancy. Vitamin E supplements during pregnancy may decrease the risk of the offspring developing a brain tumour during childhood by 65 per cent.

How Much You Need

The EC RDA is 10 mg per day. Many experts now believe a daily intake of at least 40 to 50 mg vitamin E is needed to provide good antioxidant protection. This means taking supplements – which should ideally be natural source vitamin E (d-alpha-tocopherol), not synthetic dl-alphatocopherol, which is less biologically active. Taking extra vitamin E during pregnancy (such as 67 mg, equivalent to 100 IU) seems reasonable and will help to keep your skin in good condition, possibly even reducing the risk of stretch marks.

Good Dietary Sources
- vegetable oils – of which wheatgerm oil is the richest
- avocado
- margarine
- eggs
- butter
- wholemeal cereals
- seeds
- nuts
- bread
- oily fish
- broccoli

Vitamin E is unstable when frozen – up to 80 per cent of the vitamin E content is destroyed. Heating destroys around 30 per cent vitamin E content. Fresh raw foods, and supplements, are therefore the best sources.

VITAMIN K
Vitamin K is a fat-soluble vitamin made in your liver.

Why Your Baby Needs Vitamin K at Birth
Vitamin K is essential for the formation of blood-clotting factors in the liver. Deficiency of vitamin K leads to prolonged bleeding. When your baby is born, his vitamin K level will be low, as the vitamin does not cross the placenta in great amounts. This is thought to have a protective effect in the womb – nature's way of preventing blood clots in your baby's tiny, developing blood vessels. Also, some proteins involved in the way cells develop into different types may depend on low levels of vitamin K.

Vitamin K deficiency in the first week of life causes bleeding in 1.7 per cent of newborn babies, as their blood cannot clot enough to protect against internal bleeding. This is known as classic early haemorrhagic disease of the newborn. Five out of every 100,000 children go on to have major bleeding into the skull between the 3rd and 12th week of life. This is known as late haemorrhagic disease of the newborn. Vitamin K supplementation (by injection or by mouth) is therefore recommended for your baby soon after birth. This will prevent at least 40 children in the UK from having an intracranial haemorrhage (stroke) each year. As babies who are breastfed are more likely to be vitamin K deficient than formula-fed infants, this preventative is especially important for them. A recent controversial trial suggested a link between giving vitamin K by injection (but not by mouth) and an increased risk of developing childhood leukaemia before the age of 10. This was recently disproved, but still causes some anxiety among new parents. Vitamin K by injection virtually eliminates the risk of early or late haemolytic disease of the newborn. Oral vitamin K decreases the risk of late disease, but infants may still be at risk of early haemorrhage. The best advice is to let your baby have vitamin K – preferably by injection. If you have any worries, discuss these fully with your midwife and obstetrician before your baby is born to help put your mind at rest.

Mothers who have epilepsy and have to take anti-epileptic drugs during pregnancy have an increased risk of having a baby with congenital abnormalities such as facial deformity due to faulty production of nasal cartilage. Some research suggests that this risk is reduced if women with epilepsy take vitamin K supplements early on in their pregnancy.

How Much You Need
There is no RDA at present, as vitamin K is made in your liver, unless you have a long-term liver disease.

Good Dietary Sources
☺ green leafy vegetables such as broccoli, cabbage, lettuce
☺ the richest source, liver, should be avoided during pregnancy
   due to the risk of vitamin A toxicity

Minerals for a Super Baby

Essential minerals are inorganic, dietary substances that are just as important to health as the essential vitamins. Those that are needed in amounts of more than 100 mg per day are usually referred to as minerals, while those needed in much smaller amounts are often known as trace elements.

Nutrient	EC RDA*	Average Intake
Calcium	800 mg**	726 mg
Iodine	150 mcg	171 mcg
Magnesium	300 mg	237 mg
Zinc	15 mg	8.4 mg

Nutrient	UK RNI (pregnant women)	Average Intake
Copper	1.2 mg	1.23 mg
Iron	14.8 mg	10.5 mg
Selenium	60 mcg	39 mcg per day

* New EC RDA for adults, which in most cases is greater than the former reference nutrient intake (RNI) for pregnant women. Previous RNIs for iron, copper and selenium are quoted, as these are either greater than the standard EC RDA for adults (iron) or no EC RDA yet exists (copper, selenium).

** The UK National Osteoporosis Society recommends higher amounts: 1,200 mg calcium per day during pregnancy and 1,250 mg daily when breastfeeding.

Lack of minerals is even more common than lack of vitamins, with widespread deficiency of most. The intakes quoted are only averages, which means that 50 per cent of women are getting even less than these amounts. The average adult obtains only:

68 per cent of the RDA for iron
53 per cent of the RDA for zinc
78 per cent of the RDA for magnesium.

In addition, 40 per cent of people obtain less dietary calcium than recommended, and selenium intakes have halved over the last 20 years.

Recommended Daily Intakes For Essential Nutrients During Pregnancy (US, 1989)

Nutrient	Non-Pregnant Women	Additional Requirements for Pregnancy	Total
Calcium (mg)	800	+400	1,200
Iron (mg)	15	+15	30
Zinc (mg)	12	+3	15
Iodine (mcg)	150	+25	175 mcg

MINERAL SUPPLEMENTS

All women who are planning a baby or already pregnant should consider taking a multinutrient supplement containing vitamins and minerals as well as eating a healthy diet. As a result of modern farming practices, soil mineral shortages mean that, unless you are eating organic produce that has only recently been harvested, the nutrient content of fruit and vegetables – especially their mineral content – is falling.

Mineral deficiencies have been linked with increased risk of stillbirth, miscarriage and some neural tube defects. It is important not to take high-dose supplements, however, as some are potentially harmful. Choose one containing vitamins and minerals especially formulated for pregnancy.

CALCIUM
Calcium is an important mineral of which 99 per cent of body stores are found in your bones and teeth.

Why You Need It During Pregnancy
Calcium is needed during pregnancy for the growth and development of strong, healthy bones and teeth. It is also essential for nerve conduction and passing electrical messages from one brain cell to another. Muscle contraction – including that of the heart – relies on calcium, as does blood coagulation, the production of energy and the immune system. Research suggests that calcium supplements reduce the risk of pre-eclampsia (high blood pressure) during pregnancy by more than 60 per cent – they also significantly lower blood pressure in women who have developed pre-eclampsia. Babies born to mothers with a poor calcium intake tend to have a low birthweight and to develop more slowly than normal.

Research suggests the optimal intake of calcium during pregnancy and breastfeeding is 1,200 – 1,500 mg per day. Calcium supplements during pregnancy may decrease the risk of the offspring developing a brain tumour during childhood by almost 60 per cent.

How Much You Need
Adequate calcium intakes are important throughout life. Dietary deficiency at any stage significantly increases the risk of developing osteoporosis. The EC RDA and UK RNI for calcium is 800 mg per day – surprisingly, no extra is recommended during pregnancy, although an extra 550 mg per day is suggested when breastfeeding. The UK National Osteoporosis Society suggests an intake of 1,200 mg during pregnancy (1,250 mg per day when breastfeeding).

Good Dietary Sources
- milk
- dairy products such as cheese, yoghurt, fromage frais
- green leafy vegetables such as broccoli
- salmon
- nuts and seeds
- pulses
- white and brown bread – in the UK, white and brown flour are fortified with calcium by law – but not wholemeal flour
- eggs

Vegetarian mothers-to-be need to pay special attention to their dietary intake of calcium, especially those who do not eat dairy products or eggs.

It is relatively easy to increase your calcium intake before pregnancy. The best way is to drink an extra pint of skimmed or semi-skimmed milk per day. This provides as much calcium as whole milk but without the additional saturated fat. By law in the UK, white and brown flour must be fortified with calcium – but this does not apply to wholemeal flour. So, if your calcium intake is likely to be low (for example, if you don't like milk or milk products), brown bread is the better choice.

Vitamin D is needed for absorption of calcium from the intestines. Usually, only a small fraction of dietary calcium is taken up (typically less than 40 per cent); the remainder is lost in bowel motions. Interestingly, calcium absorption from the intestines seems to be more efficient during pregnancy. This is secondary to a natural increase in blood levels of vitamin D – without any obvious increase in intake or increased exposure to the sun.

CHROMIUM
Chromium is a trace element whose only known function is to form part of a complex called Glucose Tolerance Factor (GTF) that also contains vitamin B_3 (niacin) and three amino acids.

Why You Need It During Pregnancy

As GTF helps to control blood sugar levels, chromium may help to protect against gestational diabetes. Interestingly, chromium levels are relatively high in newborn infants but slowly decrease with age. This may reflect a dietary deficiency and it has been suggested as one reason why diabetes becomes increasingly common with age.

How Much You Need

The optimum chromium intake is unknown. The US National Research Council suggests 50–200 mcg per day for an adult. The average intake is below 50 mcg, and it is thought that only 2 per cent of this intake is in an absorbable form. Deficiency is therefore common, especially among pregnant women. The importance of this is not yet fully understood. Some experts suggest obtaining an additional 100 mcg of chromium per day during the pregnancy, starting during the preconceptual care period.

Good Dietary Sources

- brewer's yeast
- egg yolk
- red meat
- cheese
- fruit and fruit juice
- wholegrains
- honey
- condiments such as black pepper, thyme
- vegetables

The chromium found in brewer's yeast is already in the form of GTF, which is 50 times more effective than other sources. Most refined carbohydrates have had their chromium content removed.

COPPER

Copper is a trace element.

Why You Need It During Pregnancy

Copper is essential in small amounts for healthy brain function and is required for the production of several brain chemicals (neurotransmitters) such as noradrenaline. It also forms part of an antioxidant enzyme system (cupric zinc superoxide dismutase) that is vital for protecting the brain from damage due to exposure to the metabolic chemicals and free radicals (see page 175) produced during the rapid developmental process in the womb. This enzyme may provide some protection against cerebral palsy. Copper is also needed for the production of collagen, of the skin pigment melanin, and of the red blood pigment haemoglobin, which carries oxygen to your baby's brain. It is involved in maintaining healthy bones, cartilage, hair and skin – especially their elasticity.

How Much You Need

The UK RNI is 1.2 mg copper. An extra 0.3 mg is recommended when breastfeeding, and some researchers suggest an extra 0.5 mg during pregnancy as well.

Good Dietary Sources

- brewer's yeast
- olives
- nuts
- pulses
- wholegrain cereals
- green vegetables grown in copper-rich soil

Potential Problems

Absorption of copper is decreased by the presence of raw meat or excessive vitamin C, zinc and calcium in the intestines. Copper and zinc antagonize one another, and symptoms of copper deficiency (anaemia, low white blood cell count, subfertility, elevated blood cholesterol, thinning bones) have been seen in patients taking zinc supplements in large amounts for over a year. In general, you need a zinc to copper intake ratio of 10 zinc:1 copper, so an intake of around 15 mg zinc and 1.5 mg copper is ideal. Copper is toxic in excess.

IODINE

Iodine is a trace element of which you only need a tiny amount per day – this small quantity is vital for the healthy development of your baby's brain, however.

Why You Need It During Pregnancy

Iodine is essential for making thyroid hormones. Adequate supplies of iodine are essential for the development of your baby's brain and nervous system during the first 3 months of life in the womb. Lack of iodine leads to an underactive thyroid, which shows up after birth as a condition known as cretinism. As well as an underactive thyroid, the child's brain cannot develop properly, leading to severe mental retardation. This is a serious problem in some parts of the world, including parts of Europe, New Zealand, Brazil and the Himalayas. In some areas, iodine deficiency affects 9 out of 10 of the population. In Indonesia, for example, there are currently an estimated 1.5 million severely mentally retarded children and 800,00 with cretinism. This is a devastating condition that is entirely preventable if expectant mothers are given injections of iodized oil – preferably during the preconceptual period. Treatment must be given before the 6th month of pregnancy, however, to protect the brain against the effects of iodine deficiency. When treatment is not given until the last 3 months of pregnancy, it does not seem to improve brain function. In the Western world, newborn babies are screened for cretinism as part of the heel prick test carried out soon after delivery.

How Much You Need

The EC RDA is 150 mcg, and the UK RNI 140 mcg with no extra suggested for pregnancy. US recommendations, however, suggest that requirements rise by 25 mcg during pregnancy, from 150 mcg to 175 mcg per day.

Good Dietary Sources
☺ marine fish such as haddock, halibut, salmon, tuna
☺ seaweed (such as kelp)
☺ iodized salt
☺ milk (in many countries, cattle feed is also iodized)
☺ crops and cattle reared on soils exposed to sea-spray

Potential Problems
Gross iodine deficiency leading to swelling of the thyroid gland (goitre) is now rare in the UK since the introduction of iodized salt. People who restrict their salt intake and who do not eat iodine-rich foods (such as seafood) are at risk of iodine deficiency, however. Selenium plays a role in the metabolism of thyroid hormones, and the effects of iodine deficiency are exacerbated by low selenium intakes.

IRON
Iron is one of the best-known minerals, needed for the production of the red pigments haemoglobin and myoglobin (found in muscle cells). World-wide, iron deficiency is the most common nutritional disease, with most cases going unrecognized.

Why You Need It During Pregnancy
Iron is an essential component of haemoglobin, the red blood cell protein which carries oxygen from the lungs to the tissues. Iron from your diet is also needed to produce your baby's blood pigment, which is slightly different from yours and known as haemoglobin F (F for fetal). Haemoglobin F binds to oxygen more easily than your own adult haemoglobin, so that oxygen quickly passes from your own bloodstream into your baby's blood within the placenta. Oxygenated blood arriving from the placenta and umbilical cord is carried straight up to your baby's

brain to ensure it receives adequate supplies during development. During pregnancy, your iron requirements increase as you produce 30 per cent more red blood cells and haemoglobin.

Many enzyme systems also rely on iron, including those involved in the production of energy from carbohydrate, fat and protein. It also forms part of an antioxidant enzyme system (iron catalase) that is vital for protecting the brain from damage due to exposure to the metabolic chemicals and free radicals (see page 175) produced during the rapid developmental process in the womb. This enzyme may provide some protection against cerebral palsy. Iron also has a role in boosting immunity. White blood cells destroy invading micro-organisms using powerful iron-containing chemicals. In iron deficiency, there is an increased susceptibility to infection, with sufferers being especially prone to recurrent thrush, especially during pregnancy.

A common symptom of iron deficiency during pregnancy is a craving for strange foods such as soil or coal. This is known as *pica*. If it happens to you during pregnancy, start taking a supplement containing iron immediately – ask your pharmacist or doctor for advice on dosage. Your doctor may also want to perform a blood test to check your iron stores. Long-term deficiency of iron during pregnancy and during childhood can lower your baby's intelligence.

Iron deficiency increases the risk of growth retardation in the womb and low birthweight. Taking iron supplements during pregnancy may halve the risk of the offspring developing a type of brain tumour (astrocytoma) during childhood.

How Much You Need
Overall, an extra 550 mg of iron is needed throughout pregnancy – 300 mg for your baby, 50 mg for the placenta and 200 mg to offset the blood lost during childbirth. As you have stopped having periods while pregnant, however, your iron losses are less than usual. US Recommended Dietary Allowances suggest that iron requirements should double during pregnancy from 15 mg to 30 mg per

day. The EC RDA for adults is 14 mg, while the UK RNI is 14.8 mg per day. The UK does not suggest any additional iron during pregnancy unless a woman previously had heavy periods (putting her at risk of iron deficiency anaemia). As the average iron intake for British women is only 10.5 mg per day, however (30 per cent lower than recommended) – and as 50 per cent of women obtain less than 9.8 mg per day – a supplement specially formulated for pregnancy and containing some iron is a good idea.

Good Dietary Sources
🍽brewer's yeast
🍽offal (liver, kidney, heart)
🍽red meat
🍽fish, especially sardines
🍽wheatgerm
🍽wholemeal bread
🍽cocoa powder
🍽egg yolk
🍽green vegetables
🍽parsley
🍽prunes and other dried fruit

Vegetarian mothers-to-be need to pay special attention to their dietary intake of iron.

The form of iron that is most easily absorbed is organic haem iron found in red meat. Vegetarians, and those who eat little red meat, are therefore at increased risk of iron deficiency. Their intakes are dependent on absorbing inorganic non-haem iron, and food supplements are essential.

Overboiling vegetables decreases their iron availability by up to 20 per cent. Vitamin C increases the absorption of inorganic iron, while calcium- and tannin-containing drinks (such as tea) decrease it. Coffee can reduce iron absorption by up to 39 per cent if drunk within an hour of eating. Your absorption of dietary iron generally becomes more efficient during pregnancy, however.

Potential Problems

Avoid taking too much iron, as this can cause constipation or indigestion, and excess is toxic. Iron supplements given alone can decrease the absorption of zinc and other essential minerals (such as manganese, chromium and selenium), so some specialists advise that iron should be given in combination with these.

MAGNESIUM

Magnesium is increasingly recognized as an important mineral, of which 70 per cent of body stores are found in your bones and teeth. It is the third most common mineral inside the body cells of you and your baby, after potassium and phosphorus.

Why You Need It During Pregnancy

Magnesium is vital for every major metabolic reaction from the synthesis of protein and genetic material to the production of energy from glucose. Few enzymes can work without it, and magnesium is now known to be vital for healthy tissues, especially those of the muscles, lung airways, blood vessels and nerves. It is vital for the integrity of all body cells. Special salt pumps maintain different ion concentration gradients across your cell membranes that allow them to hold an electrical charge and pass electrical messages from one cell to another. Magnesium is essential for these membrane pumps, for maintaining a cell's electrical stability, and for allowing brain cells to pass messages to one another. It is also important for controlling calcium entry into heart cells to trigger a regular heartbeat. Magnesium has been used as a treatment for high blood pressure during pregnancy and lowers the risk of eclampsia (fits) by over 50 per cent; it has also been used to reduce the risk of other complications for both mothers and babies. Babies born to mothers who had received magnesium supplements for pre-eclampsia have been found to spend less time in the special care baby unit.

How Much You Need

The US National Research Council recommends a daily intake of 280 mg magnesium for women, with an additional 40 mg per day during pregnancy and an extra 60–75 mg daily during breastfeeding. The UK RNI for adult women is 270 mg per day. No increment is suggested during pregnancy, although an extra 50 mg is recommended during lactation. The EC RDA for adults is 300 mg. Magnesium deficiency is common. The observed average daily intake of magnesium among British women is 237 mg per day, which is well below recommended levels. Some researchers recommend that supplements of 200 mg per day are taken during the preconceptual period and throughout pregnancy.

Good Dietary Sources

- soya beans
- nuts
- brewer's yeast
- wholewheat flower
- brown rice
- seafood
- seaweed
- meat
- eggs
- milk
- dairy products
- wholegrains
- bananas
- dark green leafy vegetables
- chocolate
- drinking water in hard-water areas

Processing foods removes most of their magnesium content.

Potential Problems
Lack of magnesium is exacerbated by pregnancy; some researchers believe deficiency contributes to miscarriage, premature delivery and painful contractions during childbirth.

Excess magnesium causes diarrhoea.

MANGANESE
Manganese is a trace element found mainly in your bones, soft tissues, the pituitary gland of the brain, and in the liver and kidneys.

Why You Need It During Pregnancy
Manganese is needed for synthesis of an important brain neurotransmitter, dopamine, which passes messages between many important groups of brain neurons. Manganese is also essential for normal structure, growth and development. It is involved in many metabolic functions, including the synthesis of amino acids, carbohydrates, sexual hormones, blood-clotting factors and cholesterol. It also acts as an antioxidant.

How Much You Need
The optimal intake of manganese is unknown. The US National Research Council suggests that a daily intake of 2 – 5 mg is adequate, while up to 10 mg per day is safe. There is no UK RNI. The observed average intake among British women is 5.5 mg for pregnant women, but only 3.3 mg among non-pregnant women.

Good Dietary Sources
- tea
- wholegrains
- nuts and seeds
- fruits
- egg
- green leafy vegetables/herbs
- offal
- milk

Potential Problems
Manganese is one of the least toxic minerals, as when excess is consumed in the diet, absorption is very low while excretion (via bile and kidneys) is high. Lack of manganese is associated with poor fetal growth, birth defects and stillbirth in animals and is likely to have similar effects in humans.

SELENIUM
Selenium is an important mineral antioxidant, but is only required in minute quantities.

Why You Need It During Pregnancy
Selenium is essential for cell growth and immune function. It is involved in the synthesis of hormone-like substances known as prostaglandins, and in antibody production. Research suggests antibody synthesis increases up to 30-fold if supplements of selenium and vitamin E – which work together as powerful antioxidants – are taken. It also forms part of an antioxidant enzyme system (selenium glutathione peroxidase) that is vital for protecting the brain from damage due to exposure to the metabolic chemicals and free radicals (see page 176) produced during the rapid developmental process in the womb. This enzyme may provide some protection against cerebral palsy. Selenium levels fall during pregnancy, and recent research suggests that women who miscarry have significantly lower selenium levels than normal. Low levels of selenium seem to increase the risk of congenital defects such as spina bifida, suggesting that selenium plays an important role in the early development of the brain and spinal cord. Selenium may be important in preventing cot death. Studies suggest that a quarter of babies who die from sudden infant death syndrome were found to be deficient in selenium and/or vitamin E.

How Much You Need
There is no EC RDA for selenium. The UK RNI is 60 mcg with an additional 15 mcg suggested during breastfeeding. Selenium

intakes in the UK have halved over the last 20 years to just 29 – 39 mcg per day.

Good Dietary Sources
🐮broccoli
🐮mushrooms
🐮cabbage
🐮radishes
🐮onions
🐮garlic
🐮celery
🐮wholegrains
🐮nuts
🐮brewer's yeast
🐮seafood
🐮offal
🐮butter

The selenium content of vegetables depends on the soils in which they are grown.

Potential Problems
Lack of selenium lowers immunity, reduces production of antibodies by as much as 30-fold, and seems to double your risk of certain cancers. Excess is toxic.

ZINC
Zinc is an important metallic mineral.

Why You Need It During Pregnancy
Zinc is essential for the proper function of over a hundred different enzymes. It forms an integral part of the enzyme which interacts with the genetic code (DNA) to switch on a gene in response to hormone triggers. By switching on a gene, it initiates synthesis of the specific protein that gene codes for. Zinc is therefore vital in

the development of your baby's brain. It also forms part of an antioxidant enzyme system (cupric zinc superoxide dismutase) that is vital for protecting the brain from damage due to exposure to the metabolic chemicals and free radicals (see page 175) produced during the rapid developmental process in the womb. This enzyme may provide some protection against cerebral palsy. There is some evidence that optimal zinc status is linked with a larger head circumference and lower risk of low birthweight – in fact, some researchers have been able accurately to predict a baby's birthweight and head circumference simply by analysing placental content of zinc. Zinc is also important for general growth, sexual maturity, wound healing and immune function.

Although your zinc requirements steadily increase throughout pregnancy, zinc deficiency is common. It is linked with many congenital defects of the brain and spinal cord, including mental retardation and learning difficulties. Zinc is needed during the metabolism of essential fatty acids (see Chapter 6), and zinc deficiency makes the effects of lack of essential fatty acids worse. Lack of zinc also increases the risk of miscarriage, pre-eclampsia, anaemia, preterm delivery, congenital defects and difficult delivery due to inefficient contractions during labour. Babies born to mothers with low zinc levels are more likely to have learning difficulties.

Taking a daily zinc supplement during pregnancy boosts infant weight and increases head circumference – a direct indication of an increase in brain size.

Recent research has shown that babies given low-dose zinc supplements after birth grew significantly faster than babies fed normally. This difference was mainly noted in boys. The authors of this research concluded that infants breastfed for more than 4 months may show a slower rate of growth due to zinc deficiency. Other studies have suggested that zinc increases the size of the penis and testis in growing boys.

Zinc supplements seem to reduce some of the central nervous system effects of excess alcohol during pregnancy which are associated with developmental delay and intellectual impairment. It seems to help reduce the malformation of synapses between brain cells which are caused by excess alcohol.

How Much You Need

The US National Research Council recommends a daily intake of 12 mg zinc for non-pregnant women, 15 mg per day during pregnancy and up to 19 mg per day during lactation. The UK RNI is only 7 mg, but recommends an extra 6 mg during pregnancy and 2.5 mg when breastfeeding. The EC RDA is 15 mg per day for adults. Studies show that most pregnant women obtain less dietary zinc than recommended and that maternal blood zinc levels fall by around 30 per cent during pregnancy. Your baby's zinc levels are usually double your own. Maternal zinc levels are significantly lower in mothers who have low birthweight babies. Some researchers feel that zinc supplements are essential during pregnancy.

One of the earliest symptoms of zinc deficiency is loss of taste sensation. This can be tested for by obtaining a solution of zinc sulphate (5 mg/5 ml) from a pharmacy. Swirl a teaspoonful in your mouth. If the solution seems tasteless, zinc deficiency is likely. If the solution tastes furry, of minerals or slightly sweet, zinc levels are borderline. If it tastes strongly unpleasant, zinc levels are normal.

Good Dietary Sources
☙red meat
☙offal
☙brewer's yeast
☙wholegrains
☙pulses
☙eggs
☙cheese

Food processing removes most mineral zinc from foods.

Potential Problems

Soya products and foods rich in iron reduce the absorption of zinc from the intestines. They are best avoided within 2 hours of taking zinc supplements.

Lack of zinc is linked with increased risk of miscarriage, pre-eclampsia (high blood pressure in pregnancy), anaemia, abnormally prolonged pregnancy and difficulty during delivery.

Multivitamins and Minerals

The best way to obtain extra vitamins and minerals during pregnancy is to eat a healthy diet and to use sensible amounts of supplements as a nutritional safety net. A recommendation to take folic acid is a start, but is too conservative. A good multinutrient, which includes folic acid, is essential. Choose one especially formulated for pregnancy, however – your pharmacist will advise on the brands available.

Taking a multivitamin and mineral supplement has been shown to reduce the risk of:

- all congenital developmental defects in general
- urinary tract abnormalities by 85 per cent
- neural tube defects by at least 50 per cent
- facial abnormality, cleft lip or cleft palate by 25 – 50 per cent
- some limb abnormalities by 35 per cent
- heart defects by 35 per cent
- low birthweight
- maternal night cramps during pregnancy

Antioxidants and Free Radicals

Antioxidants are protective dietary substances that help to protect your cells from damaging chemicals (free radicals) produced by the normal processes of metabolism and by exposure to pollutants, alcohol, smoking and drugs. The best-known antioxidants are vitamins A, C, E and betacarotene plus the minerals selenium, zinc, copper and manganese.

WHAT ARE FREE RADICALS?

A free radical is an unstable molecular fragment that carries a negative electrical charge. This makes it unstable and it quickly tries to lose this charge through collisions with other molecules in your body. In these collisions, the free radical either steals a neutralizing, positive electrical charge from the other molecules, or offloads its own negative one. This process is known as oxidation. Body proteins, fats, cell membranes and your genetic material (DNA) are constantly under attack. It is estimated that every cell in the body is subjected to 10,000 free radical oxidations per day. Oxidation of fats increases the risk of hardening and furring up of your arteries, while oxidation of genetic material increases the risk of abnormalities during division. During pregnancy, this may trigger congenital defects – especially during the first few weeks of pregnancy. It may also increase the risk of future cancers. One reason why smoking is so harmful is that it generates massive numbers of free radicals.

Antioxidants protect against free radical attack by mopping these unstable fragments up, and neutralizing their electrical charge, before they can do any harm.

To protect your baby's development in the womb, consider taking a multivitamin and mineral supplement during pregnancy, rather than just taking folic acid.

8

Exercise, Relaxation and Stress

It is important to maintain a gentle exercise programme during pregnancy. Your should reduce your exercise level to 70 per cent of what you were doing before pregnancy, however.

Sensible levels of exercise help to improve your circulation so that more blood and nutrients pass through your placenta to reach your baby. There is some preliminary evidence that the vibrations and noises your baby experiences during exercise act as a form of prenatal stimulation that can enhance maturation of your baby's brain. Exercise also helps you to maintain a degree of strength, stamina and overall fitness so you cope with the rigours of childbirth more easily. Having stronger abdominal muscles also helps with pushing during labour. Over-exertion, however, will divert blood away from your womb to your muscles (to supply oxygen and energy) and to your skin (to cool you down). This can affect neurological development and lead to low birthweight. Here are some general rules:

☺ Avoid prolonged periods of aerobic exercise.

☺ Don't start a strenuous exercise regime.

☺ Aim for gentle exercises such as walking, swimming, using an exercise bike.

☺ Try to exercise at least 3 times a week for at least 15 minutes each time.

☺ Don't let your pulse rise above 120 beats per minute.

☺ Don't let your body temperature rise above 37.8°C (100°F).

☺ Don't let yourself become dehydrated.

☺ Stop if you become uncomfortably short of breath, or feel faint or tired.

☺ Seek medical advice about whether you can continue exercising if you develop any complications linked with your pregnancy (such as vaginal bleeding, contractions, abdominal or chest pain).

☺ Do not use a Jacuzzi as there are risks of overheating and of an air embolus (air bubble in the bloodstream; rare)

☺ Avoid water-skiing, as water can be forced up into the vagina and may potentially cause problems.

☺ From the 4th month of pregnancy onwards, avoid high-impact sports such as jogging, sprinting or advanced aerobics and activities such as skiing or horse-riding where falling is a possibility.

☺ Avoid abdominal exercises from 5 months onwards, as your stomach muscles are already stretched and further strain may do more harm than good.

☺ Avoid exercising flat on your back from the 5th month onwards as this can affect your circulation and cause dizziness.

☺ Slowly decrease your level of exercise from around the 6th month of pregnancy, as you grow larger, your centre of balance changes and your ligaments start to soften and stretch in later pregnancy.

Working

Try to stop work by around the 28th – 30th week of your pregnancy. After this time increased rest is vitally important for the health of both you and your growing baby. Prolonged standing, for example, is linked with an increased risk of preterm delivery and a low birthweight baby. More than 8 hours of physical work per day during the last 3 months of pregnancy has the same damaging effect on fetal development as heavy smoking, with babies weighing around 100 g ($3\frac{1}{2}$ oz) less than those of women working 20 hours a week or less. Employers are usually flexible and will change your work obligations so you can sit down for most of the day. They also have an obligation to ensure you are not exposed to potentially harmful industrial chemicals, gases or radiation. There is no evidence that using a computer terminal, or sitting in front of a VDU screen, is harmful during pregnancy. It is important, however, to:

- ensure your chair, desk and screen are ergonomically adjusted for you
- have good back support from an adjustable chair
- use a wrist rest
- use a foot rest
- use a paper holder
- sit up straight and avoid crossing your legs or ankles
- take a regular screen break every 15 minutes by getting up, walking around and stretching your arms and legs
- try to keep regular hours and to avoid nightshift work and jet lag.

Stress

During pregnancy, mothers produce their own, natural tranquillizer – a substance known as pregnanolone. This is because the effects of stress can be harmful to your developing baby. If you are exposed to excessive stress, your natural reserves of pregnanolone may not be able to cope. Babies of mothers who are excessively stressed or anxious during pregnancy have a higher risk of low birthweight, small head size, impaired neurological development and preterm delivery. In fact, some of these risks due to stress during pregnancy are of the same magnitude as those linked with smoking cigarettes.

Babies born to mothers who were stressed during pregnancy are also more likely to have learning difficulties and to become anxious and depressed themselves in later life. Exposure to excess maternal stress hormones during development seems to increase sensitivity of the fetal brain to their effects, so the baby's behavioural response to stress is magnified. Stress hormones also cause constriction of blood vessels and may reduce the blood supply to the fetus. Both these effects can lead to hyperactivity in the womb, and in later life. During an earthquake in Italy, for example, mothers who were from 18 to 36 weeks pregnant happened to be having ultrasound scans at the time. The mothers were intensely frightened and their babies responded by moving excessively for the next 2 to 8 hours. There is some evidence that male babies are more sensitive to these effects than female offspring. In rats especially, maternal stress during pregnancy is linked with lowered aggression, impaired sexual behaviour and general demasculinization.

Rest

Whenever you stop, sit or lie down and relax, the muscles of your abdominal wall and uterus relax, too. This increases blood flow to the uterus and increases the amount of oxygen and nutrients your baby receives. It also gives your baby more space to move around and the baby recognizes this and likes it. This may be why a mother sitting down and relaxing while listening to music or reading a story aloud to her infant gives him a feeling of pleasure that he learns to respond to. Research suggests that mothers who take part in prenatal relaxation classes such as yoga have few obstetric complications and have a lower risk of having a low birthweight baby than mothers who do not relax regularly throughout pregnancy. It is therefore important to sit down for increasing periods of time as your pregnancy progresses. From around 30 weeks of pregnancy it is also important to lie down for at least an hour mid-morning and mid-afternoon. Lying down relaxes the uterine muscles as well as boosting circulation through the placenta. Standing for long periods of time decreases blood flow to the uterus and is linked with low birthweight and preterm delivery.

One of the many advantages of taking part in a prenatal stimulation programme is that it encourages you to sit or lie down twice a day while interacting with your baby. When wearing the BabyPlus unit, for example, take the opportunity to lie down on your bed, or sit on a sofa with your feet up and relax for an hour.

How to Get a Good Night's Sleep

A good night's sleep is vitally important for you and your growing baby. While lying down, your kidneys find it easier to flush excess fluid and wastes from your system, and blood flow to your placenta increases. Sleep is also a time when you secrete more hormones involved in the growth, repair and regeneration of your tissues. Even though rest is so important, most women have difficulty sleeping during pregnancy – especially in the last few months.

One of the most common sleep problems is difficulty getting comfortable. As your womb enlarges, lying on your back interferes with blood flow through the large vessels (aorta, inferior vena cava) running down your back. As well as affecting the blood supply to your baby, this can lead to fluid retention and also make you feel faint. Lying on your stomach puts pressure on the womb and becomes impossible after the first few months. Your only option is to lie on your side, although the weight of your stomach can pull you over and make it difficult to relax.

If you are not used to sleeping on your side, start practising in early pregnancy. It helps to use a few extra pillows. Put one behind you so you don't roll onto your back during the night, or get your partner to snuggle up close. Place another pillow between your knees or fold it in half and place it in front of your legs. You can then roll forwards slightly, with your bent upper leg resting on the pillow. This stops you rolling fully onto your front.

Later in pregnancy, when you produce a hormone (relaxin) that softens your ligaments, backache can be a real nuisance, especially if you are sleeping on a mattress that is too hard or too soft. Swiss and US scientists have perfected the ideal sleeping surface for pregnancy – a visco-elastic polymer that is heat- and pressure-sensitive and naturally moulds to your body. A mattress overlay made of this material (or full mattress if you prefer) gives firm support and lets you sleep comfortably on your side without needing extra pillows – your hip sinks into the polymer just enough to support your tummy and make your bulge feel almost weightless. And when the baby moves, it feels likes he's wriggling in the mattress rather than in you, which is much less likely to disturb your sleep. For further information – and a 30-day fully-refundable trial – UK readers should contact Medical Agency Systems on 0645 556678. It goes under the brand name Integra in the UK and Australia; Confor-Plus in the US.

If you are planning to hire a TENS machine for pain-relief during delivery, you may find it helpful to use it earlier to relieve backache, too.

OTHER IRRITATIONS
Some women suffer a stuffed-up nose (rhinitis) during pregnancy so that difficulty breathing stops you sleeping soundly. This is due to increased blood flow which makes the lining of

your nose swell. Try using a humidifier or a negative ionizer in your bedroom.

Another sleep-robber is 'restless legs syndrome'. This tends to occur when you are tired and when drifting off to sleep – you have a sudden irresistible urge to move your legs, which wakes you up again. It is thought to be linked with lack of iron, and may indicate that you need to take a supplement.

Itchy skin can also keep you awake scratching. This is often due to lack of essential fatty acids. Eating more fish – especially oily fish such as salmon, sardines, mackerel and herrings – will help, as will taking evening primrose oil. Adding Balneum Junior to your bath will help moisturize your skin without leaving an oily residue.

Other tips to help you sleep include:

- Eat a healthy, wholefood diet with plenty of unrefined, complex carbohydrates (such as wholegrain cereals, brown bread, wholewheat pasta, brown rice) plus fruit and vegetables for vitamins and minerals. Avoid hunger, as this will make you more alert – but avoid rich, heavy, fatty meals in the evening.
- Avoid substances that interfere with sleep such as caffeine (coffee, tea, chocolate, colas) and nicotine – a warm, milky drink just before going to bed will help you to relax. Hot milk is better than hot chocolate, which contains some caffeine.
- Try to take gentle exercise during the day, as active people sleep better.
- Take time to unwind from the stresses of the day before going to bed – read a book, listen to soothing music or have a candle-lit bath.
- Get into the habit of going to bed at a regular time each night and getting up at the same time each morning.
- Set a bed-time routine such as brushing your teeth, bathing and setting the alarm clock to set the mood for sleep.
- Make sure your bed is comfortable, and your bedroom warm, dark and quiet – noise and excessive cold or heat will keep you awake. A temperature of 18 – 24°C (64 – 75°F) is ideal.

✥ If you can't sleep, don't lie there tossing and turning. Get up and read or watch television for a while. If you are worried about something, write down all the things on your mind and promise yourself you will deal with them in the morning, when you feel fresher. When feeling sleepy, go back to bed and try again.

✥ Drinking a soothing, herbal tea is often all that's needed for a good night's sleep. Choose ones containing gentle herbs such as limeflower, lemon balm or rosehips. *NB* Avoid teas or supplements containing fennel, passionflower, cinnamon, camomile oil or hops during pregnancy.

✥ Relaxing homoeopathic remedies include:
  • Coffea 6c: if your mind is over-active
  • Nux vomica 6c: for sleeplessness leaving you irritable and unrefreshed
  • Arnica 6c: if you are overtired and can't get comfortable
  • Take the dosage recommended on the label half an hour before going to bed; repeat every half hour as necessary.

✥ Aromatherapy oils that can induce sleep and are safe to use during pregnancy include: Mandarin, Lemon, Sandalwood or Neroli oils

  NB Lavender or Camomile oils are often recommended for insomnia, but should *not* be used during the first 3 months of pregnancy – use sparingly in later pregnancy and avoid totally if there is a history of miscarriage.

After following these tips, you should enjoy a much better night's rest. Once your baby is born, you will delight in once more being able to sleep on your front or back. For at least the first few months, however, your sleep will be broken by night feeds. Interestingly, if you breastfeed research shows that producing milk hormones help you to sleep better after waking in the night than if you give a bottle-feed.

Another excellent tip is to use a Bed-Side-Bed. This cot has an adjustable base and a removable side and acts as an extension to your own bed. It lets your baby sleep at the same level as you, making it easy to tend to him and breastfeed him in the night without getting out of bed. For more information, readers should contact tel. 0181–989 8683 (if outside the UK, tel. 011 44 181 989 8683). *NB* If itching skin is severe, always seek medical advice.

9
Prenatal Factors that Can Harm Your Baby's Intelligence

Changes in your womb environment – especially during the critical first 12 weeks of development – can play havoc with the carefully choreographed movements of the cells in your baby's brain and nervous system. Harmful factors include malnutrition, lack of vitamins, minerals and essential fatty acids, exposure to cigarette smoking, alcohol, drugs and infections. These can lead to congenital defects, lower intelligence, mental retardation, autism, epilepsy and even schizophrenia as a result of cells moving into the wrong position, being wired up incorrectly or being deprived of some of the oxygen and nutrients they need.

At least 15 per cent of babies born with developmental abnormalities – and possibly many more – are thought to be related to avoidable exposures to drugs, alcohol, smoking and environmental toxins. Avoiding these harmful factors during pregnancy is one of the simplest ways in which you can help your baby's brain, nervous system, intelligence and emotional well-being reach optimum potential.

Smoking

Most babies are exposed to cigarette smoke from the moment of conception. Chemicals from cigarette smoke have been found in the placenta, amniotic fluid and fetal bloodstream of both actively and passively smoking mothers.

Surveys suggest that around 30 per cent of mothers smoke at some stage during pregnancy, with 25 per cent smoking through-out. Only 5 per cent of pregnant women manage to give up. Even if you don't smoke yourself, the risk to your baby is increased if someone else in your household does. Two-thirds of non-smoking adults – including pregnant women – are exposed to the equivalent of at least one hour of passive smoking per week.

Stopping smoking at any stage of pregnancy is better than continuing to smoke all the way through. Up to 4,000 different chemicals are present in tobacco smoke, of which many are highly toxic. Women who smoke during pregnancy have a 30 per cent higher risk of miscarriage, stillbirth, neonatal and sudden infant death than babies born to non-smoking mothers. It is estimated that eliminating smoking in pregnancy could prevent 5 per cent of stillbirths and deaths associated with delivery.

Nicotine is concentrated in the dividing fertilized egg (blasto-cyst) and may have a direct effect on implantation and early embryonic development.

Babies exposed to cigarette smoke in the womb are also more likely to suffer genetic abnormalities leading to childhood cancer, as well as problems with the immune system leading to increased risk of asthma, eczema, glue ear and recurrent infections.

Smoking during pregnancy is linked with malfunction of the placenta:

☞ nicotine causes spasm and narrowing of blood vessels throughout the body, including the womb and placenta
☞ smoking generates carbon monoxide – a molecule that displaces oxygen from haemoglobin in red blood cells so blood becomes less oxygenated.

These two factors mean that up to 20 per cent less oxygen is supplied to the baby of a mother who smokes. As a result, low birthweight is common. Babies born to smoking mothers are on average 200 g (7 oz) lighter than babies born to non-smokers and have a 10 – 15 point IQ disadvantage. It is estimated that eliminating smoking in pregnancy could prevent 20 per cent of low birthweight babies and 8 per cent of preterm deliveries.

In one study, 800 smokers were followed throughout their pregnancy – with their tobacco consumption accurately measured. Mothers who quit smoking during the pregnancy gave birth to infants that were an average of 241 g (8½ oz) heavier than babies born to mothers who continued to smoke, and 167 g (6 oz) heavier than babies born to mothers who managed only to cut back.

SMOKING AND YOUR BABY'S BRAIN
During the last 3 months of pregnancy, your baby makes many breathing movements with the muscles in his chest wall as he practises for independent life after birth. If he receives less oxygen from your placenta due to excess maternal smoking, however, he will stop making these practice breathing movements in an attempt to conserve both oxygen and energy. In the womb, he therefore stops breathing when oxygen levels are low. After he is born, however, his behaviour must change to the opposite –

when oxygen levels are low, he needs to respond by breathing more quickly and deeply to draw more oxygen into his lungs. The 'low oxygen = stop breathing' response in the womb is under the control of a small area of neurons in the brain that must be over-ridden and deactivated immediately after birth to ensure survival. In some babies, it is thought that this inborn instinct is not over-ridden, and continues after delivery, so that lack of oxygen triggers an inappropriate lack of breathing and an increased risk of sudden infant death syndrome (SIDS, also known as cot death). Exposure to cigarette smoke during fetal life seems to strengthen the 'stop breathing' response, which may explain why maternal smoking is linked with an increased risk of SIDS. This is currently under investigation.

The chemicals generated by smoking cigarettes are harmful to your baby's developing brain. Less oxygen, plus the toxic effects of other chemicals in cigarette smoke, mean that babies born to mothers who have smoked during pregnancy are more likely to have a smaller head, a smaller brain and a lower intelligence than expected – by 10 to 15 IQ points. They are also at greater risk of developmental problems such as difficulty reading, solving problems and interpreting information. They are also twice as likely to display delinquent, sociopathic behaviour – probably as a result of brain damage caused by smoking during early development – as babies born to non-smoking mothers, and are almost 3 times more likely to have attention deficit hyperactivity disorder. Overall, 50 per cent or more of babies born to mothers who smoked at least 20 cigarettes per day during pregnancy had abnormal central nervous system development with developmental delay and learning difficulties. There is no doubt that smoking during pregnancy lowers the intelligence of your baby.

Apart from the effects on the baby's growth and potential intelligence, children born to mothers (or fathers) who smoke are twice as likely to suffer a childhood cancer, including leukaemia and some types of brain tumour.

Research suggests that women who smoke during pregnancy have lower intakes of several vitamins and minerals, including:

- thiamin (B$_1$)
- riboflavin (B$_2$)
- vitamin C
- calcium
- iron.

Pregnant women who smoke also tend to have a higher fat consumption and overall their diet is much less nutritious than that of non-smoking pregnant women.

Smoking liberates dangerous chemicals including gases and condensed tar particles which generate free radicals in the body. These damage cell membranes and are partially mopped up by dietary antioxidants. As a result, smoking lowers your blood levels of vitamins C, E, betacarotene, several B group vitamins – including folic acid – and the mineral selenium. Cadmium, a toxic metal found in tobacco, antagonizes selenium and zinc so they become less available. These effects make a nutritionally poor diet worse. If you are unable to stop smoking during pregnancy – which is your main priority – please take a good vitamin and mineral supplement, especially formulated for pregnancy and including folic acid – and in addition take extra antioxidants (vitamin C, at least 500 mg per day, and vitamin E, at least 100 mg per day) as well as increasing your intake of fresh fruit and vegetables.

STOPPING SMOKING

Nicotine is addictive, which is why it is difficult to give up smoking. Withdrawal symptoms of tension, aggression, depression, insomnia and cravings can occur. You have a strong incentive, however – the well-being and future potential of your baby.

The good news is that, within 48 hours of giving up smoking, levels of clotting factors in your blood start to fall. This will improve blood circulation through your placenta and reduce the risk of placental insufficiency, growth retardation and low birth-weight in your future child. Falling levels of chemicals from the cigarettes will also reduce the toxicity to your baby's developing brain.

- Name the day you're going to give up and get into the right frame of mind.
- Find support – stopping smoking is easier with a friend or partner.
- Get rid of temptation – throw away all smoking paraphernalia – papers, matches, lighters, ashtrays, spare packets, etc.
- Take it one day at a time and concentrate on just getting through each day.
- Take extra gentle exercise, which will help to dampen nicotine cravings.
- Find something to occupy your hands, such as decorating the nursery, knitting clothes or toys for your baby, painting watercolours, learning origami.
- Identify situations where you would usually smoke and either avoid them or plan ahead on how you will overcome them.
- Ask friends and relatives not to smoke around you.
- Keep a chart and tick off each successful cigarette-free day.
- Plan a reward for every week of cigarette-free success.
- Picture a growing baby in your mind, receiving its life blood through healthy vessels in the placenta. Now imagine these vessels constricting with every puff on a cigarette. See the blood supply to the baby slow down to a trickle. Now think positive again – you are going to give up, your baby is going to have the best possible start in life.
- Save the money previously spent on cigarettes in a special fund to buy something special for you or your baby.
- Learn to say 'No thanks, I've given up' and mean it.

When you have an urge to smoke, try:

- sucking on an artificial cigarette or herbal stick, available in pharmacies
- sucking on celery or carrot sticks
- eating an apple
- cleaning your teeth with strong-flavoured toothpaste
- going out for a brisk walk, swimming, cycle-riding or jogging
- taking a supplement containing oat straw (*Avena sativa*), which can reduce cravings
- try hypnosis, which has an average success rate of 30 per cent for helping smokers to quit, and acupuncture, which has a success rate of 24 per cent.

An aromatherapy device impregnated with 19 essential oils (Logado – available from pharmacies) can be sniffed or inhaled so cigarette cravings disappear for up to 30 minutes. To non-smokers, the device smells like an old ashtray, but to smokers it is a delicious combination of tobacco and aromatic scents that make you feel as if you've just had a cigarette. The aromatherapy scents help to relax you and also block your sense of smell – so even if you do smoke, the cigarette will taste insipid. In trials, one in three smokers using Logado regularly gave up, and a further one in four cut the amount they smoked by half.

If withdrawal symptoms are particularly strong, try the following breathing exercise to help reduce your stress levels:

- Breathe in slowly and deeply.
- When you reach your limit of breathing in, immediately start to breath out – without holding your breath – to empty your lungs as much as possible.
- Repeat 5 times without holding your breath in-between.

Alcohol

Alcohol is the most widely available drug in the world. Ninety per cent of Western adults indulge – even if only occasionally. Alcohol can seriously damage a developing baby. If a woman regularly drinks more than 12 units of alcohol per week (for example, 2 units per day) during pregnancy, her baby will suffer growth retardation and birthweight will be lower than normal.

Women have a lower alcohol tolerance than men due to their higher percentage of body fat – around 30 per cent body weight compared to 15 per cent in the male. Pregnancy is also a time when your body fat stores increase by an average of 10 per cent. Fatty tissue absorbs alcohol like a sponge and slowly releases it into the circulation. Alcohol therefore stays in your body longer than in the average male, as it is only slowly transported to the liver for processing.

When you drink alcohol it is rapidly absorbed from your stomach and small intestines into your bloodstream. Before your body has time to break it down, it will pass from your circulation into the placenta and straight into your baby's system. Your baby will also receive a constant alcohol infusion, as the alcohol absorbed by your fatty tissues is slowly released.

During early embryonic life, alcohol will enter the rapidly dividing embryonic cells and start to interfere with some of the enzymes responsible for early metabolic reactions. This results in increased levels of acidity within your baby's circulation (metabolic acidosis) and is highly toxic. In adults, alcohol is broken down in the liver to a poison, acetaldehyde. If this accumulates in adults, it is a potent trigger of nausea and vomiting – as anyone who has ever suffered a hang-over will recognize. When it accumulates in your developing baby, it can trigger congenital defects or even a miscarriage.

Because of the way alcohol is distributed throughout your body fluids, if you drink alcohol during pregnancy your developing baby will develop a higher blood concentration of alcohol than you. Alcohol will also stay in your baby's tissues longer – including his developing brain – as once it reaches his body, his liver is less efficient at breaking down alcohol than yours. And as the tiny liver bud only develops during the 4th week after conception, your baby is most vulnerable to alcohol damage in the first month after conception – often before you even know you are pregnant. Unless you take positive steps to avoid alcohol during the months *before* trying to conceive, as well as during pregnancy itself, you may have affected your baby's future brain potential.

BINGE DRINKING

A woman who has an alcoholic binge during pregnancy (for example to celebrate a birthday, or Christmas) can cause as much harm to her developing baby as if she drank regularly. A study of over 1,000 pregnant women showed that those who drank 10 units of alcohol on a single occasion were more likely to have damaged offspring than those who avoided alcohol. This has important implications. Many women are happy to give up alcohol as soon as their pregnancy is confirmed. By this time, however, their developing baby may be anything from 3 – 12 weeks old or more. A single evening's drinking during these important early stages, when a mother doesn't know she is pregnant, can affect her baby for life.

HOW ALCOHOL AFFECTS YOUR BABY'S BRAIN

In the developing brain and spinal cord, the toxic effects of alcohol can result in the death of some neurons, as well as acting like a general anaesthetic to damp down the way brain cells conduct electrical signals. The net effect may be to alter the way some neural pathways are laid down. Excess alcohol also causes synapses to be malformed, although to some extent taking a supplement that includes zinc seems to help protect against this. Drinking alcohol during the first 8 weeks of pregnancy, when your baby's face and brain are forming, can cause malformations.

Drinking alcohol after this time can lead to a small baby whose brain is smaller and weighs less than it otherwise would. Alcohol seems to damage neurons in the cerebral cortex (where intelligence is regulated), the limbic system (where emotions are controlled) and the brain stem (where vital functions such as breathing and heart rate are organized) most of all.

Bingeing is most harmful – especially in the first 3 to 4 weeks in the womb – often before the mother even knows she is pregnant. Another critical stage of brain development occurs between 10 and 18 weeks after conception when neurons start making connections with each other and the scaffolding for future nerve pathways are sketched out. Alcohol interferes with this process, resulting in connections that are wired up incorrectly – or not at all. This has been linked with future behavioural problems including antisocial behaviour, psychiatric problems and an increased tendency towards violence. Sadly, babies with fetal alcohol syndrome (see below) often have poor speech and their average IQ score is below 80. If alcohol is taken together with drugs – especially painkillers, anti-depressants, anti-epileptic medications and illegal drugs, the risk of serious damage increases.

According to some researchers, exposure to alcohol during the earliest stages of pregnancy could account for a large proportion of the murders, mental illness and violence afflicting society. A third of inmates on Death Row in the US are said to have suffered from fetal alcohol syndrome.

FETAL ALCOHOL SYNDROME

Babies born to women who drink excessively during pregnancy are at risk of fetal alcohol syndrome (FAS), linked with an increased risk of stillbirth and neonatal death. Those who survive are likely to have low birthweight, reduced intelligence and to suffer emotional and developmental problems. Other abnormalities linked with FAS include:

- a narrow, receding forehead
- a short, upturned nose
- a receding chin
- asymmetrical, poorly formed ears
- thin lips
- an unusually long distance between the nose and lips, with flattened or absent skin folds
- short-sightedness
- squint
- heavy epicanthic folds between the nose and eyes
- slanted eyes
- congenital heart disease
- small brain
- low intelligence.

If a woman regularly drinks 2 or 3 units per day throughout pregnancy, she has an 11 per cent chance of her baby developing fetal alcohol syndrome. This risk rises to 19 per cent with 4 units per day, and 30 per cent in women who drink more than 5 units daily. A pregnant woman who regularly drinks more than 9 units of alcohol per day is almost certain to have an affected child. Babies of women who are pregnant over the age of 30 seem to be especially vulnerable to the effects of alcohol and to developing fetal alcohol syndrome.

1 unit alcohol is equivalent to each of the following:

= 100 ml (one small glass) of wine (there are 7.5 units per bottle of wine)
= 50 ml (one measure) of sherry
= 25 ml (single tot) of spirits
= 300 ml (½ pint) of normal-strength beer.

NB In the US, a unit of alcohol is called a drink.

HOW MUCH ALCOHOL IS ACCEPTABLE DURING PREGNANCY?

Recent studies suggest that low intakes of alcohol (up to 8 units spread throughout the week) are not linked with birth defects. The effect on intelligence is less clear, however. It seems sensible to avoid such a potent toxin altogether during pregnancy if possible. Many women find they go right off the taste of alcohol during pregnancy, anyway, in one of nature's spectacular ways of protecting the unborn child. If you find it difficult to go without alcohol altogether, then accepted opinion is that 1 or 2 units of alcohol once or twice a week during the last 3 months of pregnancy is unlikely to do serious harm. There does seem to be an increased risk of spontaneous miscarriage, however, even when amounts are this low.

Caffeine

Caffeine is a stimulant drug found in coffee, tea, cola drinks, chocolate and a variety of over-the-counter medications. Caffeine is metabolized more slowly during pregnancy, especially during the last few months. It affects the way your body handles thiamin and calcium, crosses the placenta, and is also found in breastmilk. Many women find they develop a sudden loathing of coffee or tea during pregnancy and naturally avoid it. Some researchers have found that a relatively low intake of 800 mg caffeine (equivalent to around 4 to 5 cups of coffee) per day is linked with an increased risk of miscarriage, low birthweight, smaller head size and preterm labour. New research suggests drinking three or more cups of coffee per day inceases the risk of miscarriage, whilst drinking four or more cups per day increases the risk of sudden infant death syndrome. It is therefore advisable to limit your intake as much as possible.

Drugs of Abuse

It is estimated that more than 10 per cent of pregnancies in some Western countries are exposed to illegal, mind-altering drugs of abuse such as cannabis, amphetamines, cocaine, crack and heroin (diamorphine). These drugs will affect your growing baby's brain and can cause permanent damage to neurons and the pathways connecting brain cells, leading to emotional problems and lowered intelligence in the future. They also significantly increase your risk of congenital abnormalities, miscarriage, stillbirth and low birthweight babies. Babies born to addicted mothers are addicted too, and have to go through a process of withdrawal which has over a 30 per cent risk of death in the perinatal period. Babies exposed to cannabis, cocaine and crack tend to be small for dates, highly strung and irritable and to have problems sleeping. Women who inject have an increased risk of potentially lethal problems such as blood poisoning (septicaemia), hepatitis B and HIV.

COCAINE

Cocaine can have a devastating effect on your baby. It does not even have to get into the baby's circulation to cause damage, as taking cocaine or crack can shut down the blood supply to the uterus almost completely, depriving the baby of oxygen and other essential nutrients. Using cocaine during the first 3 months of pregnancy increases the risk of bleeding into the placenta, miscarriage, preterm labour and severe, congenital abnormalities. Cocaine can also get into your baby's brain to make it smaller than normal, lower intelligence and cause long-term mental deficiencies. In particular, it will affect his emotional development, so he is less likely to feel pleasure, bond to people, make emotional judgements or to control outbursts. He is more likely to cry and become irritable if exposed to new stimuli and experiences, rather than enjoying and learning from them. Sadly, babies exposed to cocaine in the womb are also more likely to be stillborn or suffer sudden infant death syndrome. Damage to your baby can occur within 3 days after conception, so stop using cocaine several weeks before you stop using contraception. The combination of cocaine and alcohol seems particularly harmful.

HEROIN
Heroin addiction is linked with a 3-times greater risk of miscarriage or stillbirth, a 4-times greater risk of premature labour and a significant risk of intrauterine growth retardation, resulting in a low birthweight baby. Prolonged exposure to heroin in the womb has harmful effects on your baby's future growth, behaviour and intellectual development.

AMPHETAMINES
Exposure to amphetamines in pregnancy may cause heart and other defects. Long-term use increases the risk of poor growth, preterm delivery, stillbirth and death soon after birth. Withdrawal symptoms can also occur.

CANNABIS
Babies exposed to heavy use of cannabis in the womb are more likely to be born premature and to have a low birthweight. They may also display abnormal behaviour, with tremor, ready startling and altered visual responses – which all indicate harmful affects on brain development.

Prescription Drugs

Avoid all over-the-counter drugs during pregnancy unless absolutely necessary – even those you might think are safe such as aspirin, paracetamol, ibuprofen and cough medicines can cause problems. If you are considering taking a drug, always check first with a pharmacist whether that particular medication is known to cause any problems during pregnancy.

Surveys suggest that as many as 90 per cent of women take one or more over-the-counter or prescription drugs during pregnancy. The vast majority take as many as three drugs with the potential to harm their developing baby, without realizing the risks involved. There is an average 1 in 20 risk of conceiving a child who will be born with a developmental abnormality, although many of these problems are non-serious. A mother who takes at least one prescription drug during pregnancy has a risk that is 3 times higher – that is, 1 in 7 – of giving birth to a baby with a congenital defect.

Avoid as many prescription-only drugs as possible during pregnancy. Make sure the prescribing doctor knows you are pregnant, and ask him or her what problems any particular drugs are known to be linked with during pregnancy. Drugs are sometimes essential during pregnancy for the well-being of the mother. Nevertheless, it is often possible – when treating epilepsy, for example – to reduce the number of drugs you are taking to the bare minimum needed to control your symptoms. Women suffering from epilepsy and who are taking certain epileptic drugs do face a particular problem during pregnancy, as their medication may interfere with the action of folic acid – increasing the risk of a neural tube defect unless large doses of folic acid supplements are taken. This in turn interferes with their medication, increasing their risk of a fit. It is therefore vital to seek specialist advice from a consultant gynaecologist and/or neurologist before trying to conceive.

If taking any form of medication for a medical problem, always seek advice about the possible effects of the drug on pregnancy before trying to conceive.

Environmental Pollutants

The environment is full of toxins such as lead exhaust fumes, mercury, industrial chemicals and pesticides. These enter the food chain and may contaminate a large percentage of our diet, whether we are vegetarians, 'fishitarians' or carnivores.

Most environmental toxins cross the placenta and pose a risk to the developing fetus. A study by the UK Woman's Environmental Network suggests that up to 8 per cent of British children suffer from poor responsiveness and memory loss because of toxic damage in the womb. They may also have reduced intelligence in later life. Even if only 1 per cent are affected, this still represents thousands of children per year.

CADMIUM

Cadmium is a common pollutant linked with increased risk of congenital abnormalities (including cleft palate, hare lip, limb deformities), low birthweight, small head, reduced intelligence, miscarriage, preterm delivery and stillbirth, especially when coupled with high lead and low zinc levels. Your main sources of exposure to cadmium are:

- cigarette smoke
- processed foods
- water that has coursed through galvanized mains
- industrial waste
- shellfish from polluted waters
- burning fossilized fuels.

Zinc seems to be important in counteracting some of the adverse effects of cadmium exposure.

LEAD

Lead is associated with an increased risk of miscarriage, congenital abnormalities, fits, delayed development, reduced intelligence, stillbirth and neonatal death. You are exposed to lead from a number of sources:

- exhaust fumes from lead in petrol
- water that has coursed through old, lead water pipes, old, lead-glazed earthenware mains or copper piping with alloy joins containing lead
- unlined tin cans
- food grown in polluted soil
- smoking tobacco treated with lead-containing insecticides.

Lead is rapidly carried across the placenta to your baby and can build up to cause lead poisoning from as early as 12 weeks of pregnancy. In one study, babies' blood levels of lead were assessed both before and after birth, and regularly up to the age of 7 years. When these children took part in IQ tests between the ages of 11 and 13, it was found that IQ was related to lead levels, and seemed to fall by 3 points as concentration of lead doubled. Other studies have also confirmed that exposure to lead can reduce IQ by averages varying from 3 to 9 points. Some research suggests that lead interferes with the way some brain communication chemicals (the neurotransmitters glutamine and dopamine) function. Others believe that it leads to low levels of oxygen within brain cells.

MERCURY

Mercury is a toxic metal that crosses the placenta and is concentrated in your growing baby, so his mercury levels may be as much as 20 times higher than your own. Mercury toxicity is linked with impaired neural development in babies exposed to mercury in the womb, leading to an increased risk of cerebral palsy, small brain, mental retardation, blindness, fits, preterm delivery and stillbirth. Your main sources of exposure to mercury are:

- pesticides and fungicides
- fish (especially tuna) from polluted waters (reputable fish oil supplements are screened for contaminants)

🐢industrial waste
🐢dental amalgams.

It is important to avoid having mercury amalgam tooth fillings removed or inserted during pregnancy if at all possible.

ORGANOPHOSPHORUS AND OTHER PESTICIDES

Pesticides are powerful chemicals that affect specific biological systems (such as fungi, caterpillars, whitefly) in low concentrations but can build up to cause harm in humans – especially during pregnancy – as they can easily cross the placenta to enter the developing baby and trigger congenital malformations. Many of the most harmful chemicals are fat-soluble, and become concentrated in animal fat products.

PCBS

Polychlorinated biphenols (PCBs) are an environmental pollutant that has been linked with lowered intelligence in infants and young children. In 1968, contamination of rice oil in Japan led to babies being born with developmental abnormalities, lower body weight, hyperactivity, behaviour problems and lower intelligence scores.

In one study, women exposed to PCBs as a result of eating contaminated Lake Michigan fish had blood and breastmilk levels assessed, and their children were followed up at regular intervals. Children exposed to the highest levels of PCBs were three times more likely to have a low average IQ score, and twice as likely to be at least two years behind in reading ability than those not exposed. This suggests that the developing brain may be sensitive to PCBs. The researchers concluded that exposure to slightly higher concentrations of PCBs than occur in the general population can have long-term effects on intelligence. Tests showed prenatal exposure to high PCB levels reduced verbal IQ scores by 7 – 16 points, performance IQ scores by 10 – 18 points, and overall IQ by 9 – 18 points. The differences remained throughout the 6 years of follow-up.

The use of PCBs are now banned, although they are difficult to eliminate as they were so widely used in industry and are resistant to biodegradation.

To reduce your exposure to environmental poisons:

- Eat organic wholefoods where possible.
- Cut down on your consumption of animal fats.
- Avoid tinned foods, processed foods and excess salt.
- Eliminate all dietary additives.
- Wash all vegetables, fruit and salad stuff thoroughly, and peel as many as possible.
- Eat garlic, yoghurt, bananas and pectin-containing fruits to help reduce absorption of dietary toxins.
- Avoid heavy traffic and inhaling exhaust fumes – keep car windows closed in traffic jams.
- Avoid burning waste rubbish, especially newspapers, magazines and plastics.
- Switch to lead-free petrol and a car fitted with a catalytic converter.
- Avoid any sheep-dipping activity or contact with dipped sheep.

DETOXIFICATION

Hair mineral analysis may indicate whether you have a particular toxic metal problem. You can also have your domestic drinking water analysed for toxic metals such as lead.

Ensure an adequate intake of antioxidant vitamins and minerals – especially vitamin C, E, betacarotene, zinc, selenium, chromium and manganese. Vitamin C can lower body cadmium levels. Vitamin C, E, zinc and calcium can help reduce lead levels.

A new generation of mineral supplements are now available which contain nutrients bound to humic acid complexes (such as Humet-R). These complexes boost absorption and can also bind toxic heavy metals in the intestines, removing them from the body.

It is worth considering the use of a water filter during pregnancy. An activated-carbon filter will extract chlorine, while a reverse-osmosis water treatment system is needed to remove nitrates and dissolved metals such as lead, aluminium, cadmium, mercury and traces of hormones. Alternatively, consider drinking bottled water from a source that provides an analysis or certification of purity.

Infections

Many different infections can have a devastating effect if contracted during pregnancy.

GUM DISEASE

New research suggests that gum disease (periodontitis) may be a significant risk factor for low birthweight, premature babies. It may even cause almost one in five premature births before 37 weeks of pregnancy and weighing less than 2,500 g (5½ lb). This makes gum disease even more of a danger than smoking or alcohol. It is thought that the mouth bacteria that cause gum disease release toxins into the mother's circulation which interfere with fetal growth. Low-grade chronic infection also stimulates production of 'sticky' inflammatory proteins and hormone-like prostaglandins – these chemicals can make the cervix dilate and trigger contractions of womb muscle, precipitating premature delivery. It seems that the risk of preterm birth is seven and a half times higher in women with gum disease than in those without.

It is therefore worth having your dental health sorted out as early as possible during pregnancy – and preferably during the preconceptual period. Avoid having mercury amalgam fillings disturbed or inserted, however.

LISTERIOSIS

Listeriosis is a bacterial infection common in cattle, pigs, poultry and the soil. In humans it can cause a flu-like illness up to 6 weeks after exposure. Over 70 per cent of the population have antibodies indicating past exposure to Listeria, although many cases of infection are thought not to develop symptoms. The disease is usually self-limiting, but those with lowered immunity – including pregnant women and newborn babies – are at risk of serious illness. Listeriosis can be passed from mother to child at any stage during pregnancy. Treatment involves hospitalization and high-dose antibiotics.

Listeriosis is linked with an increased risk of miscarriage, still-birth, preterm delivery, and severe illness in the newborn such as meningitis or pneumonia. Listeria is usually destroyed by pasteurization but can continue to reproduce at 4°C (39°F) – the temperature found in a domestic refrigerator. It is therefore important to cook all foods thoroughly to destroy the organism, *before* refrigeration. To reduce your risk, avoid foods that can contain Listeria, including:

- ripened soft cheeses such as Brie, Camembert, Cambazola
- blue-veined cheeses such as Stilton, Roquefort, Blue Shropshire, Blue Brie, Dolcelatte
- goat or sheep cheeses such as fetta, Chèvre
- any unpasteurized soft and cream cheese
- any under-cooked meat
- cook-chill meals and ready-to-eat poultry unless thoroughly re-heated
- all types of paté
- ready-prepared coleslaw and salads
- unpasteurized milk or dairy products
- all foods past their 'best by' date
- rolls or sandwiches containing any of the above.

Listeria can also be passed on through contact with infected live animals.

TOXOPLASMOSIS

Toxoplasma infection can affect all mammals and birds, but it reproduces in cats. A cat first becomes infected when it starts to hunt; it then produces infective feces for about 3 weeks, after which the cat itself is immune. It is estimated that 25 per cent of pork and 10 per cent of lamb eaten by humans is infected with Toxoplasma, but these are killed by thorough cooking and by freezing. A pregnant woman can catch Toxoplasma by eating raw or undercooked meat, unwashed fruit and vegetables, drinking unpasteurized milk or by handling cat's feces. In the UK, 20 per cent of people have a protective level of antibodies against Toxoplasma by the age of 20. Toxoplasma infection often passes unnoticed, but may cause a sore throat or a flu-like illness. Infection during pregnancy is associated with congenital abnormalities, miscarriage, stillbirth and:

- hydrocephalus
- eye defects and blindness
- physical and mental retardation
- convulsions
- unusually small head
- calcification (hardening) of parts of the brain
- enlarged liver and spleen
- increased risk of death during infancy.

If infection occurs during the second half of pregnancy, damage to the fetus is less severe. Sadly, around 12 severely damaged babies are born in the UK each year. An infected baby remains at risk after delivery and may suffer irreversible damage, with future learning difficulties. Monthly antenatal screening for toxoplasmosis is therefore mandatory in France and Austria, but is discouraged in the UK. To reduce your risk of Toxoplasmosis:

- avoid emptying cat litter trays
- if having to handle cat litter, use thick, disposable gloves and wash hands thoroughly afterwards with an antiseptic solution
- avoid close contact with sick cats
- always wash hands thoroughly after handling cats, or after contact with other animals or soil
- wear gloves when gardening
- wash hands thoroughly after handling raw meat
- avoid eating raw meat or fish and their products
- cook all meat thoroughly – avoid eating meat that is still pink
- avoid barbecued meat
- wash fruit and vegetables
- avoid unpasteurized milk – especially goat's milk and goat milk products
- avoid contact with sheep and lambs – especially pregnant or milking ewes and newborn lambs – women farm workers and shepherds should handle work clothing with gloves even when washing it and keep this clothing away from kitchen work surfaces.

CHICKENPOX

Chickenpox is uncommon during pregnancy, but can cause abnormalities known as Varicella Syndrome if caught during the first 3 months of gestation. These abnormalities are similar to those of Rubella Syndrome and include:

- cataracts and other eye defects such as blindness
- small head
- physical and mental retardation
- developmental difficulties
- intrauterine growth retardation
- excess cerebrospinal fluid (hydrocephalus)
- skin pock marks.

Although most adults are immune to Chickenpox, avoid anyone who has chickenpox, or shingles, while you are pregnant. Shingles is caused by reactivation of dormant chickenpox virus and causes a patch of infectious blisters on the skin. If you do come into contact with a person who has chickenpox or shingles during pregnancy, seek medical help straight away. An injection of anti-Varicella zoster antibodies will help to protect you and your unborn child.

RUBELLA

Rubella (German Measles) is a viral illness that can have devastating effects if contracted during early pregnancy. If the mother is infected during the first few weeks of pregnancy, there is a greater than 50 per cent chance that her baby will be affected, too. During the third month of pregnancy, the risk is 17 per cent; from the fourth month onwards, the risk is low. Generally, the earlier Rubella is contracted in pregnancy, the more seriously the fetus is affected. Problems associated with congenital Rubella syndrome include:

- miscarriage
- cerebral palsy
- mental retardation
- deafness
- cataracts, eye defects and blindness
- heart defects
- bone deformities
- facial abnormalities
- skin bruising (*purpura*)
- stillbirth
- a 20 per cent risk of death during early infancy
- continued shedding of Rubella virus in urine, feces and saliva for up to a year after birth.

Thanks to Rubella immunization programmes, congenital Rubella is now less common as it is entirely preventable. When planning a baby, and before conceiving, all women should ideally request a blood test to assess their level of anti-Rubella antibodies – even if they are known to have previously had the disease or received inoculation, as antibody levels may still be low. If your test shows you are at risk of Rubella infection, you should be vaccinated *before* becoming pregnant, and continue using contraception to prevent pregnancy for the next 12 weeks. After inoculation, your antibody levels should be checked by a subsequent blood test to ensure protection before trying to conceive. The vaccine cannot be given during pregnancy, as it contains the live, albeit inactivated, virus.

Rubella is passed from person to person by airborne droplets containing infectious viral particles. Symptoms develop after an incubation period of two to three weeks to cause a mild rash on the face which spreads to the trunk and limbs. This usually disappears within a few days. There is sometimes a slight fever and enlargement of lymph nodes at the back of the neck. Often, however, the illness passes unnoticed, although adults usually fare worse than children and develop headache, fever and sometimes painful joints.

It is wise for all women who are pregnant, or planning a pregnancy, to avoid contact with any person who is ill or has a rash, to minimize the risks of infection. If a non-immune woman who is, or might be, pregnant comes into contact with anyone thought to have Rubella, she should immediately seek medical advice. In such cases, passive immunization with pooled antibodies (immunoglobulin) may help to protect the fetus from infection in the womb.

CYTOMEGALOVIRUS
Cytomegalovirus (CMV) is another infection that can be passed from mother to child during pregnancy, with devastating results.

It may cause a mild, flu-like illness, but in many cases goes unnoticed. Infection is linked with an increased risk of:

- miscarriage
- preterm labour
- small head
- physical and mental retardation
- developmental difficulties
- intrauterine growth retardation
- progressive hearing problems
- jaundice
- chest and eye infections.

VACCINATIONS

Women who are pregnant should avoid immunization with any vaccines containing live viruses. Live vaccines should only be administered during pregnancy when the benefits are thought to outweigh the risks.

10

Avoiding Preterm Birth

Any baby born before 37 weeks of pregnancy (35 weeks gestation) is classed as premature or preterm. A low birthweight baby
is one weighing less than 2.5 kg (5½ lb) at delivery. Very low
birthweight newborns are those born weighing less than 1.5 kg
(3 lb 5 oz), and extremely low birthweight babies weigh less
than 1 kg (2 lb 3 oz) at birth. Most babies who are preterm also
have a low birthweight. Some babies born at the normal time
(term) have a low birthweight, too, due to factors such as poor
maternal nutrition or the effects of alcohol, smoking cigarettes
or drugs.

Premature Birth

In the Western world, as many as 1 in 8 deliveries results in a preterm, low birthweight baby. This is one of the biggest health risks a developing baby faces. Although 1 in 8 babies is premature, preterm babies account for 75 per cent of birth-related deaths and 50 per cent of long-term problems due to damage of the brain and nervous system. More babies die from being premature than from any other cause.

Despite advances in the care of preterm infants, they still do not achieve the same equivalent growth during the first year of life as babies born at the normal time. These differences are significant from around 2 months after the expected date of delivery. Preterm infants on average remain smaller than normal after the first year of life, have a smaller head circumference and show poorer mental and physical performance.

As birthweight falls, there is an increased risk of developmental problems affecting the brain. Low birthweight babies have three times the risk of cerebral palsy, for example. All the evidence suggests that many cases of cerebral palsy are linked to events occurring prenatally before delivery begins. Poor nutrition and exposure to toxins probably play an important role.

There are many different causes of preterm birth. These fall into four main groups:

1   those that have no obvious cause (25 – 50 per cent of cases)
2   early rupture of membranes (10 per cent of cases)
3   elective delivery due to a maternal or fetal problem (such as high blood pressure, placental insufficiency, placenta covering the cervix, diabetes, urinary tract or other infection) where the benefits of delivery outweigh the risks of continuing the pregnancy (15 – 40 per cent of cases)
4   emergency delivery due to an obstetric emergency such as bleeding (25 per cent of cases).

In the majority of cases there is no obvious cause for preterm labour. The main known causes include:

- multiple pregnancies (twins, triplets, etc.)
- smoking cigarettes
- exposure to others' cigarette smoke (passive smoking)
- alcohol
- illicit drug use
- weak cervix
- asthma, especially poorly controlled asthma
- uterine fibroids
- an abnormally shaped womb
- urinary or reproductive tract infections.

The safest place for your baby is inside your womb, so it is important to avoid factors that are associated with an increased risk of preterm labour and low birthweight.

Once a preterm baby is born, he will usually be whisked into an intensive care unit for round-the-clock life support. It is vital that premature babies are kept in an environment that is as quiet, soothing and non-stressful as possible. However, those who are stimulated through rocking, massage and regular stroking for 15 minutes 4 times a day thrive better, put on weight 50 per cent faster and develop improved co-ordination and ability to learn compared with babies who are not touched and massaged.

FREE RADICAL ATTACK

Preterm babies do not have all the antioxidant systems and enzymes in place to help protect them from the harmful effects of chemicals produced by metabolism. These chemicals, known as free radicals, are produced in large numbers during times of rapid growth. Free radicals are unstable and highly reactive, interacting with delicate cell structures – including the genes – to cause damage. Our main protection against free radicals are dietary antioxidants, of which the most important are vitamins

A, C, E, bioflavonoids and the mineral selenium. We also have some inborn protective measures that are not fully developed in small babies. Premature babies quickly use up the antioxidants supplied by their mother, and are then exposed to the damaging effects of free radicals before their own protective mechanisms are fully developed and in place. At 28 weeks gestation, for example, a baby's own antioxidant enzyme systems are only half as active as they will be at 38 weeks gestation. This is thought to be one of the causes of lung damage in babies born too early. Free radicals can also damage the delicate blood vessels in a preterm baby's brain and increase the risk of cell death and bleeding into the brain.

The body substances that are most sensitive to oxidative damage are fats. Your baby's brain is composed of 60 per cent fat, with up to 20 per cent of brain cell weight composed of the long-chain polyunsaturated fatty acids (LCPs) DHA and AA. This means brain cells, which are 60 per cent fat, are particularly sensitive to free radical attack – but only if there are lower-than-optimal levels of DHA and AA. Paradoxically, optimal levels of DHA and AA in the fatty membranes of blood vessels and brain cells seem to strengthen these cells and protect against oxidation. This seems to be because an important antioxidant enzyme system (superoxide dismutase, also known as SOD) is activated by DHA and so provides extra protection. AA is important for making strong, flexible, elastic blood vessel walls which reduce the risk of bleeding into the brain, especially in premature infants.

Unfortunately, very premature babies often have low levels of DHA and AA. As they are no longer receiving essential fatty acids (EFAs) from their mother, their blood levels of DHA and AA – which are vital for healthy eye and brain development – fall dramatically within the first 3 weeks after birth: levels are only one-third of what they were at birth. Levels can be replenished by feeding on breastmilk, or on formula milk that is supplemented with these LCPs.

In one study, babies born at an average of 30 weeks gestation were fed either their mother's milk or formula milks containing different concentrations and types of a variety of essential fatty acids. The electrical activity of the back of their eyes (retinas) in response to seeing a light was then recorded. By 6 weeks after birth (that is, 36 weeks after conception) the infants who received mother's milk or formulas containing DHA in amounts similar to mother's milk achieved the best score – their eyes and the nerve connections involved in seeing had matured and were functioning best of all. This advancement was still present 30 weeks after delivery, with improved learning ability, problem-solving skills, speech, word capacity and ability to think in the abstract. This provides strong evidence that DHA at concentrations found in breastmilk are essential nutrients for the proper development of a premature baby's eyes and the nerve–brain connections involved in sight. As a result of many similar studies, formula feeds designed for premature babies are now routinely supplemented (since around 1991) with careful blends of LCPs to maximize their brain and eye development. Even so, preterm babies fed human milk have better brain development when assessed at 18 months of age, and higher intelligence than similar babies fed formula milks.

Premature babies fed with mother's milk through a tube have been found to have an 8.3 IQ point advantage at age 8 years, compared with similar, matched babies who did not receive breastmilk. Children whose mothers wanted to provide breastmilk but were unable to do so had the same IQ as those whose mothers had elected not to provide breastmilk. Although these results may be affected by parenting skills and genetics, adjustment for these factors indicates that human breastmilk provides a significant advantage to the brain development of preterm infants (see Chapter 13).

DHA levels of premature infants are positively related to their head circumference, birthweight and birth length. This suggests that increasing their DHA status may promote fetal growth and improve the outcome for preterm infants, as those born with a higher birthweight usually do better.

One of the richest dietary sources of LCPs is fish oil. Research in which mothers were given fish oil supplements, olive oil supplements or no supplements starting from the 30th week of pregnancy showed that babies of mothers receiving fish oils were healthier in that they weighed, on average, 107 g (3 ¾ oz) more than other groups and stayed in the womb for an average of 4 days longer. The extension of gestation time in the womb was thought to be due to fish oils' ability to inhibit the production of the hormone-like substances (prostaglandins) that help to trigger labour, or to inhibit the production of other prostaglandins that help to relax uterine wall muscles.

Multiple Pregnancy

Prematurity is more common where there is a multiple pregnancy – especially where twins are identical and share the same placenta, rather than each having a placenta of their own. Over the last few years it has been realized that twins sharing a single placenta suffer 5 to 10 times the risk of brain damage or death. This is partly because one twin may not get all its share of nutrients from the placenta, or may not receive as much blood, so that low blood pressure decreases oxygen supply to the brain.

Poor growth, which occurs when a baby is malnourished, is accompanied by slowed activity and slowed breathing movements as the baby tries to conserve his energy. These muscle movements are important for stimulating the baby's brain development. So, in growth retardation, malnourishment leads not just to a smaller than usual brain, but the accompanying lack of stimulation and activity leads to fewer synaptic connections being laid down and may lead to increased death of brain cells that are not fully wired into the neural net.

Low Birthweight

Some babies are born too small for their gestation period. This is known as intrauterine growth retardation and is characterized by low birthweight. Size is not everything, however, and this may not matter as long as good nourishment in early life lets your baby catch up in the physical sense. What does matter, however, is how his brain was nourished in the womb. It is brain growth that is significant for his future potential.

Your baby responds to lack of oxygen or glucose by increasing blood supply to protect his brain at the expense of his other organs. He may therefore be undersized but still have a brain that was well protected. The outcome is not always poor. The figures quoted in the following studies are average outcomes – some will do better.

Babies born at optimum birthweights (3.5 – 4.5 kg/7 lb 12 oz – 9 lb 15 oz) have the lowest risk of developmental disorders such as those of the central nervous system. Average intelligence seems to increase up to a birthweight of around 4.2 kg (9 lb 4 oz), whereafter it slightly decreases. Unfortunately, however, those born with low birthweight have a higher risk of physical or mental handicap, with up to 8 per cent suffering severe disorders such as:

- cerebral palsy
- mental retardation
- faulty development of the lungs
- blindness
- deafness
- epilepsy.

A study of babies born weighing less than 1.75 kg (3 lb 14 oz) found that, 4 years later, of the survivors sadly 16 per cent were severely disabled, 47 per cent had cerebral palsy, 11 per cent were deaf and 7 per cent blind. Their performance in school was generally poor and was found to correlate to their weight at birth.

Studies have shown a significant relationship between size of a baby at birth and maternal diet at or around the time of conception. These first few weeks of gestation are a time of rapid division of cells. The central nervous system (brain and spinal cord) are often fully developed before the pregnancy is even recognized. Babies of teenage mothers are particularly at risk. Studies show their diets are low in iron, calcium, vitamin A and riboflavin (vitamin B_2), particularly if they're trying to lose weight with inappropriate slimming diets.

Studies comparing babies born with a low birthweight with babies born at a healthy weight show the lower birthweight babies are more likely to have a lower intelligence when language, spatial, fine motor, touch and attention skills are tested at 6 and 13 years of age. Performance was found to improve as birthweight increased to well over 3 kg (6 lb 10 oz). Half of babies born weighing less than 1.5 kg (3 lb 5 oz) had special educational needs and language problems.

Other studies that compared low birthweight babies with adult intelligence found an increase in average IQ of at least 10 IQ points between those who were born weighing less than 2.5 kg (5½ lb) and those weighing more. The risk of mental retardation is 2.8 times greater for low birthweight babies than those of normal birthweight.

The good news, however, is that early intervention and stimulation of these children during the first 3 years of life can improve their performance by around 4 IQ points, especially for babies born weighing 2 – 2.5 kg (4 lb 6 oz – 5½ lb).

New research also suggests that low birthweight babies are more likely to develop high blood pressure, coronary heart disease, stroke and insulin-dependent diabetes in later life. In fact, low birthweight quadruples the risk of heart disease in later life compared with larger babies.

To reduce the risk of low birthweight:

- ☺Stop smoking – ideally before you become pregnant – or at least cut down as much as possible (see Chapter 9).
- ☺Avoid alcohol as much as possible, especially during the first 3 months of pregnancy (see Chapter 9).
- ☺Have your dental health checked and any gum disease treated – preferably before you become pregnant.
- ☺Eat a healthy diet with plenty of fresh fruit, vegetables and oily fish.
- ☺Consider taking supplements of essential fatty acids designed for pregnancy.
- ☺Consider taking a multivitamin and mineral supplement designed for pregnancy.
- ☺Increase your intake of garlic and possibly take garlic powder tablets, especially if you have a family history of pre-eclampsia (pregnancy-associated high blood pressure).
- ☺Take gentle exercise (see Chapter 8).
- ☺Take time for regular relaxation sessions.
- ☺Reduce your exposure to excess stress.
- ☺Have a sexual health check-up – preferably before becoming pregnant – to rule out infections and bacterial imbalances (such as bacterial vaginosis) linked with an increased risk of miscarriage and preterm delivery.
- ☺Decrease your exposure to environmental toxins (see Chapter 9).

11

Safe Delivery of Your Super Baby

The process of birth is an endurance test for both mother and baby. It is also a relatively dangerous part of pregnancy. While many cases of cerebral palsy are thought to have their origins in prenatal development, profound lack of oxygen at the end of pregnancy can also cause brain damage.

The following statistics show how many babies are damaged due to lack of oxygen during delivery, and make frightening reading:

🐸 1 in 500 babies dies during the last 2 weeks of life in the womb due to lack of oxygen.

🐸 1 in 5,000 babies dies during labour due to lack of oxygen.

🐸1 in 1,750 babies has an epileptic fit after birth due to lack of oxygen.

🐸1 in 4,000 babies suffers cerebral palsy as a result of oxygen lack during birth.

It has been suggested that the risks of brain damage due to natural delivery are around 1 in 360. This is 3 times greater than the risk of sudden infant death syndrome (cot death), which sadly affects 1 in 1,200 babies. In contrast, the risks associated with an elective (planned) Caesarean section are much lower – in the region of 1 per 50,000. It is therefore not surprising that the rate of Caesarean section is increasing – what is surprising is that this increase is being condemned.

Caesarean Section

A Caesarean section is by far the safest option for both you and your baby, and it is not surprising that rates are on the rise. In the US it is becoming increasingly common for women to request an elective Caesarean – known as a vaginal by-pass. While it is not yet accepted practice in the UK to elect a Caesarean when there is no medical indication, it is probably not far away. In 1996, a study showed that, given the choice, 31 per cent of female obstetricians and 17 per cent of male gynaecologists would prefer to have their own baby delivered by Caesarean. The main reason was the risk of damage to the mother's pelvic floor during natural delivery, but 40 per cent were also concerned about the effect of natural delivery on their baby.

Interestingly, babies born by Caesarean have a higher intelligence on average. This may be partly because having a baby with a larger brain and head size will increase the chance of his mother needing a Caesarean. It may also be because fewer brain cells die, as can occur when there is even just a transient lack of oxygen during vaginal delivery.

Interestingly, prenatal stimulation seems to lead to shorter, less painful labours, lower numbers of Caesarean sections and non-traumatic births. Increased maturity of the fetal brain may be a factor, as researchers now know it is your baby's brain that dictates when he will be born.

It seems that hormone signals are sent from your baby's brain to the placenta to increase output of the female hormone, oestrogen. As oestrogen levels increase, they overcome the natural damping-down effect of progesterone (the pregnancy hormone) on the uterus so that muscular contractions start.

Eating During Labour

Many problems with vaginal delivery occur when the mother is exhausted and not allowed to eat or drink anything to fuel her labour. Low blood sugar levels can reduce efficiency of uterine contractions and prolong labour. Low glucose levels may also affect the unborn child. There is a growing argument in favour of allowing women to have light snacks during delivery.

If the mother receives dietary energy, her contractions become more efficient so labour is shorter. This in turn means she needs less pain relief and her baby is likely to be in a better condition after delivery. One study found that women who were allowed to eat light meals while labour was induced had a labour that was shorter by as much as 90 minutes compared with mothers who were not allowed to eat anything. This in turn meant that interventions such as pain relief, forceps and Caesarean delivery were less likely. When the babies were born they were also pinker and more active, with better breathing and heart rates than those born to mothers in the unfed group.

One hospital in New York City allowed women to eat a light diet and drink as they wished during normal deliveries. During this time, 88 per cent of mothers had spontaneous vaginal deliveries, just over 2 per cent needed instrumental help (as with forceps) and 9 per cent had Caesarean sections. A change in policy then meant that for 6 months, all women were routinely fasted during labour. As a result, the use of drugs to induce labour rose by 500 per cent, the use of forceps increased by 35 per cent and the rate of Caesarean sections increased by 38 per cent. The chance of a newborn baby needing to spend time in the special care baby unit also rose by 69 per cent. Not surprisingly, when these effects became clear the previous policy was quickly reinstated, women were once more allowed to eat or drink as they wished, and the delivery statistics reverted to their previous levels.

THE DOWNSIDE OF EATING DURING LABOUR

The reason that starvation is traditionally advised during labour is in case you need a general anaesthetic. If your stomach is full you are more likely to vomit while unconscious and inhale acidic juices into your lungs. This is a serious condition known as Mendelson's syndrome. Secretion of stomach acids continues even if you are starved, however, and Mendelson's syndrome has been known to occur in women who have had nothing to eat for at least 36 hours – so this argument is no longer valid.

It is still the policy of many hospitals to ban eating or drinking during labour, and to put up a drip to provide fluids and glucose once the mother starts to flag or her contractions start to decrease. Having a drip in your arm limits your movements, however, and makes it less easy for you to change your position as and when you wish. It can also lead to swings in blood glucose levels, salt imbalances and fluid overload, all of which are potentially harmful for your baby.

IMPORTANCE OF ANAESTHETIC SKILL

The most important factor for avoiding Mendelson's syndrome is good anaesthetic technique. When eating and drinking were first banned during labour, anaesthetics were primitive and involved giving gas via a mask over the nose and mouth. If vomiting occurred, inhalation into the lungs was therefore highly likely. With modern anaesthetics, a cuffed breathing tube is inserted directly into the airway so stomach contents cannot be inhaled. A further technique involves an anaesthetic assistant pressing on the front of the throat to stop stomach contents rising upwards. These two factors make Mendelson's syndrome unlikely today. In addition, new drugs are available that reduce stomach acidity and speed stomach emptying, so vomiting is less likely. General anaesthesia are also increasingly being replaced with regional pain relief (epidural or spinal analgesia) so that you can remain awake while your baby is delivered by Caesarean section. This reduces the risk of inhaling stomach contents even further.

Many experts now feel there is no longer any firm evidence to justify withholding food or drink during a time when nourishment is essential for both mother and baby. Even if a modern anaesthetic is needed, there is little evidence that light snacks to boost your energy levels during delivery does any harm.

Midwives and obstetricians in some hospitals are now actively encouraging women to eat or drink during labour as they wish:

☺ ask your midwife and doctors for their views on eating or drinking during labour
☺ find out what the policy is in your local hospital, and whether they would allow you to eat a light diet, drink glucose solutions or suck glucose tablets during labour
☺ when you first go into labour, considering having a light snack at home before venturing to the hospital – you may have hours of starvation ahead of you
☺ if you decide to have something to eat, try a light snack such as low-fat yoghurt, a banana, soup, toast or bread, cereals, jelly, ice-cream or even scrambled eggs
☺ keep a note of the time you ate, so your anaesthetist will have an accurate estimate of how long you have been without food if a Caesarean proves necessary

☙if you have eaten or drunk during labour, consider using a method of pain relief other than a narcotic drug such as pethidine; once pethidine is used you should not eat or drink anything other than sips of water

☙if you do require a Caesarean operation, having regional anaesthesia (epidural or spinal) will reduce your risk of Mendelson's syndrome to a minimum.

Apgar Score

When your baby is born, his overall condition is quickly and easily assessed using the Apgar score – named after the American anaesthetist who devised it. Five different features are scored from 0 – 2 as follows:

Sign	Score: 0	1	2
Colour	Blue, pale	Body pink, hands/feet blue	Pink all over
Spontaneous breathing	Absent	Weak cry or irregular breathing	Good, strong cry and regular breathing
Muscle tone	Floppy	Bends some limbs	Active movement of all limbs
Responsiveness	No response	Pulls face when oxygen blown on nose	Good, lusty cry
Heart rate	Absent	Slow	Normal (over 100 beats per minute)

The Apgar score is assessed both at 1 minute and 5 minutes after birth. The most important features are breathing and heart rate – if these are satisfactory, the other features are usually OK as well:

- a (combined) low score of 0 – 3 means a baby needs urgent resuscitation
- a (combined) Apgar score of 4 – 6 suggests the baby may need some medical help
- a (combined) high score of 7 – 10 means the baby is fit and well.

If a mother obtains some nourishment during a long labour, it seems that her baby's Apgar is likely to be higher than a mother who has starved for hours.

Bonding

Keeping to a prenatal programme and communicating with your baby during pregnancy have the additional benefit of helping you bond with the newest addition to your family.

By the time your baby is born, he will know the sound of your voice, your pattern of speech and your smell so that he can instantly recognize you after delivery. Early contact, and putting your baby to the breast within an hour of birth, seem to help the bonding process between mother and child.

Aim to put your baby to your breast within his first hour of life so he can use his instinctive skills to suckle.

12

What Your Newborn Senses in the World Around Him

Your baby is a complex being with a number of highly tuned, but only partially developed, senses with which he has to make sense of the world around him. His brain stem is completely wired so that vital functions like heartbeat and breathing can occur spontaneously, but other connections are still waiting to be strengthened and used – or, if not used, to be pruned.

Over the next few months, quadrillions of new connections will form between dendrites and axons, and new dendritic spines and axon telodendria will form like buds awakening on the branches of trees in spring. A baby who was stimulated in the womb already has a head start in life, as he tends to:

☺ be calmer
☺ be more alert
☺ be happier and cry less
☺ be more empathic
☺ have a longer attention span
☺ hold your gaze for longer
☺ be stronger
☺ lift his head up earlier
☺ stand earlier
☺ have better co-ordination
☺ walk earlier
☺ talk earlier
☺ have more self-confidence.

Prenatal stimulation will have given him the best possible start in life.

Reflexes

Your baby is born with over 70 primitive reflexes designed to protect him in the early days of life. Some disappear in the first 1 or 2 days after birth, while others last from a few weeks to 3 months. These reflexes include:

☺ a rooting reflex – if you place your baby on your naked chest, he will root around until he finds your nipple, locating it through smell and turning towards anything that touches the side of his cheek or mouth (such as your nipple).
☺ sucking reflex
☺ blinking reflex – his eyes close momentarily in response to light, loud sound and touch.

- 🐸 a false crawling reflex – if you place your newborn baby on his stomach, he will naturally curl up with flexed arms and legs so he looks as if he will crawl off. He may also make crawling movements.
- 🐸 false walking reflex – if you hold him upright so his feet just touch a firm surface, he will make deliberate stepping movements, placing one foot in front of another while you support him.
- 🐸 false swimming reflex – if supported horizontally in water, he will start to make swimming motions with his arms and legs.
- 🐸 breath-holding reflex – newborn babies automatically hold their breath when immersed in water (don't try this, however).
- 🐸 false grip – if you stroke your baby's palm with a finger, he will grasp tightly enough to almost support his weight, and when you try to remove your finger, the grip will tighten.
- 🐸 startle reflex – if your baby feels himself moved suddenly, or if he is startled, he will fling out both arms and legs in fright, then flex them violently as if clutching for support. This is known as the Moro response and is very upsetting for your baby.

Sight

Your baby can see well and focus clearly on objects within 25 cm (10 inches). He can tell the difference between shapes and patterns; tests suggest newborn babies prefer stripes and angles to circles. Normal binocular vision does not start to develop until your baby is about 1 month old. If a squint develops, it must be treated as soon as possible, otherwise the brain will suppress images from the affected eye and the brain will learn not to see them so that blindness will develop in that eye (cortical blindness). Faces are the most fascinating object to your newborn baby.

For more information on what your baby can see, how his vision develops and how you can stimulate him through this sense, see Chapter 14.

Hearing

Your baby already knows your voice – and that of your partner – from the speech patterns he heard while in the womb. If you listened to music during pregnancy, he will recognize that, too. He will be soothed by soft, gentle, rhythmic noises similar to those of your heartbeat.

Your baby recognizes your voice after he is born partly by your pattern or rhythm of speech. If a baby hears his mother whisper in one ear, and his father whisper in the other, he will usually turn towards his mother – he recognizes your pattern of speech even though the tones are not there. Similarly, if he hears his father whisper in one ear, and an unknown male whisper in the other, he will turn towards his father 4 times out of 5.

For more information on what your baby can hear and how you can stimulate him through this sense, see Chapter 14.

Smell

Your baby quickly learns to recognize your smell and that of your milk. Three-day-old babies can even tell the difference between their own mother's milk and someone else's. Special sweat glands around the nipple produce secretions that attract a newborn baby to the breast and encourage feeding. A newborn baby will quickly learn to recognize the smell of your own milk. If a new mother washes one breast and nipple, but leaves the other unwashed, her newborn baby will invariably root out the unwashed nipple – he already recognizes the smell of breastmilk at birth, or at least finds it attractive.

Sleeping, breastfed babies were exposed to the smell of a series of pads held a few centimetres from their nose. One pad had been placed inside their mother's bra for 3 hours, one inside another mother's bra for 3 hours, and one that was simply left clean but moist. Babies smelling breastmilk in their sleep made sucking movements in response to the odour when tested at 2 days, 2 weeks and 6 weeks after birth. By 6 weeks, most babies had a stronger sucking response when smelling their own mother's milk, and some cried and jerked away from the pad containing the smell of another mother's milk. Other studies have shown that babies start showing a preference within the first week of life.

For more information on what your new baby can smell, and how you can stimulate him through this sense, see Chapter 14.

Maternal Depression

After you have given birth, it is very common to suffer so-called 'baby blues'. Feelings of low mood, unhappiness, tearfulness, irritability, anxiety and extreme tiredness appear 4 – 5 days after giving birth in 50 – 80 per cent of new mothers. Symptoms usually improve within a week or two and are due to the rapid adjustments in hormone levels occurring at this time.

More severe postnatal depression affects 1 in 10 new mothers, with many cases going undetected. Most problems are short-lived, but some persist for months, even into the next pregnancy and beyond. The cause remains uncertain. A personal or family history of depression seems to increase the risk, as do vulnerability factors such as lack of confidence, lack of social support and a poor relationship with the baby's father. A recent study suggested that postnatal depression may be linked with thyroid antibodies, which occur in 12 per cent of child-bearing women. Half of these women will develop depressive symptoms, so screening for thyroid antibodies may help to identify women at risk. Another theory is that postnatal depression is due to a relative progesterone imbalance which is prolonged and may trigger changes in the level of certain brain chemicals. Symptoms of postnatal depression include:

☻despondency
☻lack of interest in your baby or yourself
☻feelings of not being able to cope
☻feelings of guilt, inadequacy and rejection
☻irritability
☻anxiety and panic attacks
☻difficulty sleeping
☻difficulty concentrating
☻loss of appetite
☻loss of interest in sex
☻obsessive behaviour
☻difficulty bonding with, or feeling love for, your baby.

Even more serious is a postnatal psychiatric disorder known as puerperal psychosis. This occurs in one or two out of every 1,000 deliveries and is most common after a first pregnancy and Caesarean section. Symptoms include:

☻excitability and euphoria
☻over-activity
☻disjointed thoughts and speech
☻feelings of not being able to cope
☻feelings of guilt, inadequacy and rejection
☻irritability
☻anxiety and panic attacks
☻lack of concentration
☻poor memory
☻sleep problems
☻aggressive behaviour
☻using obscene language

☺delusions
☺hallucinations
☺feelings of persecution
☺wanting to harm yourself or your baby.

Puerperal psychosis is a medical emergency and mother and baby usually need to be admitted to hospital for their own safety. There is a 1 in 5 risk of the condition recurring in subsequent deliveries.

HOW POSTNATAL DEPRESSION CAN AFFECT YOUR BABY

Postnatal depression has a severe effect on mother–baby interactions. Compared to well women, depressed mothers are less sensitively tuned to their baby's needs and stimulate their babies less. As a result, babies whose mothers were depressed at 2 months after delivery had significantly poorer cognitive development at 18 months. A study of over 170 children showed that if their mother remained depressed throughout their first year, they scored around 10 per cent lower on IQ tests at age 3–4 years than those whose mothers were well during the first year of life. This result was reliable, even when other factors such as birthweight, parental IQ, family environment and breastfeeding were taken into account.

If the mother's depression remains undiagnosed and is prolonged, her baby will also find it more difficult to learn positive emotions such as joy, pleasure and laughter. This is especially likely if the mother's illness leads her to ignore her baby, fail to interact with him or be irritable. If a depressed mother is given adequate support and is encouraged to make attempts to interact with her baby, cuddle him, and show love and affection, this will make all the difference to his development and alleviate her feelings of inadequacy. Research shows that if a depressed mother gets better before her baby is a year old, her baby is more likely to learn positive emotions – even if his mother was severely depressed and did not interact with him before.

☺ If you think you are developing depression after your baby is born, it is vital for the well-being of both you and your baby that you seek help. If you have postnatal depression it must be diagnosed and treated as early as possible. Treatment involves close emotional support. Antidepressant drugs or hormone treatment may be needed.

☺ Even when you are feeling low, try to interact with your baby – give him attention and play games with him to stimulate him.

☺ Try to have someone with you most of the time – a close friend or relative for example – both to help you, and to inter-act with your baby.

☺ If you find it difficult to interact with your baby, don't be afraid to ask your GP or health visitor for advice. Many mothers experience postnatal depression; keeping your feelings to yourself will only make you feel worse.

Interestingly, mothers who take part in a prenatal stimulation programme, and who use the BabyPlus unit, seem less likely to develop baby blues or postnatal depression. This may be due to the fact that they have a calmer, happier baby.

13

The Importance of Breastfeeding for Your Baby's Brain Development

This chapter concentrates on only one aspect of breastfeeding – why it is best for your baby's developing brain and intellectual potential. Every woman who is pregnant should also read *Breast is Best* by Drs Penny and Andrew Stanway (Pan) for a complete picture of breastfeeding, including why it is best for you and your baby, hints and tips on how to get started, how to do it successfully and how to overcome any problems – especially in the daunting, early days when you and your baby are learning how to do it properly.

Breastmilk is without a doubt the most nutritionally complete food you can offer your newborn baby. It contains:

- essential fatty acids (EFAs)
- long-chain polyunsaturates (LCPs) including DHA and AA which are vital for your baby's brain development (see Chapter 6)
- nerve growth factors that influence growth and maturation of brain cells
- intestinal growth factors
- antibodies to protect against disease
- active scavenger immune cells
- natural antibacterial and antiviral substances
- amino acids in the right quantity and ratio for human babies
- milk sugars (such as lactose)
- nucleotides that act as building-blocks for genetic material and which are important for immunity
- all the energy your baby needs for his first 6 months of life.

The ideal way to breastfeed is to supply your baby with milk whenever he needs it – that is, on demand. New UK Government guidelines recommend putting your baby to the breast within an hour of birth, and breastfeeding exclusively for the first 4 – 6 months of your baby's life. Breastmilk should then continue to be given after weaning onto solids, up until at least your child's first birthday. Many children continue to enjoy the benefits of breastfeeding until the age of 2 years or beyond.

Your baby knows the smell of your milk, as there is a great similarity with the smell and taste of your amniotic fluid. The processes that flavour your amniotic fluid are similar to those that flavour milk, and to the secretions of modified sebaceous glands (Montgomery's tubercles) that develop on the pigmented skin surrounding your nipples. Dietary factors such as garlic, spices and meat influence these odours and flavours. If your diet changes immediately after birth, you may have difficulty establishing breastfeeding as your milk will taste different from your amniotic fluid. As noted in Chapter 3, this has been observed in Indian mothers used to eating spicy, garlicky curries who were admitted to hospital and had to eat bland, Western hospital food instead. As a result, their babies do not seem to recognize the smell or taste of their breastmilk so well.

Breastmilk and DHA

When a baby is born, his brain weighs around 350 g (12 oz) – 10 per cent of his total body weight. During the first year of life, a baby's brain will almost triple in weight to 1,000 g (2 lb 3 oz). This growth spurt is remarkable when you consider that his brain will only weigh a little more – around 1,300 g (2 lb 14 oz) – at puberty and a total of 1,400 g –1,500 g (3 – 3 lb 5 oz) by the time he reaches adulthood. Around a fifth of your baby's brain weight is made up of long-chain polyunsaturated fatty acids (LCPs). Because of this rapid growth, 60 per cent of the calories your baby needs during his first year of life outside the womb are used to build new brain cell membranes and coat his growing nerve fibres with a fatty (myelin) sheath. Much of this energy will come from the fat in human milk and infant formulas.

The essential fatty acid (EFA) content of human milk includes linolenic acid, AA and DHA. DHA is especially important, as babies are unable to make their own DHA from linolenic acid until they are around 4 – 6 months old. The LCP content of your breastmilk is much higher than that in cow's milk. It is dependent on your diet and therefore varies widely from mother to mother. It is estimated that the diet of as many as 80 per cent of pregnant women is deficient in EFAs. This can result in low levels of DHA in breastmilk – 0.05 per cent compared with as much as 1.4 per cent in women who regularly eat oily fish or who take supplements. The amount of DHA in the breastmilk of vegan women is lower than that in fish- and meat-eating women, but is still significantly greater than that found in cow's milk formulas that have not been enriched with LCPs:

- breastmilk of vegan women has an average DHA content of 0.14 per cent
- breastmilk of vegetarian women has an average DHA content of 0.30 per cent
- breastmilk of women who eat meat has an average DHA content of 0.37 per cent.

This may not seem like much, but the total EFA content of breastmilk (AA, DHA, linoleic and linolenic acids) makes up 10 – 12 per cent of total energy content. In comparison, protein only accounts for around 6 per cent of the energy content of breastmilk. As less than half the amino acids found in the protein fraction are 'essential', the total EFA content of breastmilk is in fact significantly greater than the total essential amino acid content of breastmilk. These quantitative relationships are not generally realized, as the EFAs are thought of in comparison with the total fat content of breastmilk, which is present as the major energy source of milk (60 per cent). Weight for weight, fats provide more than twice the energy (9 kcal/gm) of protein (4 kcal/gm) or sugars (4 kcal/gm) and are therefore the most compact and efficient energy source available.

Taking a fish oil supplement especially formulated for pregnancy can increase levels of DHA in human breastmilk by up to 69 per cent. This in turn increases the blood levels of DHA in breastfed babies by up to 40 per cent. Taking supplements can therefore enrich your baby's supply of DHA so he is more likely to incorporate optimum amounts into his brain cell membranes and synapses.

Eating foods rich in essential fatty acids and taking fish and evening primrose oil supplements can significantly improve the quality of your breastmilk when it comes to feeding your baby's brain. Supplements are now available over the counter that are specifically enriched in EFAs and LCPs to suit women who are pregnant or breastfeeding. As well as benefiting your baby, they will help to ensure your own continued good health by reducing your risk of symptoms linked with essential fatty acid deficiency (see Chapter 6).

Breastmilk also changes to adapt to your growing infant's changing needs. Over 9 months of breastfeeding, the proportion of long-chain polyunsaturated essential fatty acids slowly decreases, while that of long-chain saturated and monounsaturated fatty acids (such as nervonic acid) increases. The latter are preferentially laid down in your baby's axons during myelination, so breastmilk adapts from the early months when brain cell division is important, so that it is more suitable once myelination of axons becomes important. This finding is fascinating.

Sadly, only around 30 per cent of mothers in the UK breastfeed their baby until the age of 3 months. In Scandinavia and New Zealand, however, thanks to educational and health initiatives, around 80 per cent of mothers breastfeed until at least the age of 6 months.

Neuro-developmental Benefits of Breastfeeding

Infants who are breastfed have a significantly greater amount of the long-chain polyunsaturate docosahexaenoic acid (DHA – see Chapter 6) in their cerebral cortex than infants fed standard, non-enriched milk formulas. DHA is important for the transmission of signals from one brain cell to another and is found in especially high concentration in the areas of membrane forming synaptic connections between one brain cell and another. When DHA is in short supply, it is replaced in the synapse by other fatty acids that are less optimal for brain function. As a result, transmission of nerve signals from one brain cell to another is impaired. In contrast, an optimum supply of DHA ensures rapid communication between brain cells, which boosts neural development and intellectual potential.

A variety of studies have shown the beneficial effects of breastmilk on a baby's emotional, physical and intellectual development. By the age of 3 months, the IQ of babies who are breastfed is 3 points higher than those fed on formula, and those who are breastfed until 6 months have an IQ that is 6 points higher than those receiving formula. Some studies suggest that babies who are breastfed for at least 6 months enjoy a 10-point IQ advantage over non-breastfed children when assessed in later childhood. Even breastfeeding for just 3 weeks can improve your child's long-term IQ by an average of 4 points, as it supplies important building-blocks for the brain at the time when it needs them most.

Research shows that breastfeeding improves hand-eye co-ordination, visual development, language and social skills. By the age of 7 years, children who were breastfed as babies were found to be less timid, nervous, jealous and spiteful than similar children who had been bottle-fed. This may link in with observations that young babies who are held or carried by someone for most of the time, breastfed on demand, and who slept with their parents are far less likely to cry and are more content and secure than babies left alone in their cot for long periods of time.

Other studies suggest that breastfeeding has such beneficial effects on brain development that it seems to protect against the future development of dyslexia, schizophrenia, multiple sclerosis and other neurological problems. This is on top of the benefits in reducing allergies (such as asthma, eczema), glue ear, sudden infant death syndrome, autoimmune diseases (such as ulcerative colitis, Crohn's disease, juvenile rheumatoid arthritis), infections, diabetes, high blood pressure and coronary heart disease in later life.

Breastfeeding is by far the best option for your baby. It is especially important for preterm and low birthweight babies. Those fed human milk have better brain development when assessed at 18 months of age, and a higher intelligence score at age 8 years, compared with similar babies fed formula milks.

Enriching Your Diet While Breastfeeding

When it comes to the brain potential of your developing baby, the essential fatty acids in your diet are equally as important as your vitamins, minerals and energy supply. Your blood levels of EFAs during pregnancy, and the concentrations found in breast-milk during lactation, vary depending on how much of the essential fatty acids you obtain from your food.

The richest sources of EFAs include oily fish (such as mackerel, herring, salmon, trout, sardines, pilchards), nuts, seeds, wholegrains and dark green leafy vegetables. Some research suggests that the balance of EFAs in rapeseed oil may be better for brain development than safflower or sunflower seed oils, so it may be worth switching to rapeseed oil for cooking and to use it in salad dressings.

Many researchers have reported that the essential fatty acid status of full-term infants is marginal – the mother's diet rarely contains enough for optimal brain growth of her baby unless she regularly eats oily fish, nuts and seeds (see Chapter 6). Research shows that in mothers not taking EFA supplements, their EFA status (especially that of DHA) becomes poorer with each subsequent pregnancy. This suggests that her stores are not easily replenished after pregnancy and breastfeeding, and that supplementation is likely to be important.

If the fetus does not receive enough DHA he will start to leach it from his mother's richest supply – her own brain. This may account for the slight shrinkage (2 – 3 per cent) in maternal brain size seen in some pregnant women, and may cause the poor concentration, forgetfulness and vagueness that many women experience during the last few months of pregnancy. It seems sensible to ensure adequate dietary intakes, and to take supplements to help prevent this. Anecdotal evidence suggests that women taking these dietary and supplementary measures do not develop problems with concentration.

If levels of EFAs and LCPs are marginal during pregnancy, deficiency will be even more marked during breastfeeding. Breastfeeding is often associated with intense thirst, and this is one of the cardinal signs of dietary deficiency in essential fatty acids. By making dietary changes and by taking a supplement designed for pregnancy and breastfeeding, you can help to maintain optimal breastmilk levels of DHA which will in turn feed your baby's developing brain.

While diet should always come first, not every new mum wants to increase her intake of oily fish, for example. Supplements containing essential fatty acids (from fish oil and evening primrose oil) therefore provide an important dietary alternative. To suggest they are not needed – as some people have – is a grave disservice to the many mothers and babies who would benefit from them. Their importance is such that formula milks are now being fortified with them, too.

Losing Weight

Nature provides you with at least an extra 4 kg (9 lb) of fat reserves during pregnancy to ensure you have reserves to help see you through the early breastfeeding period. It is important not to try to lose weight while you are breastfeeding, or the quality and quantity of your milk will decrease. Sixty per cent of the calories in breastmilk consist of fat, and your body stores are essential to give your baby good quality milk in the quantities that he needs. You may find that your weight naturally falls while feeding your baby – but don't try to hasten the process. Put your bathroom scales out of sight until you decide to stop breastfeeding. Then you can take stock and lose any remaining excess weight slowly through a sensible regime of healthy eating and regular physical exercise.

Enriched Formula Milks

While breastmilk is still the food of choice for a Super Baby, formulas containing LCPs are the next best option available. If DHA-enriched milks are not given, then a formula-fed baby shows a fall in brain levels of DHA during the first 40 weeks of life outside the womb, rather than the increase that occurs with breastfed babies.

DHA levels in your baby's brain steadily increase from around 20 weeks gestation in the womb. They are important for the fluidity of membranes at the synapses, and for fast transmission of electrical signals, so this observed fall in brain levels of babies fed unenriched formulas is likely to be non-optimal – if not detrimental – as it slows synaptic transmission of information. Researchers have stated that the structure and function of cell membranes in a baby's cerebral cortex are likely to be extremely important during early development, and failure to maintain intakes of fatty acids similar to those provided by breastmilk may cause permanent adverse effects.

Manufacturers are now starting to enrich formula milks with LCPs for mothers who are unable or unwilling to breastfeed. Several random, double-blind prospective studies of developmental quotient in healthy, full-term infants have been performed. When breastfed babies are compared with those randomly assigned to receive standard formula or LCP-enriched formula milk, psychomotor developmental assessments show that a baby's DHA levels are directly related with his developmental advancement. No other fatty acid shows the same relationship. The results are the same when babies' visual acuity is assessed. Researchers have concluded that, when breastmilk is not available, the use of a formula containing LCPs is the most effective way to achieve DHA levels beneficial for early brain development.

Research also shows that adding LCPs to formula milks during the first 30 weeks significantly improves a baby's sharpness of vision compared with babies not receiving LCP-enriched formulas. Trials are ongoing to see if enrichment also boosts intelligence. At present, it seems that breastfed babies, and those receiving formula enriched with LCPs, may have up to a 10-point IQ advantage on children not receiving LCPs during early development. Breastfeeding also confers additional advantages such as nerve growth factors, which influence brain growth and maturation.

Not surprisingly, there is considerable controversy at present concerning these findings. If a mother is unable or unwilling to breastfeed, however, she is well advised to stake her baby's intellectual future on an enriched formula. At the worst, it can do no harm. Chances are it will provide a significant intellectual benefit.

If you decide to give your baby a formula milk, check the labels and choose one supplemented with LCPs. These are now becoming more widely available. At first, LCPs were only routinely given to premature infants (since around 1991). They were expensive and difficult to extract in a pure form, but new technology means they can be produced more cheaply. For example:

☺ DHA may now be extracted from vats of algae that naturally synthesize it, or from eggs
☺ AA is extracted from fungi that naturally produce it.

Ideally, an LCP-enriched formula should be given to term infants for at least the first 4 – 6 months of life after birth – until your baby can start making DHA himself in adequate quantities from other dietary essential fatty acids. After this age, continue either giving him formula enriched with LCPs or with linoleic or linolenic acids to ensure his intake of DHA building-blocks. Some milk formulas now have added nucleotides too, molecules needed for the production of new genetic material and for healthy immunity.

Cow's Milk

Cow's milk is quite different from human breastmilk, and contains three times as much protein, four times as many minerals and only a quarter of the essential fatty acid content. This is because a calf's greatest priority is building his body, not his brain.

Cow's milk should not be introduced until your child is at least 12 months of age. Up until the age of 2 years, your infant should only receive cow's milk that is full-fat – he needs the extra calories. Fifty per cent of a child's energy should come from fat during the first 2 years of life, with this level only declining to 35 per cent by the age of 5 years. Semi-skimmed milk can therefore be introduced from the age of 2 years, but fully skimmed milk should not be given until 5 years of age.

Vitamins and Minerals

Consider giving your child vitamin and mineral drops designed for his age group. Sadly, many nutrients, but especially vitamin A, calcium, iron and zinc, are missing from the diets of 85 per cent of children under the age of 4.

Some evidence suggests that a vitamin and mineral supplement boosts the speed at which children process information and can give an IQ advantage of at least 4 to 5 IQ points.

Your baby needs the right amount of vitamins and minerals to grow properly. Too many can be just as harmful as too few, however, so always give the right dose.

SUPPLEMENTS

0 – 6 months

🐸Most babies do not need supplements during the first 6 months of life.

🐸Breastfed babies are sometimes given supplements from the age of 1 month if their mother is not well nourished.

6 – 12 months

🐸Babies who have formula milk as their main drink usually do not need supplements – formulas are already fortified with good levels of vitamins and minerals.

🐸Babies who have breastmilk as their main drink after the age of 6 months should receive extra vitamins A, C and D.

1 – 5 years

🐸All children need supplements of vitamins A, C and D unless their diet is known to be rich in these.

🐸Moderate exposure to sunlight allows your child to make vitamin D in his skin – but make sure he doesn't get sunburned.

At present only one in five children aged 18 months to 4½ years is given dietary supplements.

14
Enriching the First Year of Your Child's Life

During the first few years of life after birth, each of your baby's 200 billion brain cells forges new connections with thousands of other neurons. As well as forming new dendritic spines, the axon of each cell also makes an increasing number of connections with other cells – including those it is already linked up with. These extra couplings help to amplify the electrical signal passing from one cell to another, so it is more likely to reach the stimulation threshold of its target. Each time your baby is stimulated – through sound, colour, touch, taste or emotional interactions – thousands of new connections are made. The more he is stimulated, the more he eventually learns.

Pathways that are used regularly receive nourishment in the form of nerve growth factor (NGF) secreted along with the chemicals that send information across the synaptic cleft. NGF ensures that a particular pathway is maintained, strengthened and preserved. Connections that are rarely used receive little NGF and are eventually pruned away as genes coding for synapse-destroying enzymes are switched on. Pruning is a vital process that sorts the brain wheat from the chaff.

One of the most important years for your baby's brain development is his first – in terms of both the nourishment and stimulation he receives. Rich experiences – especially when coupled with breastmilk, which contains nerve growth factors and essential long-chain polyunsaturated fatty acids – undoubtedly produce the optimum conditions for the development of your baby's brain.

In a well-stimulated child, new synaptic connections are continually forming so that, despite selective pruning, the number of synaptic connections continues to increase until puberty. Within the first 6 months of life, for example, the average number of synapses connecting a single neuron to your baby's visual cortex increases by a factor of 10 from around 2,000 to 20,000 synapses per cell. The highest average number of synapses per neuron throughout your baby's cerebral cortex is reached at around the age of 2 (15,000 synapses per cell). An enriched, stimulating environment boosts the number of synapses made by each neuron by as much as 25 per cent. After his first year of life after birth, your baby's brain should contain twice as many synapses, and consume twice as much energy, as your own.

The complexity of dendritic connections also increases, so that more and more dendritic trees split into two, branches which in turn each split into a further two branches. By the age of 6 months, third- and fourth-order branchings occur; and by the second year of life, babies receiving the most stimulation – and who are the most intelligent – develop increasing numbers of fifth and sixth or more orders of branching. Experience and an enriched environment therefore help to shape your baby's brain after birth.

In a neglected, under-stimulated child however, the formation of new synapses and destruction of the old become unbalanced. Researchers have found that children who are not played with and who are rarely touched or stimulated develop a brain that is up to 30 per cent smaller than expected for their age.

Windows of Opportunity

New research suggests that attempts to boost intellectual potential must start during the first 3 years of life, especially the first year after birth, as brain development during this time is more extensive than previously believed. As we have already seen, the brain is shaped by stimulation, use, play and experience. Stimulation needs to occur during the right time period when the appropriate part of the brain is developing, however. The time slots during which your baby's brain can acquire particular new skills are known as critical periods or windows of opportunity. During the first few years of life after birth, there are a number of critical windows when your baby's brain can best learn new skills. Once these periods are passed, particular parts of the brain will have become hard-wired and less able to make new connections so the skills they are associated with are less easily learned.

With the right input, at the right time, almost anything is possible. The right input at the wrong time, however, may miss the cortical development boat.

It is important not to hot-house your child, however, or push him in ways he is reluctant to go. Don't fall into the trap of forcing him to overachieve. In the long run this will do more harm than good. Learning and environmental enrichment should be fun, not a chore. As soon as he seems bored with a particular activity, let him stop. The aim is to widen your child's experience and his learning opportunities so his future potential is enhanced. Do not try to force him to acquire particular skills, as this will start to imprint dislike and reduce his motivation. Let him choose what activities he participates in as much as possible.

Emotions

The parts of the brain that handle emotions are among the first circuits that develop during life after birth. Up until the age of around 8 weeks, babies experience simple states of upset or content. Emotions develop in layers, each more complex than the last, and are mostly in place by the age of 10. Eventually, your baby will know more sophisticated feelings as he starts to recognize himself as a person – joy and sadness, envy and empathy, pride and shame. These complex feelings form the basis of your child's individual personality. Experience will continue to modify his emotions throughout the rest of his life, however.

Happy feelings develop most easily in a loving, caring environment where there is a lot of emotional warmth and touching. In some cultures, the mother holds her baby next to her skin night and day, sleeping with the baby so she is alert to his every need.

Positive emotions are reinforced if you mirror your child's responses. If, for example, he squeals with delight when he builds a tower and you respond with delight and claps, this will help to hard-wire his senses of pleasure and achievement. If you always react in a 'So what, don't bother me now, I'm busy' kind of way, he will lose the opportunity to learn joy and instead may sense an emotional anticlimax that leads to passivity.

Staying attuned to your child and mirroring his positive emotions will help to reinforce them. This is especially important during early life, as your child's critical 'window' for learning emotional control starts to close soon after the first year of life after birth.

Attention

Babies do not look around at random, but will seem to study parts of their surroundings longer than others. By observing a baby's patterns of attention, researchers have discovered more about how an infant views the world. One method is to record the direction and duration of a baby's look when different visual stimuli are presented side to side. If a baby consistently looks at one more than the other, it shows he can distinguish between them. Researchers have also found that babies get bored with repeated stimuli, just as adults do. If he is given the same picture to look at repeatedly he will be disinterested. If he is then shown a new stimulus in the form of a similar but sufficiently different picture, he recognizes it is different and perks up again, becoming more attentive. By showing babies squares, circles, stripes, faces, bull's eyes and so on in either black and white or colours, researchers can work out what a baby can see at different ages. A baby under 4 weeks can distinguish stripes of 3 mm (at 25 cm/10 inches away); by 6 months, he can distinguish stripes of less than half a millimetre wide.

Vision

Normal vision is essential for normal development. It is by seeing objects that your baby will want to learn their name. His motivation to reach out, roll over, crawl and walk also comes from his curiosity and his wish to explore what he sees around him. In the first 2 months of life, your baby can see best at close range.

At birth, your baby's field of view is more restricted than your own. He is most likely to look at objects falling within a 60-degree arc straight in front of him (that is, 30 degrees left or right from straight ahead), within 10 degrees above or below his line of sight, and within 90 cm (3 ft) of his body. He can naturally focus on objects around 17 – 20 cm (6 – 8 inches) away – the distance between his face and yours when he is lying cradled in the crook of your arm feeding at the breast. He can usually recognize his mother's and father's face by 2 weeks of age. His visual acuity is between 10 and 30 per cent less acute than your own, so that fine lines are harder for him to perceive. He see them as a blurred grey. Newborn babies find high-contrast black-and-white striped patterns more fascinating than colours, as his rods (cells in the retina that detect dim light and see in black and white) are working better than his cones (cells that detect colour in bright light) at this stage. He prefers straight or angular lines to those that are curved or wavy. He is attracted to simple pictures of faces, however.

By the age of 6 weeks, he can focus clearly on objects about 30 cm (12 inches) away and will usually start to smile around this age. Babies who have been stimulated in the womb often smile within 1 – 3 weeks after birth, however. He is especially attracted to drawings of faces and targets (concentric lines). He will also look more closely at the outside edges of patterns rather than the insides.

The number of synapses between neurons in the visual cortex involved in interpreting information from the eyes start to increase during the first 2 months of life after birth.

Between 2 and 4 months after birth, the number of synapses then suddenly explode by at least a factor of 10. This corresponds with a sudden improvement in your baby's vision around this time and an ability to start tracking objects with his eyes or turning to stare in the direction of sound. He starts to prefer patterns of increasing complexity (such as 4 concentric circles rather than 2) and prefers curved lines and shapes to ones that are straight or angular. He also shows signs of remembering what he sees.

Many infants can distinguish colours by 2 months of age as the cone cells in their retina start to work properly. He may not be able to see the colour blue as effectively as red or yellow until 3 months of age, however.

By 4 months, your baby can see in full colour and can adjust his focus to see near and far objects, too. He will love to watch you and other people – especially children – to see what you are doing. He continues to prefer curved lines to straight ones and looks for increasing complexity of design. He also develops depth perception so that, by 4 – 5 months of age, he will start to reach for an object he sees. By 7 – 8 months, he will successfully grab the object and bring it to his mouth. Prenatally stimulated babies often do all these things much earlier.

A baby given a visually enriched environment tends to be calmer, quieter and more attentive when he is awake than a baby deprived of stimulation. If your baby is unable to see out of one eye – because of a congenital cataract, for example, then rapid surgical correction is vital. Otherwise the brain rewires itself to ignore input from the retina of the affected eye. If correction is not carried out until later in childhood, sight in that eye will never be restored, even though the corrected eye is now func- tionally normal. The eye remains blind because the brain can no longer see from it. This is known as cortical blindness. This rewiring will not occur if the cataract develops in later life, how- ever, when correction will restore normal sight.

The number of synapses in the visual cortex peaks at 8 months old, stays high until 4 years, then begins a gradual decline over the next 5 years, during which their number halves as a result of selective pruning.

Interesting new research suggests that baby boys can recog- nize each other at just 3 months of age, even when fully clothed – a feat that many adults are unable to do. Researchers per- formed psychological tests on 60 3-month-old babies who were shown pictures of male and female babies wearing identical clothing, plus pictures of trucks, dolls and older children. Baby boys were more interested in looking at pictures of other baby boys the same age. In contrast, baby girls spent as much time looking at other boys as they did looking at girls.

Binocular vision continues to develop throughout your baby's first 4 years of life, by which stage it is fully complete. In contrast, while visual acuity is virtually complete by 5 years of age, it continues to develop until around the age of 10 years.

Hearing

By 3 months of age, the parts of your baby's brain involved in hearing (auditory cortex) become more active. Your baby learns about sounds by seeing which objects make which noise. At birth, your baby will already know the sound of your voice – and that of your partner – from patterns heard while in the womb. Newborn babies respond to sound and should become startled by loud, sudden noises. By 8 weeks he will start attending to continuous sounds such as a vacuum cleaner. At 3 months he will react to the sound of your voice even if he cannot see you. By the age of 6 months, your baby will recognize the vowel sounds that are the building-blocks for his native language – if exposed to more than one language, he will recognize a wider variety of sounds and speech patterns. By talking to your baby a lot, and using a high-pitched, rhythmic, sing-song intonation – called 'parentese' – you can help to imprint the sounds of your language on your baby's brain so that he learns to connect words and objects more quickly. Your baby's heart rate will change when listening to this melodious form of speech. By 14 months, he will show a response to his own name.

Your baby's hearing will be tested by your health visitor between 7 and 9 months, but let her know at any time if you think your baby is not hearing properly, as this will have a serious effect on his learning ability.

Language

Recognition of language and speech starts from before birth and continues up until around 10 years of age. The optimum time for learning a foreign language is before the age of 6, however. It then becomes increasingly difficult to master the new sounds that form the basis of different cultures.

A baby starts babbling sounds together to make nonsensical phrases by the age of 8 weeks. The more words your infant hears, both in the womb and during early life after birth, the faster he will learn his native language. The basic sounds that make up the words of a particular language are hard-wired into the brain by the age of 1 year. Neurons that respond to different sounds are spaced apart according to how similar the sounds are. In English for example, 'Rrr' and 'Lll' sound quite different and are programmed apart so they are more easily recognized. In Chinese, 'Rrr' and 'Lll' sound very similar and are programmed in to neurons sitting close together. As a result, a child brought up in a home where Chinese is spoken will find it more difficult to distinguish between these two sounds should he later learn to speak English in secondary school. Similarly, English-speaking children will find difficulty in rolling their Rs as the French do, as this is not a sound they are accustomed to.

If you have the opportunity to expose your child to the sounds of a different language, as from a bilingual parent or an au pair, do so from as early an age as possible. Preferably from birth. It is much easier for your child to learn a second language along with the first, than to learn it afterwards when he is older.

Speak to your baby as much as possible. Explain what you are doing when you are making his breakfast, putting on his clothes or doing housework. Immerse him in the sounds of words as much as possible – although remember that quiet periods offering time for reflection are important, too. If you are concentrating on something and are unable to interact with your baby for a while, put on the radio so he can still hear some background conversation and music. Research shows that the number of sounds made by a 3-month-old baby is increased if an adult responds and talks back to the infant. Similarly, by the age of 2 years, babies whose mother spoke and read to them frequently knew over 300 words more than those from a less stimulating environment. Interestingly, it did not seem to matter what words the mother used – hearing simple words seemed to be just as good for laying down 'sound' circuits in the brain as hearing complex words. These circuits then act as the internal dictionary that starts to absorb more words.

Yet more research shows that babies and infants who were talked to a lot from an early age had significantly higher IQ scores than those who received less parental communication. They also had significantly more advanced creativity, reading, writing, problem-solving and decision-making abilities.

The size of your child's vocabulary will continue to increase throughout life as long as you encourage him to retain his innate love of words and word games such as *Scrabble* or crosswords.

New research suggests that children whose parents read to them at a very young age will perform better when learning to read, write and do arithmetic. Children introduced to books from 9 months of age significantly outperform those who were not read to, and are better able to concentrate in the classroom. This was independent of social class or environmental background. Families of 300 9-month-old children were given a free book, a poetry poster and information on how to join their local library. By the age of 30 months and by the time of starting school, they were reassessed and were significantly ahead in reading, listening and speaking ability, using numbers and handling shapes, spaces and measures than were similar children not exposed to books at an early age.

Non-verbal Communication

Before he can communicate with words or gestures, your baby will give you non-verbal clues that he is interested in what he is watching. If he is paying attention, ready to play, or finds his environment/activity interesting and fun he may:

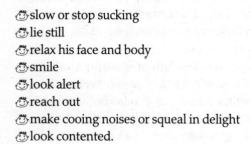slow or stop sucking
lie still
relax his face and body
smile
look alert
reach out
make cooing noises or squeal in delight
look contented.

If he has had enough, not interested or wants you to stop the stimulation, he may:

begin to suck furiously
wrinkle his face
hold his body rigidly or become limp
stare vacantly without focusing
look bored
seem drowsy
start to yawn
look away
turn his head firmly away so he can't see
start to squirm
start to cry.

By looking for these non-verbal clues, you can tell when your baby is happy to receive stimulation and when he would prefer to rest or to have the stimulus changed.

Logic

The circuits that deal with mathematics and logic are laid down during the first 4 years of life after birth. Interestingly, they develop near those involved in appreciating music. Teach your child simple mathematical concepts from as young an age as you like, by playing counting games – number the stairs as you climb to bed, count spoons as you lay the table, count bricks as you build a tower, etc. Learning numbers while music is playing in the background may help to imprint the information more easily. Music also helps the development of spatial skills – understanding where things are in relation to each other and the self. This can be demonstrated using a simple maze game. This process has been taken one stage further in using background classical music to help adults learn new languages. Some researchers believe it is beneficial to listen to Mozart when learning mathematical concepts.

Logic also seems to be linked with mobility. Babies who crawl early are more likely to be able to find objects hidden under a cloth or enclosed in your hand, compared with babies who have not started crawling. Interestingly, using a baby-walker seems to have a similar beneficial effect on spatial awareness – suggesting that it is mobility itself that is important. It therefore seems helpful to encourage your child to move by providing him with a baby-walker.

Music

A love of music is imprinted at an early age – during the prenatal stage in the womb, and during the first 4 years of life after birth. The earlier your child is exposed to music, the more synapses will be laid down to help him appreciate melodies in later life. Interestingly, the earlier a child starts to learn a musical instrument, the more of his cerebral cortex he will set aside to master that skill and the more adept he is likely to become with practice. Music can also be used to help your baby sleep – try *Sound Asleep for Babies* by Dr Elizabeth Scott. This cassette contains classical music which becomes progressively softer and slower to lull your baby to sleep (see Further Reading for supplier).

Touch

By 3 months of age, the part of your baby's brain involved in detecting touch is becoming more active.

The healing power of touch means that babies who are massaged regularly are more active, fall asleep better and gain more weight than unmassaged babies – as well as being better tempered, more sociable and less likely to cry.

🍥Only start to massage your baby when he is in good health and has passed his 6-week health check.

🍥Wash your hands thoroughly before you start and remove any jewellery and your watch.

🍥Play some quiet, relaxing music. Show your baby lots of love and affection during the massage and talk or sing quietly to him throughout, maintaining eye contact as much as possible.

🍥Make sure the room is warm, wrap your naked baby in a fluffy towel and place him on a soft changing mat on the floor.

🍥Pour a little baby oil or lotion onto your hands and rub them together to warm them.

🍥Gently stroke your baby's chest using sweeping, gliding motions that are firm enough not to tickle but gentle enough not to hurt. You can also make small circular motions with your thumbs.

🍥Repeat the massage on his arms, tummy, legs and back.

🍥Be careful holding your baby afterwards as he will be slippery!

Some babies get upset during their first massage. If so, wrap your baby in the towel and cuddle him close. Try again another day. Special classes to show you baby massage techniques are available in many areas – ask your health visitor or midwife.

Movement

Your baby has started to move his limbs since around the 7th week after conception. It is not until the 16th week of gestation that some of the motor nerves start to connect up and the process of myelination of nerve fibres (when axons gain their fatty, insulating outer layer) begins. The more your baby moves, the more his cerebellum – the part of the brain at the back that controls posture and movement – develops. Babies who are pre-natally stimulated have been observed in the womb to be moving their limbs and body rhythmically in time to music or repetitive rhythms, which helps to increase muscle strength. Prenatal stimulation has a beneficial effect on strength and co-ordination such that these babies seem to lift their head, roll over, crawl and walk earlier than babies not stimulated, on average.

As myelination progresses, some of the automatic reflexes your baby was born with (see Chapter 11) start to disappear. You will notice that control of his arms and limbs becomes smoother, without the uncontrolled jerking that previously occurred.

Circuits involved in movement will not be fully formed until around the age of 2 years. It seems that early mobility helps to boost your baby's brain development, especially when it comes to spatial awareness and logic. Moving your baby by gently rocking him in your arms, or sitting him in a baby bouncer – the type that fits securely to a door frame, or stands alone on its own scaffold – seems to help brain development by stimulating balance- and movement-detecting cells in his inner ear.

It has been found, for example, that premature babies who are rocked, rubbed and stroked for 15 minutes, four times a day, develop improved co-ordination and ability to learn. Babies also obtain stimulation of their balance organs if you hold them in your arms and bend your knees up and down to mimic the movements felt in an elevator.

New research shows that brain-damaged children and adults can be taught to walk again – against all the odds, and even when 'written off' by the medical profession – through a process known as movement imprinting. By repetitively and passively moving limbs up and down to mimic walking, muscles are strengthened and the neural connections needed to control these movements seem to be stimulated and re-laid down. This passive imprinting has helped many people to walk again. You may have seen a similar technique – using tables that move – marketed as an easy form of exercise and toning for people wanting to lose weight. You can help your baby's brain imprint the movements necessary for crawling by literally placing him on all fours on the floor – once he can support his full weight – and gently moving his arms and legs forward to show him what to do. Evidence suggests that babies quickly get the idea and start crawling on their own earlier than otherwise expected. Similarly, babies who are held with their bare feet on a firm, flat surface and who are allowed to practise their reflex stepping movements between 2 and 8 weeks, when these reflex movements are at their strongest, began to walk earlier than usual – from around 10 months of age.

Developmental Milestones

Each time your baby gazes at your face, tries to reach for a brightly coloured toy or listens quizzically to your voice, electrical circuits in his brain buzz with waves of energy that send puffs of nerve growth factors across particular synapses, along with their electrical message. This helps to hard-wire these circuits into place.

Eventually, these circuits are strong enough to trigger a developmental milestone – the first smile, the first time your baby picks up an object, the first time he rolls over or pulls himself upright on the furniture. The following chart shows the ages when important developmental milestones occur as different parts of your baby's brain develop at different rates (the chart gives the average age for various important milestones; most prenatally stimulated babies will reach these milestones earlier than normal):

How to Stimulate Your Baby's Senses

Babies who have a stimulating environment tend to be less fussy and to stay quiet and attentive more than babies who are not given special stimulation. There is a big difference between an enriched, stimulating, enjoyable environment and one that is pressured and overtaken by the need to perform or succeed. Do not be over-ambitious for your child – feel proud of his achievements and love him for his failures as much as his successes. If your child shows signs of not enjoying an activity, stop immediately.

INTERACTING WITH YOUR NEW BABY

☺Spend as much time as possible with your child.

☺Try always to be with him during the first 5 or 6 months, so that when he wakes he hears your voice or sees you. Sleep with him in the same room in a cot next to your bed, a cot that forms an extension to your mattress (Bed-Side-Bed see addresses), or with you and your partner in your bed. This early closeness is very important for your child's sense of security and confidence. It also makes breastfeeding on demand much easier at night.

☺Rock him in your arms, hold him while bending up and down to simulate an elevator, or hold him on your knee while sitting on a swivel chair and gently turning round and round (or rocking to and fro in a rocking chair). These motions seem to stimulate the production of new brain cells and synapses.

- Draw bold stripes, zig-zags, targets and simple faces onto white card using a thick black felt-tip pen for your baby to study.
- Hang stimulating contrasting black-and-white patterns above his crib in the form of a mobile he can watch when he is awake.
- From the age of 6 – 8 weeks, introduce colours and slightly more complex patterns.
- Place a few drops of a gentle aromatherapy oil such as Lavender, Camomile, Rose or Mandarin (Neroli) on a piece of cotton wool for your baby to smell – make sure it stays out of his reach at all times. Also try placing different-flavoured liquids on the tip of a clean finger (such as honey, orange juice, carrot juice) and let him suck to stimulate his taste buds.
- Cover a torch with different coloured cloths or pieces of cellophane and move it from side to side to see if he will track it.
- Let your baby listen to light classical music such as Vivaldi's *Four Seasons* or a Mozart piano concerto.
- Tape record his voice, yours and those of other people he knows and play them back to him.
- Give him different textures to feel – make up a feelie toy by stuffing an old sock and sewing on squares of corduroy, silk, denim, cotton, velvet, towelling and tweed, etc.
- Show him his own reflection in a mirror.
- Consider taking him swimming with you if a local indoor, heated pool runs parent-and-baby sessions.
- From 6 weeks, place him on his tummy when awake and talk to him from around 3 metres (1 yard) away – this encourages him to lift his head.
- Up until 3 months of age, prop him up safely in a well-supported baby seat so he can watch what you are doing.

⊙ Spend as much time as possible with your infant but start getting him used to being on his own for short periods from the age of 6 months onwards.

⊙ Introduce him to cloth or hardboard books at an early age and point out objects to him in the stories. Let him choose which of two or three books you look at together, and let him learn to turn the pages for you.

⊙ Play peek-a-boo with him – this is often one of the first games he learns to play back, with squeals of delight.

⊙ He can communicate by sound and gestures much earlier than words – work out a personal symbolic code for different animals, cars, planes, etc. For example, pant for a dog, hiss and weave your arm for a snake, flap your arms and say tweet-tweet for a bird. It may seem silly but your baby will start communicating with you very early on so you can enter his non-verbal world and gain a great deal of pleasure in doing so.

⊙ Let him explore his world as much as possible – don't keep saying 'no' when he starts opening drawers and cupboards, for example; just ensure all items within his reach are safe to handle.

⊙ Let him make a mess so he can explore textures in the context of messy play.

⊙ Continue talking to him frequently so he learns language sounds.

⊙ Show him how different objects and actions make sounds when tapped or banged together.

⊙ Show him his own reflection in a mirror so he starts learning a sense of self.

⊙ Give him lots of physical contact with hugs, kisses and loves.

⊙ Soothe him when he is crying and hold him tight so he learns to calm himself while feeling loved and secure.

I probably don't need to remind you, but the best ways to stimulate your child are to provide him with:

- ☺ endless love, cuddles and emotional support
- ☺ a fun environment with plenty of laughter
- ☺ attention when he needs it – avoid his being on his own for long periods of time
- ☺ an environment that stimulates all the senses – touch, sight, hearing, smell, taste and balance
- ☺ an environment that is non-pressured – as soon as your child shows signs of becoming bored with an activity, switch to something else
- ☺ plenty of time to relax and play
- ☺ opportunities to choose activities, the clothes he wears that day, what music he listens to, etc.
- ☺ opportunities for messy play – splashing water, smearing food
- ☺ avoid over-stimulation – for example, only keep a few toys out at a time and change these regularly with others that have been put away
- ☺ lots of opportunities to interact with different people, especially other children
- ☺ a healthy diet with vitamin supplements as appropriate (see Chapter 13).

For further, expert guidance on how to interact and communicate with your child, you might want to read *Child Behaviour* by Dorothy Einon (Viking). This excellent guide will help you to bring up a happy, exceptionally well-adjusted child from birth through until puberty.

Stages of Development

	Age (months)								
	0	1	2	3	4	5	6	7	8
Personal and Social Skills								Recognizes people; people go away, give and take	
Fine Motor Skills		First smiles usually start at around 4–6 weeks.			Starts to reach for and grasp objects between 3 – 5 months.		Increasing co- and eye. Improving 5–8 months he will from one hand from hand to that he then Starts to feed		
Hearing, Visual and Language Skills		Listens, watches, starts to recognize people, objects and places. Jumps or becomes startled at loud sounds.			Babbles and coos. He will know how to make cooing noises by 4 months and repetitive 'ga-ga' noises by 6 months. Tracks objects with his eyes.		Makes sounds Starts to learn Knows his concept of be babbling		
General Motor Skills		Kicks, wriggles, turns his head and tries to roll. Tries to lift his head up when lying on the floor.			Chews; puts things in his mouth; rolls over; lifts his head up from the floor.		At 6 months he and shoulders and raise his arms months he can will wriggle crawl. Starts to around furniture. steps to walk.		

Age (months)

9	10	11	12	13	14	15	16	17	18

learns that things and
then come back. Learns to
objects. Plays peek-a-boo.

ordination between hand
hand control. Between
learn to pass small objects
to another, or passes them
mouth. Chooses objects
reaches for and gets.
himself with solid foods.

and tries to communicate.
what things are used for.
name. Understands the
'no'. By 9 months, he will
recognizable sounds.

By 18 months he can say between 6 and 20
recognizable single words, but will understand
many more.

can roll over, lift his head
when lying on his back
to be picked up. By 9
sit up on his own, and
along on his stomach or
pull himself up and walk
May make first tentative

Babies usually start to walk between the ages of
10 – 18 months. If he is not walking by 18 months,
talk to your health visitor. By 18 months he is also
ready to learn how to kick or throw a ball and how
to scribble with a crayon.

9	10	11	12	13	14	15	16	17	18

Useful Addresses

Smoking

ASH (Action on Smoking and Health)
109 Gloucester Place
London W1H 4EJ
0171 935 3519

QUIT (National Society for Non-Smokers)
Victory House
170 Tottenham Court Road
London W1P 0HA

UK Quitline
England: 0171 487 3000 9.30 a.m. – 10.00 p.m. daily
Scotland: 0800 848484
Northern Ireland: 01232 663281
Wales: 01222 641888
A fact sheet, *Smoking – Your Pregnancy, Your Baby – The Facts* is
also available from the UK Quitline.

Logado Consumer Advice Line
01223 426 410

Alcohol

Drinkline:The National Alcohol Helpline
13–14 West Smithfield
London EC1A 9DH
0345 320202 (local rates)

Nutrition

Eating for Pregnancy Helpline
0114 2424084 – you can speak to someone in confidence and
request an information pack.

Folic Acid Campaign Helpline
0800 665544

Efamol Information Line
01483 570248 (information on evening primrose oil and fish oil
supplements designed for pregnant women).

Garlic Information Centre
Saberdene
Church Road
Catsfield Battle
East Sussex TN33 9DP
01424 892440

Humet Healthcare Ltd
15 Little End Road
Eaton Socon
Huntingdon
Cambs PE19 3JH
01480 403769
Humet-R available.

Pregnancy Problems

Association of Spina Bifida and Hydrocephalus Helpline
01733 555 988

Twins and Multiple Births Association (TAMBA)
PO Box 30
Little Sutton
South Wirral L66 1TH
0151 3480020
Advice line: 01732 868 000 7 p.m. – 11 p.m. weekdays, 10 a.m. –
11 p.m. weekends

Association for Postnatal Illness
25 Jerdan Place
Fulham
London SW6 1BE
0171 3860868

Pre-Eclamptic Toxaemia Society
Eaton Lodge
8 Southend Road
Hockley
Essex SS5 4QQ
01702 205088

Stimulating Your Baby

BabyPlus UK Ltd
38 Caledonian Wharf
London E14 3EW
0171 5150870
BabyPlus machines may be hired for the duration of pregnancy (£125 at time of press) or purchased (£199).

Krucial Kids
28 Woodford Avenue
Ilford
Essex IG2 6XG
0181 5504933
Customer Services: 0181 2207711
Supply developmental toys for babies, and educational toys for older infants from 18 months – 8 years of age.

Johnson & Johnson Ltd
FREEPOST (SL1235)
Roxborough Way
Maidenhead
Berks SL6 3BW
Send your name and address on a postcard to receive a 'Baby Massage' leaflet.

Miscellaneous

Bed-Side-Bed
0181 9898683
Special cots that fit on a level with your own bed.

Medical Agency Systems
0645 556678
Mattress overlays for pregnancy.

Patients Against Mercury Amalgams (PAMA)
Helpline: 0171 6848407

Further Reading and Resources

Dr Sarah Brewer, *Planning a Baby? How to prepare for a healthy pregnancy and give your baby the best possible start* (Vermilion)

Dorothy Einon, *Child Behaviour* (Viking)

Dr Elizabeth Scott, *Sound Asleep for Babies*. Classical music to lull your baby to sleep. (Carma Sounds; available from W H Smith or by mail order, tel. 01253 780 096.)

Drs Penny and Andrew Stanway, *Breast is Best* (Pan)

Prenatal stimulation charts

The following chart, which can be photocopied, is designed to help you keep a record of how you stimulate your baby. The ideal time to start is from around 20–24 weeks gestation (22–26 weeks pregnancy).

PRENATAL STIMULATION CHART

Date: Gestation Week:

Day	Time	Activity	Notes (eg story read, music played, songs sung, BabyPlus programme (1 – 16) used.)
Monday	............mins ....mins ....mins		
Tuesday	............mins ....mins ....mins		
Wednesday	............mins ....mins ....mins		
Thursday	............mins ....mins ....mins		
Friday	............mins ....mins ....mins		
Saturday	............mins ....mins ....mins		
Sunday	............mins ....mins ....mins		

PRENATAL STIMULATION CHART

Date: Gestation Week:

Day	Time	Activity	Notes (eg story read, music played, songs sung, BabyPlus programme (1 – 16) used.)
Monday	............mins ....mins ....mins		
Tuesday	............mins ....mins ....mins		
Wednesday	............mins ....mins ....mins		
Thursday	............mins ....mins ....mins		
Friday	............mins ....mins ....mins		
Saturday	............mins ....mins ....mins		
Sunday	............mins ....mins ....mins		

Index

Of further interest...

THE SECRET OF HAPPY CHILDREN

Steve Biddulph

The Secret of Happy Children helps you with parent-child communication from babyhood to teens. It has received widespread praise around the world as a book which gives you heart to be more yourself as a parent – stronger, more loving, more definite, more relaxed.

Steve Biddulph, who has worked as a family therapist for over twenty years, here reveals what is really happening inside childrens' minds and what to do about it. You'll find yourself letting go of old, negative approaches, and freeing up more energy to enjoy your children and your life.

Steve Biddulph answers all of the questions he is most often asked on:

- stopping tantrums before they start
- curing shyness in your children
- the skills of fathering
- how to cure whingeing kids
- being a single parent – how to make it easier
- kids and TV
- food and behaviour
- the ten minutes that can save your marriage

RAISING BOYS

Steve Biddulph

Everyone who has boys today is concerned for them. Every-where we look, boys are having trouble with their lives. Parents want to understand better what makes boys tick, and how to help them be happy, loving and capable.

In *Raising Boys*, Steve Biddulph looks at the most important issues in boys' development from birth to manhood – and dis-cusses the warm, strong parenting and guidance that boys need. He brings his humour, honesty and practical knowledge of fam-ilies to the vital task of raising our sons.

Parents and teachers will find this a breakthrough book which changes their outlook on boys for the better, forever.

Publication date September 1998.

YOU AND YOUR NEW BABY

Anna McGrail

The National Childbirth Trust has helped thousands of parents to explore their own feelings, hopes and fears, making life with a new baby enjoyable and rewarding.

This handbook will answer all your questions and ease any fears you have about the first few months of being a family:

- adjusting to life with a baby
- learning new skills
- your body after the birth
- the growth of love
- play
- nursing and first solids
- twins
- your needs as a couple
- postnatal depression
- the wider family

In *You and Your New Baby*, new parents recount their experiences and give you the benefit of their skills and expertise to help you to adjust to being a family.

THE NATIONAL CHILDBIRTH TRUST
WORKING PARENTS' COMPANION

Teresa Wilson

This handbook will help you cope with the demands of work and home:

- childcare choices: live in or daily nanny, au pair, mother's help, childminder, nursery or créche
- breastfeeding and work
- your legal rights
- financial issues
- guilt and other feelings
- partnership pressures
- single parenting and support

In *The Working Parents' Companion* parents share their experiences and reveal how they cope with every issue, discussing the pros and cons of each form of childcare. And mothers in all types of work situations describe how they juggle their working lives with caring for their families.

THE NATIONAL CHILDBIRTH TRUST
BEING PREGNANT, GIVING BIRTH

Mary Nolan

This handbook will answer all your questions and ease any fears you may have about pregnancy, labour and your new baby:

- antenatal tests
- where to have your baby how labour begins
- choosing pain relief
- labour procedures
- having a caesarean birth
- the father's role
- the first 24 hours

In *Being Pregnant, Giving Birth,* parents share their experiences and reveal how they coped with each issue and event during pregnancy and birth. It gives you the facts you need to make informed choices and to enable you to work in partnership with the health professionals to achieve the best outcome for you and your baby.